D1570882

Government and Politics in
Kuomintang China
1927-1937

HUNG-MAO TIEN

Government and Politics in Kuomintang China

1927-1937

STANFORD, CALIFORNIA
STANFORD UNIVERSITY PRESS

1972

JQ
1503
1927
.T53

To My Parents and My Wife Amy

Acknowledgments

This study was originally a doctoral dissertation for the Department of Political Science at the University of Wisconsin, and has undergone substantial revision. I wish to thank Professors Fred R. von der Mehden, Lyman P. Van Slyke, Edward Friedman, Robert Kapp, James C. Scott, and Chow Tse-tsung for reading all or part of the manuscript and for making invaluable comments. I am also grateful to Benjamin Kerkvliet, Thomas Adams, and Paul Johnson for their help in the revision of the manuscript.

For financial aid I wish to thank the Graduate School and the Ford Foundation Committee of the University of Wisconsin, and the University of Wisconsin Center System. Without their support, especially that of the Graduate School, my research would have been impossible.

Miss Kathy Falk has demonstrated admirable patience in typing the manuscript and preparing the index. Thanks also go to Mrs. Betty Ann Gygax, Miss Christine Tominsek, Mrs. Karen Soli, and Mrs. Catherine Howley of the University of Wisconsin at Waukesha for their secretarial assistance. Finally, this book could not have been written without the love of my wife Amy and my daughter Wendy. My wife has also contributed many hours of hard work in typing the early drafts. To her and Wendy I owe an immeasurable debt and deep affection.

H.M.T.

September 1972

Contents

Tables

Government and Politics in
Kuomintang China
1927-1937

Bandit Suppression Zones, 1930–37

Introduction

THE NATIONALIST PARTY, or Kuomintang, had ostensibly ruled China for over two decades, 1927 to 1949, before being defeated and replaced by the Communists. For the last 12 years of their rule, however, the Nationalists were engaged in almost continuous warfare, first with Japan and then with the Communists. These wars brought massive problems that differed substantially from those of the prewar decade. Thus this study, which attempts to determine the effectiveness of the Nationalist party-government in unifying and ruling China, will confine itself to the years 1927 to 1937.

This book deals with patterns of political development and focuses primarily on the institutions and administrative structures, both civil and military, of the Nationalists. The material falls naturally into two areas of inquiry: the central government and the provinces. At each political level the study considers such topics as leadership, recruitment, and finances. It attempts to answer questions like the following: who were the political elites? how did they utilize authority and resources? in what kind of institutional milieu did they operate? and, most important, was China as a whole moving toward greater political and administrative integration?

Knowing that there are many useful ways to study political development in changing societies, I have chosen to stress institutional development because of the historical importance of institutions in maintaining political order in China. During the imperial rule various political institutions, notably the traditional administrative bureaucracy, served to control the people and to perpetuate their lack of political consciousness; the Confucian ideology served to rationalize

these goals. Institutional and ideological controls were especially important to the Manchu dynasty, which ruled over a vast majority of
Han Chinese. Hsiao Kung-chuan summarizes the Manchus' position
in this way:

> The government of the Ch'ing dynasty, like preceding regimes, was an
> autocracy ruling over a society in which the population was stratified into
> groups of people with unequal political, social, and economic status; and
> the interests of the rulers and subjects were divergent and to some extent
> incompatible. . . . Because they [the rulers] could not have confidence in
> their subjects or count on their loyalty, they sought to render the latter
> submissive and subservient by a variety of devices calculated to immunize
> them against all thought and action that might prove detrimental to impe-
> rial security.[1]

Geared solely to the maintenance of order and stability, the imperial system could not deal with the kind of social and economic change
China experienced after 1800. The administrative bureaucracy broke
down under the stress. Perhaps the most obvious symptom of this
breakdown was the central government's gradual loss of control over
revenues. Another symptom was the increasingly blatant corruption,
reflected, for example, in the purchase of official titles.[2] The 1911 revolution overthrew the Manchu dynasty and smashed the already shaky
imperial institutional order. With central authority eliminated, autonomous regional forces mushroomed. Whatever political forces
emerged, therefore, confronted the crucial task of establishing an
institutional framework for national development.

As a modern revolutionary party whose predecessors had been politically active for over three decades, the Kuomintang captured
power in 1927 with the explicit goal of re-creating a viable political
order. Students of modern China, overwhelmed by the Communist
victory in 1949, have not paid enough attention to China in the transitional period under the Kuomintang. Our knowledge of the Kuomintang is primarily limited to the pre-1927 period. Most available
writings on the post-1927 era are narratives and broad surveys, at
best superficial. Thus this study will focus on the Kuomintang's development after 1927, examining its membership, decision-making
structure, and internal organization. On the basis of our findings,
we can assess the party's ability to carry out social change and to
integrate diverse political forces into a new order.[3]

The most significant development in the party's power structure after 1927 was Chiang Kai-shek's rise to supremacy. Earlier, in the Kuomintang government in Kwangtung, Chiang had ruled with Wang Ching-wei and Hu Han-min. But this triumvirate was gradually broken up by political machines that enhanced Chiang's personal power. Three groups, the Blue Shirt Society, the Political Study Clique, and the C.C. Clique, were especially important in this development, and Chiang maintained patron-client relationships with their leaders. The cliques were the functional instruments of his search for power and a united political community in China. Although Wang and Hu, as senior party politicians, continued to have prestige and followers, their position was fatally weakened by the lack of stable, independent bases of power. Thus they played peripheral roles in decision making and policy implementation. Their primary importance was that their presence held out the possibility of an alternative to Chiang's leadership. Regional military and political forces could establish alliances with Wang or Hu against Chiang, thus posing a constant threat to his position. Indeed, a number of alliances like this were forged in the 1920's and 1930's. Local leaders in Kwangtung and Kwangsi were especially eager to use such tactics against Chiang.

The interplay of political forces in the Nanking decade, then, involved a struggle for influence among various pro-Chiang client factions, on the one hand, and Chiang's maneuvers to thwart possible coalitions against him, on the other. In order to maintain his supremacy Chiang mastered the art of factional politics.[4] First, he encouraged competition among political groups and tried to keep them separate from each other. Second, to this end he used patronage and awards of privilege and influence. Third, he avoided unnecessarily reckless measures threatening the existence of significant groups, since such action might create enemies willing to ally against him at any cost. Fourth, he promoted personal loyalty to him while fostering rivalries among the loyal. Finally, he would not tolerate any faction's gaining a clear predominance. The rules of this political game enabled Chiang to survive as the dominant figure in Chinese politics in the 1930's. But, ironically, the principles that upheld his leadership also placed enormous obstacles in the way of his achieving genuine power. For the pursuit of genuine power demanded the qualities of efficiency and ability, which were often incompatible with Chiang's excessive demands for loyalty. His political machines, although strong enough to assure his supremacy in the regime's power structure, were not efficient enough to support a truly totalitarian dictatorship.

Chiang's use of patronage did help him establish firm control over the military, financial, and organizational apparatus of the party. But his dependence on loyal stooges severely undermined the Nationalists' revolutionary legacy and his own claim to inherit it. The need to bargain and compromise to maintain a balance among existing political forces led him to support the status quo while chanting the party's revolutionary litany. Interaction with conservative groups opposed to social change kept him from carrying out any drastic reforms. Since upholding the status quo and rejecting major social reforms put the regime in a precarious position, Chiang found it necessary to give disproportionate emphasis to the mechanisms of control. And in the long run they proved inadequate to put down social discontent in a system that needed fundamental change. Further, the reliance on particularistic relationships tended to alienate many capable and influential elites whose services would have greatly strengthened the government's institutional ability to unite and govern China. In promoting narrowly based power vehicles, Chiang caused long-time party elites and provincial militarists to look on the Nanking regime with suspicion. Under this political system, access to the party's power center was cut off, and the chance for a broad-based consensus among ruling elites precluded.

In retrospect, Chiang's decision to use client groups as instruments of nation-building seems to have crippled the party-government's ability to develop the network of institutions necessary to govern a country as large and as underdeveloped in terms of communications as China. To prove the case I will analyze the Nanking Government's efforts to establish a centralized administrative bureaucracy and to subordinate provincial administrative machinery to its goal of national development. The government's first objective required vigorous efforts to recruit personnel and structural changes to facilitate communication and the mobilization of resources. The second objective required subduing the regional militarists, who had fortified their provinces in the decade before 1927, and then establishing uniform provincial administrations.

Administrative change in the provinces was handicapped by two Kuomintang policies. First, the policy of extensive compromise with the regional militarists helped perpetuate corrupt provincial administrations. Second, the policy of using purely military means against the Communists consumed most of the government's resources and undercut what marginal institutional reforms were made. Chiang's anti-Communist, bandit suppression campaigns undoubtedly created an area of common interest both between the central government and local rulers and among local rulers themselves, therefore making it easier for the Kuomintang to force its way into the provinces. But the subsequent failure to generate genuine reforms implied that if Chiang's military efforts failed, the provinces would again break away from the center. There were no viable institutions to maintain stability throughout the country.

During the Nanking decade Chiang and the Nationalists developed different degrees of control over various parts of China. They had fairly tight and continuous control over Chekiang and Kiangsu. In eight other provinces—Anhwei, Kiangsi, Fukien, Hupeh, Hunan, Honan, Kansu, and Shensi—Chiang's influence was initially marginal but became stronger once the anti-Communist campaigns began. Together with Chekiang and Kiangsu these provinces formed the "Bandit Suppression Zones." Finally, in the remaining provinces, Nanking's influence was nonexistent or at best nominal. Although during 1935 and 1936 the central government did manage to extend its authority to Szechwan and Kweichow, and to a lesser degree to Kwangtung and Kwangsi, this came too late to be of any significance. As this study will show, both the propaganda and the actual operations of the anti-Communist campaigns helped Nanking considerably in penetrating the provinces beyond its immediate domain of Chekiang, Kiangsu, and parts of Anhwei, Kiangsi, and Fukien. This is revealed when one examines administrative changes in provinces inside and outside the Bandit Suppression Zones. It was in the former that the Kuomintang gained more and more influence in appointing administrative personnel, promoting structural change, and controlling finances.

Unfortunately, much valuable source material for this period is still unavailable in the Kuomintang archives. Thus the evidence presented here is incomplete, and I do not pretend to hold my findings beyond dispute. Neither can I venture to offer a definite answer to the hypothetical question of whether Chiang Kai-shek's Kuomintang regime could have united China and defeated the Communists if not for the long and costly war with Japan. In the final analysis this work attempts to examine several major patterns of political development before the war. It studies what can be studied without intending to judge what has already become history.

PART ONE

The Central Government

ONE

The Establishment of the Party-State

AFTER THE COLLAPSE of the Ch'ing dynasty in 1911, China went through several decades of chaos and turbulence, in a painful search for a new sociopolitical order. The period before 1927 was characterized by "warlordism," as regional militarists maneuvered for power and wealth. Between 1912 and 1928 there were more than 1,300 warlords, who engaged in at least 140 local and regional wars.[1]

The disappearance of a legitimate central government created a vacuum of political authority in which regional militarism could flourish. Great numbers of landless peasants, victims of rural social upheavals, provided the warlords with a constant source of recruits. Since the warlords also needed constant sources of revenue to feed and supply these troops, economic factors often dictated their maneuvers. Major military objectives were control of the railways—especially the Peking-Hankow, Tientsin-Pukow, and Lunghai lines—and control of such strategic locations as the coastal provinces, the Yangtze basin, and the arsenals in Hanyang and Shanghai.[2] Warlords who held areas rich in resources used any means necessary to retain control, and those from poor regions were always alert for opportunities to attack the wealthier warlords.

The major warlords occupied either key economic areas or provinces with natural geographic boundaries. For over a decade they interacted like rulers of independent states.[3] So long as no central authority existed, each warlord found it necessary to have an army, as well as trusted elites to run the army and the administrative bureaucracy. The primary task of the administrative bureaucracies, maintained on the basis of patron-client relationships, was to extract revenues.[4] The rural peasantry was the major source of revenue and suffered greatly from the endless burden. Even the somewhat progressive warlords like Feng Yü-hsiang and Yen Hsi-shan had to resort to relentless financial squeezes in the provinces of Chahar, Suiyuan, Kansu, Honan, and Shansi.[5] Moreover, officials at the lower levels of the warlord bureaucracies, unsure of their futures and with few prospects for promotion, often lined their own pockets. In the 1930's the situation deteriorated still further in such provinces as Szechwan, Honan, Kwangtung, and Hunan.[6]

As a working political-military system warlordism was characterized by economic exploitation, social oppression, and political feudalism. The warlords established machines to channel revenues to the military, exhausting rural resources while producing at most only marginal social and economic reforms. Although the Nationalists frequently made alliances and compromises with various warlords, they looked on the warlord system as their chief obstacle in unifying China. It is not surprising, therefore, that the elimination of the warlords was perhaps the only clear point of agreement among competing Kuomintang leaders, especially after the death of Sun Yat-sen on March 12, 1925.

The Kuomintang had had a rather turbulent history; its predecessors had undergone several reorganizations to preserve the party and to adjust to the changing political climate.* The reorganization of January 30, 1924, marked the emergence of the party as a much more effective force. Only the year before, the Kuomintang had formed a united front with the Communist Party (the KMT-CCP united front);[7] and Sun Yat-sen's decision to reorganize the party along Leninist lines was apparently due to the strong influence of the Soviet Union.[8] In spite of the fact that the united front turned out to be a brief and unhappy experience—it was terminated by Chiang Kai-shek's bloody

* See Yü, pp. 7–147. (Complete authors' names, titles, and publication data for works cited in footnotes and tables are given in the Bibliography, pp. 211–20.) The development of the party under different names can be briefly sketched as follows: (1) the Hsing-Chung Hui (Revive China Society), 1894–1905, founded in Honolulu, primarily an overseas party; (2) the T'ung-meng Hui (Common Alliance Association), 1905–12, increasingly dominated by Chinese students and intellectuals; (3) the Kuo-min-tang (Nationalist Party), 1912–13, a parliamentary party; (4) the Chung-hua Ke-ming-tang (Chinese Revolutionary Party), 1913–19, an outlawed underground party; (5) the Chung-kuo Kuo-min-tang (Chinese Nationalist Party), 1919–24; and (6) the Kuo-min-tang, reorganized in 1924.

coup of 1927 and the Wuhan Government's subsequent decision to oust Communists from the party—certain Russian organizational influences were long-lasting.

The 1924 reorganization was the party's most vigorous effort to establish an institutional framework for policy making and administration. Before then, party policies had been determined largely by Sun Yat-sen, with occasional consultations with his chief lieutenants.[9] The legitimacy of Sun's authority was based on his charisma, a situation that runs counter to all institutional routines. Sun's personality cult created dissatisfaction even among his most trusted followers, notably Wang Ching-wei.[10] The reorganization, although reaffirming Sun's undisputed leadership by awarding him the permanent position of party president, nevertheless created legitimate institutional decision-making procedures, modeled on the practices of the Russian Communist Party.* It demonstrated the Kuomintang's changing attitude toward mass mobilization through party-directed grass-roots organizations.

Evidence suggests that Sun's personal wishes continued to guide the party even after its reorganization. As one writer points out, Sun disregarded the clear powers granted to the Central Executive Committee and "used it only as a minor administrative device."[11] Thus Sun left a damaging legacy to the party when he died suddenly in 1925. While he was alive a consensus could be maintained at the leadership level despite the presence of competing factions. But Sun did not live long enough to preside over a transition to institutionalized authority, as George Washington did in the United States. Much of the party's limited energy was exhausted in factional struggles after Sun's death, at a time when internal unity was most needed. In the long run, this paved the way for the transformation of the Kuomintang into a party of narrowly based political machines maintained by patron-client relationships. This development seriously undermined the chances of the party's so-called national government to become a viable political mechanism.

The territorial base of the party in Kwangtung was very shaky even before Sun's death. The survival of his military government at Canton

---

* Ch'ien Tuan-sheng, *Government*, p. 120. Party decisions were to be made by the National Congress or, in its adjournment, by the Central Executive Committee, of which Sun was a member.

depended on support from regional militarists. And even in Kwangtung the party could not count on this support, as the revolt of the
warlord Ch'en Chiung-ming in 1922 demonstrated.[12] After Sun's death
the political power of the party was to be controlled by a man whose
strength lay in his ability to subdue warlords with guns. That man
was Chiang Kai-shek. Prominent party leaders like Wang Ching-wei
and Hu Han-min found themselves unable to bring the army under
civilian control. Their political influence gradually slipped to the
point where they could exercise only minimal power.

Chiang Kai-shek emerged as a potential leader when the party decided that it must raise an army of its own. As this army became more
and more necessary to the party's survival, Chiang became the party's
most important figure. In the process he surpassed senior party leaders with longer service, higher status, and often greater ability. But
Chiang's success through military means later led him to ignore nonmilitary factors when the situation required vigorous social, economic,
and political reforms. Continuing to buttress his power in a military
structure independent of civilian control, he was able to defer issues
he chose not to face.

Chiang's career started when Sun appointed him president of the
newly created Whampoa Military Academy in 1924.[13] The academy
was set up to produce an army strongly dedicated to the party's revolutionary goals. In the political confusion in Kwangtung after Sun's
death, Chiang's few but well-disciplined Whampoa soldiers proved
to be his greatest political asset. Following a successful military expedition against Ch'en Chiung-ming, he was made commander of the
party army in April 1925, garrison commander of Canton in June, and
a member of the Military Council in July.[14] By mid-1926 Chiang had
become chairman of the Military Council, commander-in-chief of the
National Revolutionary Army, head of the party's Organization Department, and a leading figure in the Central Executive Committee.
This rise was due to his skillful manipulation of political events and
his neutralist position in the severe left-right struggle that had developed in the party.*

---

* In the aftermath of the assassination of Liao Chung-k'ai in 1925, two of
Chiang's important political rivals, Hu Han-min and Hsü Ch'ung-chih, were
eliminated. Later, in 1926, the so-called Chungshan gunboat incident brought
the downfall of Wang Ching-wei, then chairman of the State and Military councils. See Loh, "Politics," pp. 434–36, and T'ang Leang-li, pp. 214–21, 241–47.

After consolidating its territorial base in Kwangtung, the National Revolutionary Army under Chiang's command launched the historic Northern Expedition against the warlords on July 9, 1926. The army was a coalition of important military forces in South China, primarily from Kwangtung, Kwangsi, and Hunan. Students and instructors of the Whampoa Academy belonged to the First Army, under Chiang's direct command. It is important to remember that during the Northern Expedition the KMT-CCP united front was still in effect. As the military action progressed the Kwangtung and Kwangsi troops joined forces with T'ang Sheng-chih's Hunan Army, achieved a decisive victory over the warlord Wu P'ei-fu, and captured Hunan and Hupeh. The Nationalist Government in Canton moved to Wuhan on November 28, 1926.

Meanwhile, Sun Ch'uan-fang, the warlord who controlled the five provinces of Kiangsi, Anhwei, Kiangsu, Chekiang, and Fukien, was putting up strong resistance, and military campaigns against his armies were unsuccessful. Finally, in March 1927, Chiang himself directed assaults against Shanghai and Nanking and captured the two cities. He was apparently anxious to control Shanghai's enormous wealth and to gain a foothold in Kiangsu and Chekiang, two provinces where he could mobilize strong local support.[15] He organized his own Nationalist Government at Nanking on April 18, 1927, following a bloody coup against the Communists and their sympathizers in Shanghai. The left-wing Kuomintang leaders in the Wuhan Government followed suit soon after, undertaking a purge in July.*

For several months two Nationalist governments—one at Wuhan and the other at Nanking—existed side by side, each claiming to be the legitimate governing body. The Wuhan Government had theoretically inherited the legitimacy of the earlier Canton Government. It could not exercise authority without a substantial number of members of the Central Executive Committee, however, and most of the party's right-wing politicians stayed in Shanghai and were inclined to

* After the Nationalist Government moved from Canton to Wuhan, the Communists apparently increased their strength in the Kuomintang. When Wang Ching-wei returned to Hankow on April 10, 1927, to reassume a position of importance in the government, he found that the Kuomintang members of the Central Executive Committee had lost control of the situation. It appeared that unless drastic measures were taken, the Communists, acting on a new policy directive from Stalin, would take over the Wuhan Government and gain control of the area under its jurisdiction. See T'ang Leang-li, pp. 271–89.

support Chiang Kai-shek's rebellious government in Nanking. The balance of power was further complicated by the relatively even distribution of military strength. The situation was indeed a deadlock.

After a series of military confrontations and complicated political maneuvers, a united Nationalist Government was finally established in Nanking in September 1927. On June 8 of the following year, the Nationalist forces reached Peking, and the unification of China was officially announced. In October 1928 the formal government structure of the Five Yuans was established, in accordance with Sun Yat-sen's principles of government. The Kuomintang took on the role of political tutor and publicly outlawed all other political parties. Its goal was explicit: to create a single-party state in a united China.

Sun Yat-sen conceived of the party-state as a transitional government. A constitutional republic was his eventual objective, but he believed that considering China's enormous social and political problems, three stages would be necessary to achieve it. In the *Fundamentals of National Reconstruction*, he defined the stages as periods of military rule, political tutelage, and constitutional government.[16] During the stage of political tutelage, which entailed the establishment of a party-state, the party would instruct the people and guide them toward a sound, stable constitutional democracy. In assigning the party such an enormous task, Sun apparently assumed that it would be composed of highly qualified and dedicated elites. This plan resembles the Communist doctrine of dictatorship by the proletariat but differs in several important ways. The party-state, though authoritarian in nature, did not attempt a total transformation of society, as Marxist-Leninist doctrines prescribe. Further, it was to last only six years, unlike a Communist dictatorship, which may last forever if class differences do not disappear.[17] At the end of the six years, a majority of provinces were expected to have reached the constitutional stage, and a national assembly would then enact and promulgate a constitution.

Nanking's authority in 1928 was narrowly circumscribed. Regional forces continued to exist, and Chiang Kai-shek had to conciliate them. Chiang allowed branches of the Kuomintang's ruling political councils to be set up in Canton, Wuhan, Kaifeng, Mukden, Taiyuan, and Peking, in recognition of such warlords as Feng Yü-hsiang, Yen Hsi-shan, Chang Tso-lin, and Li Tsung-jen. Feng Yü-hsiang continued to rule Kansu, Shensi, Honan, and, to a lesser degree, Shantung. Yen Hsi-shan, in addition to his home province of Shansi, controlled Suiyuan and Hopei. Chang Tso-lin was still the overlord of Manchuria. And the Kwangsi warlords—Li Tsung-jen, Pai Ch'ung-hsi, and Li Chi-shen—held Kwangsi, Kwangtung, Hunan, and Hupeh, although the last two provinces were soon lost to Chiang Kai-shek. Thus Nanking had direct jurisdiction over only Kiangsu, Chekiang, and major parts of Anhwei, Fukien, and Kiangsi. Chiang Kai-shek was forced, for the time being, to offer the warlords high positions linking them to the Nanking Government. Trusted lieutenants of the warlords were made chairmen of the provincial governments under their military control.[18]

Since Feng, Yen, and Li Tsung-jen proclaimed themselves to be true believers of Sun Yat-sen's doctrines, the existence of their forces posed a direct threat to Nanking's authority and seriously undermined its claims to legitimacy. In addition, warlords who completely ignored the Nanking party-government continued to rule in the remote provinces of Szechwan, Yunnan, and Kweichow.* Nanking's authority began to penetrate these provinces in the first half of the 1930's, primarily as a result of the government's painstaking military campaigns against the Communists. Of course, the eventual decision to resist Japanese aggression by force in 1937 further strengthened the government's control over some outlying provinces.

Regionalism poses a series of conceptual problems for studying China from 1927 to 1937. How does one, in a political analysis, characterize the Nationalist Government in Nanking? Does one talk of all China in terms of one political system, or simply refer to China as a territory whose people share a similar cultural and historical heritage?[19] What unifying concept can bind together such regions as Yunnan, Sinkiang, Chekiang, and Szechwan? The traditional Chinese

---

* Like Jerome Ch'en, I prefer to use the term "residual warlordism" to describe the political situation in these provinces only. The term first appears in Sheridan's work (pp. 14–16), where it refers to the continuing existence of many regional militarists after the Kuomintang government was established in Nanking. Ch'en found the concept unsatisfactory because it failed to distinguish between warlords who practiced Sun Yat-sen's doctrines in their provinces (the reformist Kuomintang cliques) and those who did not participate in national politics or challenge Chiang directly, and who steadily declined until their submission to the central government in 1935. See Jerome Ch'en, "Defining Chinese Warlords," pp. 585–86.

bureaucratic empire was maintained by the scholar-gentry class, who provided the functional nucleus of a nationwide political community. According to Joseph Whitney:

Because of the broad range of spatial interaction in which they took part, theirs was a truly national vision, and the members of this community would have much more in common with other members in distant parts of China than they would with those from the different community in their own locality. For this bureaucratic community's loyalties were, in theory at least, directed towards the empire as a whole rather than to the local community.[20]

Whitney stresses the system-maintenance function of the bureaucratic network in imperial China. The 1911 revolution destroyed this network and the status, wealth, and power of the elites who held China together in a political community. When the Nanking Government was set up, it was apparent that its survival required the re-creation of a viable institutional framework encompassing all of China. The degree to which it was able to accomplish this is a crucial test of its legitimacy.

David Easton differentiates three levels of a political system as potential objects of support: the political community, the regime, and the authorities. His analysis provides another useful perspective in considering at what level China had a political system during the Nanking period. Easton defines a political community as the "aspect of a political system that consists of its members seen as a group of persons bound together by a political division of labor."[21] This concept is useful because "it conveys the latent notion that, underlying the functioning of all systems, there must be some cohesive cement— a sense or feeling of continuity amongst the members. Unless such sentiment emerges, the political system itself may never take shape, or if it does, it may not survive."[22] In China, of course, the degree of cohesion among the people was fairly strong, due to a common written language (Mandarin), the transmission of a great culture, and the integrative function performed by the bureaucratic network. It is at this level that we can speak of a Chinese system, supported by contending forces and individuals who shared a sense of community inherited from the past. This concept helps explain why most of the political forces antagonistic to, and independent from, the Kuomintang's Nanking regime eventually joined it in fighting a "national war" against the Japanese.

The concepts of regime and authorities as defined by Easton refer to constitutional order and government, respectively. Every political system "needs to develop a set of formal or operating constraints that are generally accepted, through quiescent indifference or positive consensus, by rulers and ruled alike, and that give at least broad indications of what are or are not permissible goals, practices, and structures in the system."[23] The regime, then, consists of values, norms, and structures of authority.[24] The concept of authorities refers to the structures and roles through which decisions are made and policies implemented in a political system. This includes both political and administrative organizations and the individuals who serve in these organizations. In Kuomintang China the regime was the constitutional order based on Sun Yat-sen's Three People's Principles. To some degree even opponents of Chiang Kai-shek, such as the Kwangsi and Kwangtung militarists, supported the Kuomintang regime. This is indicated by their continuous participation in electoral processes in order to maintain positions in such ruling organizations as the Central Executive and Central Supervisory committees. The authorities of the Nanking Government included the Kuomintang party apparatus, the governmental and administrative structures, and Chiang's military headquarters. It was at this level that support from the people and from various political forces was the weakest.

The government must be seen in its historical context. It had recently emerged from a temporary sanctuary in Kwangtung to occupy several provinces and was attempting to establish a party-state. Although it represented the predominant unifying force in China, its political support varied from province to province. In carefully examining the government's organizational development and legitimacy, I will try to assess fully the relations between Nanking and the provincial subsystems that still operated with varying degrees of autonomy.

TWO

The Organization of the Regime

THE STRUCTURE of the Nationalist Government was based on the principle of party dictatorship. The government served to implement policies made by the party organs. In theory, the authority to formulate policy was held by the Central Executive Committee (CEC) of the party, or, when the CEC was not in session, by the Political Council. The Military Council was to administer policies of a military nature, following guidelines determined by the CEC or the Political Council. The central government was headed by a president and supervised by the Political Council in the execution of public policy. In addition to policy administration the government had functions in the areas of control, examination, legislation, and adjudication.

A study of political development after 1928 reveals that the government was slow to institutionalize an administrative system to fulfill its needs. Its attempts to establish control over the provinces were often thwarted by local leaders, and central authority was usurped by the Military Council. The CEC and the Political Council were controlled by elites whose career interests and policy priorities tied them to the Military Council and its chairman, Chiang Kai-shek. Thus decisions were made largely in response to military needs. The usurpation of authority by the Military Council explains much about political development in the party-state. The way public policy was made and implemented clearly indicates the trend toward political machines rather than party and government institutions. *

The Administrative Bureaucracy

The Nationalist Government inaugurated in 1928 was based on Sun Yat-sen's constitutional theory, which defined five separate powers:

executive, legislative, judiciary, examination, and control. The five separate powers were to be exercised by five independent branches of the national government. The division of power among the Executive Yuan, the Legislative Yuan, and the Judiciary Yuan basically derived from Montesquieu's principle of the separation of power. The Control Yuan served as a watchdog over bureaucratic behavior and practice, and the Examination Yuan dealt with the recruitment, promotion, and retirement of administrative personnel. The Executive Yuan, which was to wield administrative control over the provinces, and the Examination Yuan together were responsible for creating and operating a central administrative bureaucracy. The development of such a bureaucracy was crucial in the party-government's attempt to create a national system of communication and control through which legitimate authority could be exercised.

Despite the fact that the complex personal relationships and intrigues of Chinese politics are frequently emphasized, China claims to have been the first nation to use an impersonal system of recruiting administrative officials. The system, based on a competitive examination, was initiated in the seventh century during the early T'ang dynasty. The social implications of the system were many. Above all, it tended to perpetuate the existing social structure, providing only limited social mobility. It produced a political elite that also enjoyed high social status. Politically, the system became the backbone of the Chinese bureaucratic empire and the primary instrument for maintaining order. It upheld the existing system of political belief based on Confucianism, which in turn justified the power of the administrative elites.

This competitive examination system, which promoted a sociopolitical equilibrium through the internalization of values, was adequate before China's modern contact with the West. Beginning in the late nineteenth century, however, the system became increasingly dysfunctional. In 1905 the despairing Ch'ing dynasty abolished it altogether. For the next few decades there was neither a standard recruitment system nor a merit system to measure administrative performance objectively.[1] The route to bureaucratic success was increasingly unclear, and a period of political decay ensued. The Chinese revolutionaries, who desired to create an effective central administration after 1911, clearly failed to do so. Events repeatedly proved that institutional change lagged far behind the "galloping ideals" of the revolutionary modernizers.[2] Institutional development failed to meet growing needs, and the narrow existing political machines were inherently incapable of generating widespread support.

During the period of warlordism (1916–28), provincial administrative systems were preserved primarily for the purpose of tax collection. Upper-level bureaucratic posts were held by chief lieutenants of the warlords, and most of the remaining posts by members of the powerful local elites with whom the warlords were connected. Improvements in administrative bureaucracy were difficult, if not entirely impossible, under such circumstances. With some possible exceptions in Shansi and Kwangsi, regional forces made no attempts to create adequate administrative systems based on objective recruitment standards. In this context the Kuomintang's late effort to reestablish a civil-service system was a significant development in Chinese politics during the prewar period.

In order to carry out Sun Yat-sen's instructions, the Nanking party-government elevated the civil-service recruitment apparatus to the status of an independent department, the Examination Yuan. According to its organizational law, promulgated on March 15, 1932, the Yuan was to have supreme authority over civil-service personnel in both the central and provincial governments. Throughout the 1930's the Yuan was composed of two departments: the Examination Commission and the Ministry of Personnel. The commission fixed the time and place of examinations, determined their nature and scope, prepared the forms, and issued rules to govern them. (For each proposed examination, however, the law required the appointment of a temporary Board of Examination.) The ministry performed the following major functions: it kept a register of all public officials and anyone else with the necessary qualifications for specific positions; it prepared eligibility lists of candidates who passed the examinations; and it determined the qualifications of new appointees and official incumbents.

The Yuan provided a ranking system for all Chinese administrative officials. According to this system there were four ranks, each of which was subdivided into several grades with fixed salaries.[3] The official salary scale, ranging from Ch $55 to Ch $800 a month, reveals a wide discrepancy between the upper and lower levels of the civil service. The salaries of the lower administrative personnel, who received neither allowances nor fringe benefits, were not sufficient to live on, much less attractive; and extralegal income obtained through patronage or corruption became necessary for survival. Civil-service candidates naturally could not regard the administrative bureaucracy as a ladder to success. Even achieving a level of material security was questionable unless the candidate had connections with higher bureaucrats or members of the party's power organs.

The system provided that whenever an administrative vacancy occurred, preference had to be given to candidates who had already passed the proper examination. If an appointment was made without the required examination, the candidate's qualifications had to be submitted to the Ministry of Personnel for careful scrutiny and approval; further, the appointee's initial salary corresponded to that of the lowest grade in his rank.

Three types of examinations were devised to meet the different levels of administrative requirements: the higher examination (*kao-k'ao*), the general examination (*p'u-k'ao*), and the special examination (*t'e-k'ao*).[4] Between 1928 and 1935 a total of 20 examinations were given in Nanking and some provincial capitals: 3 higher examinations, 11 general examinations, and 6 special examinations. Of the 19,118 participants, 1,585 (8.3 percent) reportedly passed.[5] The most important function of the examinations was to institute uniform standards of recruitment and administrative performance. Unfortunately, the Examination Yuan's own performance in the prewar period was far from satisfactory. As of 1931 it was estimated that there were well over 46,000 administrative functionaries in the central government; the total was between 100,000 and 200,000 when those at the city, county, and provincial levels were added.[6] The 1,585 candidates produced by the examinations would constitute at most only about 1 percent of a civil service this size. Moreover, many who had passed the examinations were not actually appointed to positions. Among the hundred who passed the first higher examination in 1931, for example, only 34 reportedly had obtained government jobs by 1935.[7] Of those appointed, an estimated 80 to 90 percent joined the central government.[8] Very few went to jobs in provincial or local governments. The second higher examination, held in 1933, selected 110 qualified candidates; during the next two years fewer than 10 percent of these were assigned positions, and only one took a provincial administrative job.[9] In short, these examinations played only a marginal role in staffing the administrative bureaucracy.

Since the examination system was not functioning adequately, the Nationalist Government tried to improve the quality of administrative personnel by examining the qualifications of all candidates for office, as well as those of all incumbents. But such an investigation posed enormous difficulties. According to an official report of the Examination Yuan in 1935:

From June 1930 to September 1931, the qualifications of over 17,000 candidates were investigated. These investigations were supposed to continue, but they were periodically postponed for some reason; finally a deadline of March 1933 was set for all administrative organs to submit lists of candidates and appointees for central investigation. Between September 1931 and March 1933, only a few of the administrative organs at all levels actually submitted lists. . . . From October 1931 [to the present], credentials of a total of 37,597 administrative candidates have been investigated; of these, 300 were determined to be qualified for the second rank, 2,933 for the third rank, and 24,746 for the lowest rank.[10]

All together, then, between 1930 and 1935 only 54,597 candidates for office at all levels had reached the Examination Yuan for official approval. Of the 37,597 submitted after October 1931, the Yuan disqualified 9,618, or 26 percent.

Although from 1930 to 1934 the Ministry of Personnel devoted much energy to the screening of incumbent officials, the results were grossly inadequate. The central authority was clearly unable to implement a policy that required a substantial overhauling of the administrative civil service. Incumbent officials perpetuated their own positions in the administrative bureaucracy and presented formidable resistance to progressive change from any source of authority. As Ch'ien Tuan-sheng points out: "This improvised arrangement had the effect of nullifying the advantages of those who later entered the civil service via the regular examinations. As a matter of fact, at all times men have been entering the civil service without passing the examinations."[11]

At higher levels the prospect of establishing a healthy administrative personnel system was constantly undercut by the practice of giving administrative posts as political rewards. This pervasive practice certainly hindered if not blocked progress toward an institutionalized modern bureaucracy. Its immediate effects on the central administrative bureaucracy were twofold. First, there was a tendency to appoint an official to several positions, each of which alone would have required his full attention.* This inevitably reduced the chances of efficient performance and severely blurred the functional boundaries of administrative positions. Second, the system tended to bring in people whose ability was highly questionable, to say the least. Certain top administrative appointments were clearly made as part of intricate military and political bargains between Kuomintang factions or between the Kuomintang and regional militarists. As a result, most of the high administrative personnel primarily responsible for implementing reforms were incompetent.

The Ministry of the Interior is a case in point. In the years 1928–37 the department had a total of 12 ministers, each serving an average of eight months. The first three years alone witnessed a turnover of five ministers. The position, like many others in the central government, was used mainly as a reward to regional militarists and their protégés who came to terms, at least temporarily, with the Kuomintang.† As one ex-civil-service man in the ministry recalls, these early ministers did virtually nothing during their terms in offiice.[12] The position served no administrative purpose; it only reflected power relationships between Chiang and provincial militarists. When Chiang's relations with Feng Yü-hsiang were smooth, Feng's leading protégé was awarded the office. When Yen Hsi-shan replaced Feng as the primary threat to Chiang's power, his men in due course replaced Feng's. Thus the unstable and uneasy political situation worked against the development of a sound administrative personnel system. The inexperience and incompetence of top administrative elites, combined with the frequency of turnover, were serious enough handi-

* Li P'u-sheng, p. 962. A survey of 176 members of the CEC and the Political Council showed that they held 895 administrative posts, with an average of five positions per man. Also, Li Chih-t'ang, pp. 77–81, reveals that 13 of the most influential party leaders held 167 official posts: Chiang Kai-shek (25 posts), Yeh Ch'u-ts'ang (17), Ch'en Kuo-fu (14), Sun Fo (13), Ch'en Li-fu (12), Chang Ching-chiang (12), T. V. Soong (12), Lin Sen (11), H. H. K'ung (11), Wang Ching-wei (10), Chü Cheng (10), Tai Chi-t'ao (10), and Yü Yu-jen (10).

† The first five ministers, for example, were Hsüeh Tu-pi, who was affiliated with the warlord Feng Yü-hsiang; Tsao Tai-wen and Yang Chai-t'ai, both affiliated with Yen Hsi-shan; Liu Shang-ch'ing, affiliated with Chang Hsüeh-liang; and Li Wen-fan, who held office for only 30 days, affiliated with the Kwangtung militarists.

caps to the party's attempts to institutionalize the central administration. And the lack of a sound personnel system at lower administrative levels further crippled the entire governmental operation.

During Wang Ching-wei's term as president of the Executive Yuan (1932–35), some of his associates sought to improve the obsolete administrative bureaucracy by introducing both procedural and structural reforms. In 1933 Vice-Minister of the Interior Kan Nai-kuang, a student of political science and economics, proposed that the central government sponsor a study of administrative problems. The Commission on Administrative Efficiency was subsequently set up, with Kan and his close associates Chang Jui (Ray Chang), Hsü Hsiang-shu, and Li P'u-sheng as its key members. The commission specified its major tasks as follows: (1) to improve methods for keeping archives and to simplify procedures for handling important official documents and correspondence; (2) to design a new, effective system for classifying and filing public documents; (3) to abolish superfluous administrative agencies in order to improve efficiency and coordination.[13]

After a period of research and discussion, the commission submitted a series of detailed recommendations to the Executive Yuan. The Yuan immediately adopted and put into operation the commission's proposals regarding the first two areas studied. As for the third the Yuan took the following steps: it amalgamated the numerous existing river conservation agencies into the National Economic Council; it abolished all agencies dealing with agricultural reforms and rural cooperatives and turned over their functions to the Ministry of Industry; it integrated the administrations of various wireless enterprises into the Ministry of Communications; and it shifted the responsibility for eliminating the opium trade from the Opium Prohibition Commission to the Military Council, headed by Chiang Kai-shek.[14]

In addition, the commission sought improvements in the publication of official documentary reports and journals.[15] Modern publication requires adequate funds, competent personnel, and, above all, reliable statistics. Needless to say, such statistics are also indispensable to the effective administration of a modern government. Some leading Kuomintang members—notably H. H. K'ung, T. V. Soong, and Wang's associates in the Ministries of Industry and the Interior—showed an awareness of this problem. By the mid-1930's most ministries had assigned personnel to take charge of statistical and accounting matters. Not surprisingly, the statistical bureaus of the Ministry of the Interior and the Ministry of Industry were the best organized and financed of these groups. Since the bureau at the Ministry of Industry was in charge of national economic development, the accuracy of its information was especially important. In 1932 the ministry began to prepare the first *Economic Yearbook*, working on a budget as low as Ch $20,000. Through a diligent search the ministry was able to recruit competent scholars to assist with the project. The members of the publication committee took great interest in making the yearbook a profitable venture, and after the first issue it was financed by the profits of previous years.[16]

Still, despite these partial successes, duplication and a lack of cooperation among personnel in different ministries generally characterized the statistical operation of the central bureaucracy. Conflicting statistical information from different departments frequently appeared. The problem was related to shortcomings at lower administrative levels. County governments simply could not handle the difficult daily paper work required by the provincial and central governments. Ch'en Kung-po, the minister of industry in the 1930's, vividly described this problem: "Once we dispatched some people to conduct a field survey in Hunan. After they had finished, county officials took advantage of the opportunity and used the information they had gathered to fill in forms from provincial and national administrative offices that had been accumulating for a long period of time."[17] Without the surveyors the county officials simply did not have the information to fill in the forms required by their supervisors. And when county or provincial authorities did submit official reports, they were often full of errors.*

Finally, the Commission on Administrative Efficiency dealt with possible reductions in daily operating costs, especially in the Executive Yuan and its subordinate ministries. For example, in 1933 the budget for vehicles for use by central government officials was approximately Ch $900,000, with an average monthly cost of Ch $180 per vehicle.[18] Some commission members, as well as other critics,

---

* Lo Tun-wei, p. 77. A county in Kiangsu, for example, reported that the number of chickens in the county exceeded the total number of eggs produced during the year.

thought this figure was much too high and attributed it to mismanagement and improper supervision. The commission hurriedly formulated a policy of retrenchment, which was adopted by the Executive Yuan. One official source contended that the new policy saved the central government over Ch $6 million during the fiscal year 1935–36.[19]

The commission undoubtedly made some positive contributions to the efficiency of the central administration. However, the limitations on what it could do or propose are clear. Reforms tended to involve noncontroversial procedural and technical matters. Unfortunately, the modernizing elites in the Executive Yuan were by and large tied to Wang Ching-wei, whose political power was slipping. Wang's peripheral role in the Kuomintang power structure prevented him from undertaking more drastic reforms in his own administrative bureaucracy. Chiang Kai-shek and his clients kept close watch over Wang to make sure that he was not adding to his own power and prestige. Further, the commission completely neglected the problems involved in building a centralized bureaucracy under which the provincial administrations could be restructured. True, administrations in provinces where Nanking's authority did not reach would have been little affected by central bureaucratic change anyway. But several provinces that were more or less controlled by Nanking gradually fell under the jurisdiction of Chiang Kai-shek's bandit suppression headquarters at Nanchang.

In sum, during its first decade the Kuomintang regime did little toward developing a modern administrative system. The bureaucracy apparently lacked the human and material resources to be effective, and random attempts at reform were insignificant. Power elites never seriously emphasized the bureaucracy as a source of authority or an instrument of national integration. What then was the regime's most effective governing institution? Where did power and resources lie, and where were policy measures actually carried out? Specifically, to what extent did the Kuomintang, which considered itself the only legitimate political party, perform as an effective institution in nation-building? This is the question we shall consider next.

The Kuomintang

After the reorganization of 1924, one of the party's main goals was to strengthen its effectiveness as a revolutionary force. This could conceivably have increased its effectiveness as a substitute for the dysfunctional administrative bureaucracy as well. One study of the party's activities in the 1928–31 period, however, has revealed that in fact the Kuomintang was organizationally weak and functionally incompetent.[20] It lacked a comprehensive, persuasive ideology capable of uniting the people behind its leadership. Sun Yat-sen had attempted to outline such an ideology in his Three People's Principles; however, this program did not have the power to arouse popular commitment or to create cohesive sociopolitical forces. Instead of fostering sociopolitical change the party increasingly accommodated its values to those of the traditional elites. As Mary C. Wright has noted, during the prewar decade the Kuomintang gradually shifted from advocating revolution to supporting the status quo in rural China.[21] This naturally increased its appeal to the privileged elements of society, who hoped it would assume the government's traditional role of maintaining order and indoctrinating the peasantry. The party's increasing dependence on such a base gradually stripped away its potential as an independent institutional force capable of transforming society.

The Kuomintang was also hampered by divergent views of its role among party elites, which often became the basis for factional struggles. Personality clashes and polarization along ideological lines overshadowed the needs of the party. This lack of consensus among leading elites sometimes threatened to tear apart the still shaky organization. For example, members of the CEC and the Supervisory Committee belonging to the conservative Western Hills Group, which generally opposed the 1924 reorganization and the KMT-CCP united front, held separate meetings in 1925 as a protest against the newly created party-government in Kwangtung.[22] Later, in 1931, Chiang Kai-shek and Hu Han-min clashed over whether or not the party-state needed a provisional constitution during the period of political tutelage. Largely because of his objection to Chiang's proposed constitution, Hu was taken into protective custody—a harsh, humiliating action that alienated Kwangtung party politicians from the Kuomintang center for many years.[23]

The events following the collapse of the first KMT-CCP united front (1923–27) and the establishment of the Nanking Government in 1927 clearly indicate the party's inadequate preparation for the problem of unifying the country. Procedures for recruiting members,

TABLE 1

Estimated Kuomintang Membership, 1932–35

Class and type of membership	1932	1933	1934	1935
Regular party:				
Regular	296,470	306,824	327,818	347,299
Probationary	66,332	79,544	114,263	149,097
TOTAL	362,802	386,368	442,081	496,396
Overseas:				
Regular	86,125	85,634	90,619	89,215
Probationary	12,913	15,510	13,940	9,959
TOTAL	99,038	101,144	104,559	99,174
Armed forces:				
Regular	435,210	445,935	462,533	491,592
Probationary	235,412	338,260	409,086	533,989
TOTAL	670,622	784,195	871,619	1,025,581

SOURCE: Yang Yu-chiung, *Chung-kuo cheng-tang shih* (A history of Chinese political parties; Shanghai, 1936), p. 200.

for instance, were so cumbersome and complex that they discouraged rather than encouraged interest.[24] By 1930 the total number of registered members, excluding those in the army and overseas branches, was estimated at not over 300,000.[25] Membership figures do vary from source to source, but one relatively reliable authority estimates party strength between 1932 and 1935 as shown in Table 1. Membership figures from the armed forces have little meaning, since party membership was often compulsory in the military. Also, it is conceivable that when an army commander joined the party, all the men under him were automatically reported to be party members. Most of the subordinates of Li Tsung-jen, Yen Hsi-shan, Chang Hsüeh-liang, Feng Yü-hsiang, and Ch'en Chi-t'ang were supposedly party members, for example, although they could and did defy Nanking's authority in support of their commanders.

Civilian membership figures, including both regular and probationary members, stood below half a million in 1935. (Overseas civilian members are excluded, since they had little to do with domestic politics except for making occasional financial contributions.) This was small indeed, considering the Kuomintang was in power in a land with a population of several hundred million. If the revolutionary goals the party had long advocated were to be realized, it was necessary to have considerably more participation and support at the grassroots level. The party's lack of interest in recruitment is reflected in the official record. According to the *Kuomintang Yearbook,* registered civilian members increased by only 24,847 between 1929 and 1934 (see Table 2). Kwangtung province, the original sanctuary of the party, together with the city of Canton, continued to provide about one-fourth of the party membership. The party-government's home provinces, Chekiang and Kiangsu, showed little gain during the five-year period. In fact, in all the provinces where the Nanking Government had significant influence, increases in party membership were at best marginal. Among the provinces and major cities only Szechwan and Nanking showed major gains, from 77 to 19,444 members and from 5,563 to 10,522, respectively.* Nanking's increase was definitely related to the fact that it was the center of the civil and party bureaucracies.

The distribution of membership implies two important characteristics of the party. First, membership was heavily concentrated in urban areas. Using figures from Table 2, we find that six major cities— Canton, Shanghai, Hankow, Nanking, Peking, and Tientsin—together accounted for 30,226 members in 1929, or 11.36 percent of the total, and 38,383 members in 1934, or 13.20 percent. Second, geographically the party's strength lay in Kwangtung and the Bandit Suppression Provinces—Hunan, Kiangsi, Hupeh, Kiangsu, Chekiang, Anhwei, Honan, Fukien, Kansu, and Shensi. Again using figures from Table 2, we find that the Bandit Suppression Provinces (including their major cities, Shanghai, Hankow, and Nanking) accounted for 135,606 members in 1929, or 50.92 percent of the total, and 147,526 members in 1934, or 50.66 percent. When we add the figures from Kwangtung province, the number of members equals about 80 percent of the total. This distribution reveals the Kuomintang's regional nature, which undoubtedly undermined whatever plans the party had for national unification and development. Even in the Bandit Suppression Provinces, the increase in membership between 1929 and 1934 was only 11,920.

* The 1934 Szechwan figure is extremely dubious. As Kapp's article reveals the Kuomintang was not able to force its way into the province until 1936. I am inclined to believe that the figure was used by the central regime as a pretext for penetration.

TABLE 2

Kuomintang Membership in the Provinces and Major Cities,
1929 and 1934

Registration location	No. of party members		Pct. of total membership	
	1929	1934	1929	1934
Canton	10,277	10,290	3.86%	3.53%
Shanghai	6,234	8,730	2.34	3.01
Hankow	5,610	5,907	2.11	2.03
Nanking	5,563	10,522	2.09	3.61
Peking	1,770	1,838	.67	.64
Tientsin	772	1,096	.29	.38
Kwangtung	62,775	63,260	23.57	21.73
Hunan	20,958	21,606	7.87	7.42
Kiangsi	20,881	21,190	7.84	7.28
Hopei	17,128	18,438	6.43	6.33
Hupeh	16,080	16,329	6.04	5.61
Kiangsu	15,508	15,556	5.82	5.34
Chekiang	12,530	14,554	4.71	5.00
Anhwei	11,961	12,006	4.49	4.12
Honan	8,060	8,112	3.03	2.79
Shansi	8,047	9,124	3.02	3.13
Fukien	7,569	7,902	2.84	2.71
Kwangsi	7,199	7,199	2.70	2.47
Shantung	7,129	8,032	2.68	2.76
Kansu	3,576	4,036	1.34	1.39
Suiyuan	1,787	1,987	.67	.68
Liaoning	1,675	—	.63	—
Shensi	1,076	1,076	.40	.37
Chahar	963	967	.36	.33
Kirin	739	—	.28	—
Yunnan	509	1,221	.19	.42
Kweichow	451	500	.17	.17
Heilungkiang	365	—	.14	—
Szechwan	77	19,444	.03	6.68
Tsinghai	—	184	—	.06
Ningsia	—	79	—	.02
Classified party cards	9,069	—	3.41	—
TOTAL	266,338	291,185	100.02%	100.01%

SOURCE: *Chung-kuo Kuo-min-tang nien-chien*, 1929, p. 739, and 1934, p. (Z)39. A dash indicates no record available.
NOTE: Percentages do not add up to 100 because of rounding.

The weakness of the party is further revealed in its inefficient communications system. Inquiries addressed to party headquarters from provincial and municipal bureaus indicate that party routines were not well understood or well established.[26] Such inquiries were often elementary questions about the party's operation and programs. One example of the striking absence of procedural routine is revealed in a survey conducted from June to October 1929 by the Central Propaganda Department. The purpose of the survey was to evaluate the propaganda activities of provincial and municipal bureaus. Although the department required regular written reports from these bureaus, only a few filed them. In fact, there were almost no reports from the entire regions of Manchuria, Inner Mongolia (including Shensi), and the southwest (including Szechwan).[27] In a joint report to the National Party Congress convened in late 1931, the CEC and the Central Supervisory Committee severely criticized the party for its failure to spread propaganda. The report found that the Kuomintang had no uniform program to promote party policy and party spirit.[28]

The joint report also pointed out the weakness of the party's training and indoctrination activities. Since the party had not developed a mass base, members had to act as a revolutionary cadre. Thus the issue of how to train members and probationary members was critical. As the report indicated, however, the central party had not yet worked out a practical training program;[29] this indeed was its major crisis. The party was also ineffective in preparing probationary members for regular membership. Between 1931 and 1933 only 11,526 civilian probationary members became regular members.[30] According to a review of the membership situation by the central headquarters in 1929, there was a wide variation in reports received from the training divisions of provincial bureaus, ranging from three reports from Szechwan to 136 from Chekiang.[31] Very few provincial and municipal branches kept the central party informed of what they were doing. From 1931 to 1934 only three cities (Nanking, Shanghai, and Hankow) and seven provinces (Chekiang, Kiangsu, Anhwei, Kiangsi, Hunan, Honan, and Hupeh—all but Honan middle and lower Yangtze valley provinces) submitted detailed reports of their training activities. This dismal situation was partly due to the fact that after 1928 the party tended to stress organizational activities over training and indoctrination programs. Thus these programs contributed little toward nation-building. In fact, the Kuomintang's failure in this area led to the increasing alienation of the people from the party.[32]

Even in the area the party chose to emphasize, organization, results were poor. By the end of 1933, at most only 11 provinces had actually established party branches.[33] The others had merely appointed a temporary party affairs directory committee or simply had a party agent. The executive and supervisory committees that normally served as forerunners of formal party bureaus were not set up in the majority of the provinces. Party development was even more limited at the lower levels of the city and the county (*hsien*). According to one official source, by the end of 1932 only six cities and 348 of China's 1,890 counties had established local party branches.[34] Significantly, seven provinces—Chekiang, Kiangsi, Kwangtung, Hunan, Honan, Hupeh, and Kiangsu—accounted for 330 county branches and five city branches, over 94 percent of the total. These figures are further evidence of the geographical concentration of the party's strength in the lower and middle Yangtze valley.

This geographical pattern reflected relations between the central government in Nanking and various regional forces. In areas where local political and military forces were unfriendly or hostile to Chiang Kai-shek's authority, party strength in terms of both membership and organizational development was quite limited. With the exception of Kwangtung, which was controlled by militarists and party politicians unfriendly to the Nanking Government, the party's domain extended only as far as Chiang's military power. It is evident that the institutional development of the party was a residual effect of military penetration. The party was not organized enough to serve as an independent political instrument for national integration.

Certainly, financial limitations were responsible to some extent for the ineffectual role of the party in the provinces. As we will see later the budget allocated for party affairs was often very small compared with other items of public spending. These allocations were especially small in light of the party's need to establish a broad-based national organization. To put it simply, party development was not considered a priority program by the central Kuomintang government or most of the provinces.

This account of the party's poor performance would not be complete without mentioning the complicated system of clique politics.

Fighting within the party was frequent. Lower-level cadres often aligned themselves with clique interests, which consequently impeded party development. Ch'en Kuo-fu and Ch'en Li-fu, who controlled the Central Organization Department from 1926 to 1936, had great difficulty establishing branch organizations in the Bandit Suppression Provinces, where, after 1931, they were opposed by Yang Yung-t'ai and his associates in the Political Study Clique. Also, from 1933 on the Ch'en's lower cadres clashed with members of the Blue Shirt Society over control of local party organizations in Chekiang and Kiangsu.[35] In Kwangtung, too, and in many other provinces, local leaders and elites fought hard to resist penetration by Nanking's party headquarters.

Party Decision-Making Structures

The limitations of the Kuomintang as an effective political institution are clear enough. It had a narrow geographic base, a fragmented structure, and few institutionalized routines. Given these limitations, it is questionable whether the party could have accomplished the task of mass mobilization even if there had been no war with Japan. One can also speculate about whether the weakness of the party tended to reinforce, if not precipitate, the growth of political machines. Problems of succession and top-level decision making created a crisis of legitimacy that further contributed to the party's paralysis.

Sun Yat-sen's domination of party decision making created severe problems after his death. As one historian has pointed out: "When Sun died in March, 1925, the Party had no routine, no administrative system, no plans for a National Congress, no organized executive committee with both a clear right to rule the Party and experience in doing so, and no clear channel of authority for the resolution of intra-Party conflicts."[36] Consequently, the party witnessed a series of intense power struggles among competing leaders and their carefully constructed political machines. The lack of a ruling structure explains why the party was never able to cultivate its legitimate status in the face of organized military power in the party-state and why Chiang Kai-shek could rise to the top by military means.[37]

The question of leadership succession and political legitimacy are critical issues in dealing with political change and development. As

Myron Rush, in a study of the problems of political succession in the Soviet Union, has perceptively observed: "The central question in political succession is that of legitimacy: by what right does the successor (if any) rule? Every revolution leaves as its legacy the questionable legitimacy of the ruler."[38] The problem of legitimate political succession in the Kuomintang was particularly acute in the absence of an institutional arrangement for succession. Every political system, according to David Easton, "has roles through which authority is wielded and some rules governing the use and exercise of this political power. The fact of occupying these roles and of abiding by the rules applying to them will normally in and of itself place the seal of moral approval upon the authorities."[39] This assumes there is no conflict over the validity of authority roles and related norms. In China during the 1920's and 1930's, however, the validity of authority roles was unclear. Moreover, there were no definite, institutionalized political structures through which the occupation of such roles could be made valid. The significance of this point will become clearer in our subsequent examination of the structure of the party-state.

Party statutes stipulated that the highest policy-making body was the National Congress or, when the congress was adjourned, the Central Executive Committee. (The Central Supervisory Committee had only disciplinary powers and nominal control of party finances.) However, the National Congress and later the Central Executive Committee gradually became simply "ratification conventions" and "sounding boards." Neither really had the power to make policy decisions. The loss of power by the National Congress is not surprising. It was always too large to be effective. In the first congress, convened in 1924, there were some 165 delegates. In the following two decades membership increased to 600. Furthermore, the party congress was never convened regularly. There were only four congresses between 1926 and 1937, instead of one every two years as required by party statutes.

The Central Executive Committee also gradually lost its effectiveness. It did convene to discuss various issues and did pass resolutions, but most of these involved rather trivial matters. Important questions regarding security, finances, and foreign policy, for instance, were rarely brought before it; and if they were, the committee made only token decisions. The committee as a whole was gradually transformed into a mere status institution, and senior party politicians whose influence was slipping were given positions on the CEC to prevent them from becoming completely alienated from the party. This trend is best shown by the body's fast-growing membership: 24 members in 1924, 36 in 1926, 71 in 1931, and 119 in 1935.[40] The plenary sessions of the committee, though more frequent than those of the congress, were held irregularly. The committee elected in 1929 held seven sessions between 1929 and 1931; the 1935 committee held only three sessions between 1935 and 1937, when the country was on the eve of a tremendous crisis. All in all, there were only 22 sessions between 1926 and 1937.

As both the National Congress and the CEC grew larger, decision-making power was often exercised by the Standing Committee of the CEC. The Standing Committee, composed of three to 15 leading party figures, was given the power to supervise party routine between sessions of the CEC, as well as to convene the CEC and the congress. Most important decisions on party affairs were to be made by this committee. It was also to supervise propaganda activities, the training of members, and the appointment and dismissal of ranking party officers.[41] Although the Standing Committee did provide an institutional base of legitimacy for party policy, as a body it was seriously handicapped in supervising party activities. For one thing, most of its members also had military or civil administrative duties, which left them little time and energy for party matters. For another, major political decisions affecting government operations and military administration were reserved for the Political Council, the party body that gradually acquired the greatest importance in the Nanking period. After 1931 the nine members of the CEC's Standing Committee served concurrently as members of the Political Council's Standing Committee.[42]

The Political Council (Cheng-chih Hui-i) had its origins in the Political Committee (Cheng-chih Wei-yuan-hui), established in 1924 as a consultative body to Sun Yat-sen, the party's undisputed leader and chairman of both the National Congress and the CEC. Sun held an absolute veto over decisions of the CEC and a suspensive veto over decisions of the congress.[43] Chiang Kai-shek was among the first 12 appointees to the Political Committee and one of only three who did not also hold a position on the CEC or the Central Supervisory Committee.

At first the Political Committee was not an official party organ; its powers were not clearly defined, and in practice it functioned only as a personal advisory body to Dr. Sun. In June 1925, however, after Sun's death, the CEC passed this resolution: "The Political Committee is to be established in the Kuomintang's Central Executive Committee to guide the progress of national revolution; political goals will be determined and executed by the Political Committee in the name of the party-government."[44] This was the first step toward the institutionalization of the committee, although its functions were still vague and unspecified. From this beginning the body eventually became the party-state's supreme decision-making organ, at least in theory, as this semiofficial statement issued in 1929 by Hu Han-min and Sun Fo reveals:

The Political Council is the guiding and directory organ for the task of national tutelage. . . . It is a party-affiliated organ for the management of party affairs. It is not a government organ; yet it initiates the government's fundamental policies. In other words, the Political Council is endowed with the power to determine fundamental goals in the period of political tutelage. It is the only link between party and government. The party's fundamental guidelines for national policy will be passed through the Political Council to the government for execution. . . . The Nationalist Government, though officially regarded as the highest political organ in the nation, has to subordinate itself to the Political Council in the matter of policy execution.[45]

In July 1926 the Central Executive Committee passed a resolution officially establishing the Political Council as a formal party body. The first 24 members were members of the CEC's Standing Committee and the existing Political Committee. The Organizational Principles of the Political Council, promulgated the same year, specified a wide range of activities that were to fall under the council's jurisdiction. It was to determine administrative guidelines, legislative principles, and the basic policies of national reconstruction; to control financial planning and military administration and policy; and to appoint high-level party and government bureaucrats.[46] The Central Political Council was first located in Canton, then in Wuhan, and finally in Nanking. Following the Northern Expedition branch councils were set up in Canton, Wuhan, Peking, and Taiyuan, reflecting the distribution of power among different political forces in the party.

By the end of 1926 the Political Council had held 57 sessions in Canton. During the first three months of 1927, 17 sessions were held in Nanchang. The name was changed back and forth from Political Committee to Political Council until March 1927, when the CEC, with the majority of members in Wuhan, settled on Political Committee. The CEC also redefined membership status, dividing the committee into voting and nonvoting members. There were 15 voting members—nine from the Standing Committee of the CEC and six others to be elected by the general session of the CEC. The number of nonvoting members was not specified; all ministers of the Nationalist Government were given this status. The committee was supposed to move to Nanking after the establishment of the government there in April 1927, but most members continued to hold meetings in Wuhan until August. Disputes between Kuomintang leaders in the Wuhan and Nanking governments prevented normal operations; and a Central Special Committee was set up, mainly through the mediation efforts of the Western Hills Group, to perform the functions of the CEC and the Political Committee from September to December 1927.[47] In 1928 the fifth plenum of the Second CEC, now composed entirely of Kuomintang members after the collapse of the KMT-CCP united front, revived the Political Council and elected 46 members. The new organizational rules adopted Political Council as the body's official name, which was confirmed by the Fourth Party Congress.

The 1929 organizational rules of the Political Council were revised several times before the Fourth Party Congress in December 1931. Attempts were made there to cut the council's size in order to improve its efficiency, but in the end the congress decided to expand its membership.[48] This was done to bring in various factions as a gesture of national unity in the face of the recent Japanese military activity in Manchuria. The council's membership thus grew to 172, including all regular and alternate members of the CEC and the Central Supervisory Committee. In 1935 the number of members was increased again, this time to 200. As the Political Council grew larger, it had more and more difficulty performing its normal functions. The regular weekly meetings were confusing and ineffectual, and the council had to rely on various subcommittees on law, finance, economics, education, diplomacy, politics, and military affairs to do its work. Even if members had wanted to devote all their time to the discussion and formulation of public policy, their other administrative and party positions would not have permitted it.

The widening scope of the council's activities was as much of a problem as its growing size. Amidst the hundreds and thousands of small problems assigned to the body, the initial purpose, to direct and supervise government policies, was gradually forgotten. Much time was given over to dealing with detailed, often inconsequential business.* Ch'ien Tuan-sheng sums up the situation like this: "As the volume of business transacted by the Political Council is enormous, the recommendations of its committees [subcommittees] are usually accepted by the council without much discussion. As far as routine business is concerned, it is rather the committees than the council that enjoy the high powers of government."[49]

One of the most important of the subcommittees was the Standing Committee, originally composed of Chiang Kai-shek, Wang Ching-wei, and Hu Han-min. In 1932 the third plenum of the Fourth CEC decided to expand the committee to include all nine members of the CEC's Standing Committee. This was done because Chiang, Wang, and Hu were frequently away from Nanking for long periods of time, which naturally prevented the committee from functioning.[50] The committee now included leading figures of the party-state representing various factions. Whether or not the body could function effectively depended on the degree of consensus and cooperation among these men. When conflicts of opinion arose Chiang Kai-shek's group usually showed little willingness to bargain or compromise with the other members, who had neither military nor client organizations to back them up. As a result, the committee, even with such a small membership, rarely met to discuss major policies in the 1930's.†

The evidence, then, suggests that the Kuomintang did not develop

---

* Still another problem was that the policies of the regional branch councils, which continued to exist until the mid-1930's, often conflicted with those of the central council.

† In the late 1930's Ch'en Chih-mai wrote perceptively of this state of paralysis gripping the Standing Committee and other party decision-making bodies. According to him, only two minor members of the Standing Committee stayed in Nanking during the summer of 1935. Chiang Kai-shek spent most of his time in Changtu (Szechwan) directing a military campaign against the Communists. Wang Ching-wei was away from Nanking on "sick leave," and Hu Han-min was abroad, showing not the slightest interest in the party-state's affairs. Sun Fo, the head of the Legislative Yuan, was taking a long summer vacation in Tsingtao, a seaport and summer resort in Shangtung. Yü Yu-jen and Ku Meng-yü stayed in Shanghai because of "illness." Ch'en Kuo-fu, the governor of Kiangsu, had to remain in Chinkiang, the provincial capital. This left only Chü Cheng and Yeh Ch'u-ts'ang, both identified as leaders of the then powerless Western Hills Group, in Nanking. Under these circumstances various government and party bodies were forced to consult Chiang or Wang by telegram on any important matters. See Ch'en Chih-mai, "Kuo-min-tang," p. 623.

institutionalized structures to govern the party-state. This is a crucial failure, considering that the theory of the party-state was based on a one-party dictatorship. There was no institutional base of legitimacy, and channels of command were irregular. Thus it was possible for various client factions to gain control of the processes of decision making and policy implementation. Unhampered by effective institutional constraints these groups were able to use governmental authority and resources in a way that seriously alienated other political groups. The institutional limitations of the party were compounded by its rudimentary efforts in spreading propaganda, recruiting members, and developing a national party organization. It simply proved incapable of reaching the great mass of Chinese. Lloyd Eastman's remark that "the Kuomintang . . . ruled over the people and permitted them virtually no independent or constructive political action"[51] overestimates the party as a ruling instrument. The size of China, its political diversity, and the complexity of its social and economic problems required a far more effective institutional framework than the party provided.

The Military

With both the party and the civil administration proving ineffectual as instruments for nation-building and policy implementation, the 1930's saw a clear tendency toward the militarization of politics and administration. This tendency was closely related to Chiang Kai-shek's rise to power and to his skillful control of the military, as well as to a series of crisis circumstances that rationalized militarization. The Northern Expedition that placed Chiang in charge of the National Revolutionary Army and the Military Council never really succeeded in uniting China. Regional military forces unwilling to comply with central authority continued to exist in the decade after 1927. Further, after 1930 the ever-present threat from Japan overshadowed other issues in the minds of Kuomintang leaders. The situation was also complicated by the Communist Party's increasing activity among the desperate peasant population. All of these factors provided a justification for the growing military control of the regime. And the man who built this control, Chiang-Kai-shek, was a master of manipulation.

To understand how the military exercised power in Kuomintang

China, we must examine its systems of command and administration and their development. The highest governing body of the military was the Military Council, first established in 1925 in Canton. Composed of eight major departments and bureaus, the council was in charge of military policy, command, and administration.[52] The creation of the National Revolutionary Army on the eve of the Northern Expedition in 1926 deprived the council of much of its power and jurisdiction, although power continued to rest with its chairman, Chiang Kai-shek, who was also the commander-in-chief of the army. After the Northern Expedition and the formal establishment of the party-government in 1928, both the Military Council and the National Revolutionary Army headquarters were abolished. A number of more diversified offices took over their functions. Powers previously held by the council, for example, were now "vested in the war ministry, the general staff, and the military advisory council."[53] According to the Nanking Government's organizational law, the military machinery would be under the authority of the president of the national government; thus as president Chiang would continue to control it. The large number of new military offices and titles served as political rewards for regional militarists who had cooperated with the Kuomintang during the Northern Expedition.[54]

After 1928 the power of the military steadily increased at the expense of both the party and the government.[55] Continuing threats to Nanking kept military priorities and influence high. In late 1931 the formal institutional basis of military power was strengthened by a dramatic reorganization of the party-government. All real power was stripped from the president of the republic, the newly appointed Lin Sen, and the president of the Executive Yuan, Wang Ching-wei, was given a wide range of administrative authority, at least on paper. This redefinition of institutional power in the central government was partially intended to eliminate internal dissension among Kuomintang leaders. But the most significant outcome was the resurrection of the National Military Council under the chairmanship of Chiang Kai-shek. By now, the Japanese had already created an incident in Manchuria; and they gave every indication of having greater territorial ambitions in North China. Also, the Kuomintang government had already engaged in a number of military campaigns against the Communists, who were active in the rural areas of the lower Yangtze valley provinces. Both these threats provided Chiang with a solid rationale for expanding his authority.

According to the theory of political tutelage, the CEC had the right to make final decisions on military matters. Since Chiang was able to gain control over the CEC, however, it merely served to authorize whatever policy measures he wanted. As the accompanying organizational chart shows, the entire military machinery now came under the direct jurisdiction of the Military Council.* In addition, the council maintained an extensive administrative apparatus of its own. Many of its administrative activities overlapped with those constitutionally assigned to the Executive Yuan in the 1931 reorganization and with those of the party's central headquarters. Through the council Chiang also appointed more than twelve commanders in the bandit suppression campaigns against the Communists. Many of these titles went to provincial militarists whose support he sought.† Since the commanders were actually appointed by the council instead of by high party bodies, they were under the council's military and administrative control.

Although the Military Council had its headquarters in Nanking, Chiang exercised its power wherever he went. After 1930, in his persistent pursuit of the Communists, he traveled frequently in Kiangsi, Anhwei, Hunan, Hupeh, and Honan. In 1932 he set up his commanding headquarters in Hankow to direct anti-Communist operations in Hupeh, Anhwei, and Kiangsi. A year later he established field headquarters in Nanchang (Kiangsi); these were later moved to Wuchang (Hupeh) and in 1935 to Chungking. In each place the field headquarters served as the supreme headquarters of military command and as an administrative center that was to exercise authority over all the Bandit Suppression Provinces through an administrative hierarchy independent of Nanking. It was in these temporary headquarters (among which Nanchang was especially important) that major mili-

---

* The Ministry of War was officially placed under the joint jurisdiction of the Military Council and the Executive Yuan. In fact, however, the ministry usually took its orders from the council, since Chiang was able to secure the ministry position for one of his political clients.

† Some regional militarists accepted the titles; others turned them down. For example, Chang Hsüeh-liang served as Chiang's deputy-commander-in-chief of the anti-Communist operations in Honan, Hupeh, and Anhwei in 1934; but Ch'en Chi-t'ang refused to accept the title of commander-in-chief of the anti-Communist campaigns in Kwangtung, Fukien, and Hunan in the early 1930's.

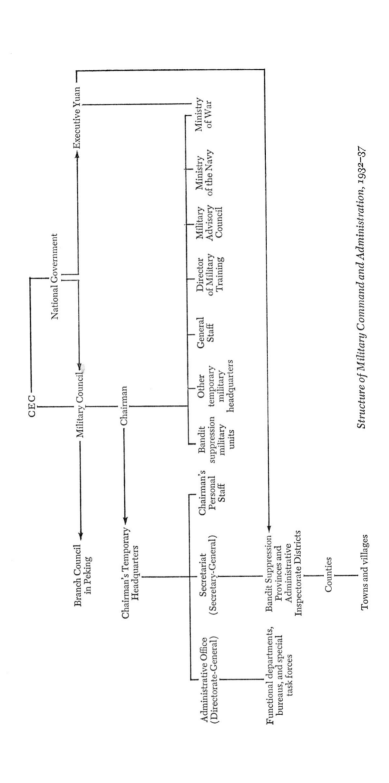

Structure of Military Command and Administration, 1932–37

tary, party, and administrative policies were actually discussed and determined; then they were submitted to Nanking for formal ratification.

This whole process can be called the militarization of the Kuomintang regime. In effect, the regime's center of authority shifted from Nanking to the locations of Chiang's military headquarters. Chiang's reliance on particularistic values and patron-client relationships resulted in the personalization of the enormous military administrative bureaucracy, which further weakened the already shaky government bureaucracy and the ineffective party apparatus. The formal party organs did not make decisions; they merely approved measures already decided on by the informal groups around Chiang. The civil administrative bureaucracy did a lot of paper work but had no real chance to implement policy.

In retrospect, our evidence reveals that the Kuomintang's efforts to build a modern party and an administrative bureaucracy were rudimentary. Although the causes of this failure are complex, the regime's concentration on military affairs undoubtedly prevented the party-state from developing nonmilitary structures. The domination of political power and financial resources by military men, namely Chiang Kai-shek and his colleagues, deprived civilian leaders of the ways and means to establish such structures. The Nanking decade never saw a healthy balance of power and influence between Chiang's military-oriented groups and the party elites. Civilian leaders whose interests lay in administrative reforms and modernization programs were inevitably alienated.

Chiang's military apparatus did attempt to provide institutional alternatives in the provinces gradually brought under its jurisdiction. Informal client groups loyal to Chiang embarked on a series of administrative reforms, which produced some results. But the achievements were by and large piecemeal. Institutional changes were too often dictated by immediate military considerations. Further, there was no genuine cooperation among Chiang's client groups themselves; they were never able to develop a systematic program of institutional change that all could support. The chief architect of the military-oriented provincial institutions, Yang Yung-t'ai, was assassinated in 1936, and the fate of his programs in the hazardous military and political circumstances after his death was unclear. Thus, even before China declared war against Japan in 1937, it was uncertain whether Chiang and his followers could fill the vacuum created by the lack of effective party and government structures. Their efforts will be examined in later chapters.

THREE

Factions in Kuomintang Politics

CHINESE POLITICS in the 1920's operated in a weak institutional milieu, and the establishment of the Nanking Government brought little change. Though it destroyed the rules of the previous political game and the institutionalized mechanisms enforcing them, the new regime soon discovered the difficulty of developing new rules and governing institutions. The absence of a functioning decision-making mechanism and the inability of the civil administration to translate authority and demands into policy contributed to the continuing reliance on informal, particularistic political processes. Factions operated in the political arena as the most sensible alternative to a system in which authority was so diffused.

There were two levels of factional politics in the Kuomintang. One level involved rivalries for control of the regime's legitimate authority and the official institutions designated to exercise this authority, the CEC and the Political Council. These struggles were often expressed in terms of who rightfully inherited the Kuomintang's revolutionary legacy; at stake was survival in the system. Chiang Kai-shek faced this kind of challenge from Wang Ching-wei and Hu Han-min at the center and from certain provincial forces—the Kuomintang leaders in Kwangtung and Kwangsi, on the one hand, and Feng Yü-hsiang and Yen Hsi-shan, on the other. The second level of factional politics involved groups within Chiang's own power structure, namely, the C.C. Clique, the Blue Shirt Society, and the Political Study Clique. These groups were competing at the level of policy implementation— one stage beyond the activities of the CEC and the Political Council and the stage where power was in fact wielded and the regime's scarce resources were allocated. The growing organizational and territorial strength of the various factions under Chiang's authority enhanced his position against his rivals in the National Government.

The status of Wang Ching-wei and Hu Han-min in the Nanking Government was the legacy of party politics before 1927. As the party's senior politicians they continued to command respect and support from the left and the right, respectively. Their presence on the political scene provided potential alternatives to Chiang's leadership. No wonder, then, that conventional analyses of Kuomintang politics in this period tend to assume that Chiang, Wang, and Hu formed a ruling triumvirate.[1] According to this line of analysis, Chiang Kai-shek had to rely on an alliance with Hu from 1928 to 1931 and on one with Wang from 1932 to 1935.[2] The political situation in the late 1920's and early 1930's substantiates this to only a limited extent, however. When there were regional forces presenting a serious challenge to Nanking's authority, Hu and Wang assumed some importance. Hu had a considerable following in Kwangtung and, to a lesser extent, Kwangsi, whose leaders were hostile toward Nanking during most of the 1930's. Wang, also from Kwangtung, attempted to form coalitions with the Kwangtung-Kwangsi generals and with the forces of Feng Yü-hsiang and Yen Hsi-shan in the north. All of these coalitions fell apart, however, partly because Chiang took skillful measures against them and partly because they were unstable from the beginning. Temporary displeasure with Nanking could not sustain a strong, permanent alliance.

Thus Chiang's leading opponents, though able to survive with a certain degree of status, were frustrated in the pursuit of genuine power. Chiang's followers tightly controlled financial, military, and party affairs, and they guarded their power with a growing police and security network. Still, although Wang, Hu, Yen, Feng, and the southern militarists posed no real threat to Chiang's supremacy, the existence of factional opposition did circumscribe his political behavior on many occasions. It narrowed his range of choices and at times compelled him to devote considerable energy to breaking up hostile coalitions. Ch'en Ch'eng's importance in Chiang's political structure lay precisely in performing this function.[3]

An emphasis on factional politics at the top does not lead us very far in comprehending the development of the Kuomintang regime.

Instead, it was the other kind of factional politics, the competition among groups within Chiang's own power structure, that was responsible for most of the political change at this time. The C.C. Clique, the Blue Shirts, and the Political Study Clique transformed the Kuomintang as a party and carried out the policies of the regime. They constituted the hard core of Chiang's anti-Communist campaigns and encouraged his obsession with them. Finally, they were better organized than other political groups and were often instrumental in Chiang's dealings with the regional militarists. For good or bad, they were the major force in Chiang's search for a formula of national integration. Since they were critical elements in China's political development before 1937, each of these factions or cliques will be examined in detail.

The C.C. Clique

The C.C. Clique, also known as the Organization Clique, was led by two brothers, Ch'en Kuo-fu and Ch'en Li-fu. There has been no official explanation of the meaning of "C.C." It could stand either for the two Ch'ens or for the Central Club, the inner core of the Kuomintang's central headquarters at the time of the Northern Expedition. At any rate, what is really important is the role of the Ch'en brothers in the development of the clique.

Ch'en Kuo-fu and Ch'en Li-fu were nephews of Ch'en Ch'i-mei, the well-known leader of the Chekiang and Kiangsu faction of the Chinese Revolutionary Party (Chung-hua Ke-ming-tang), one of the political bodies that merged to form the Kuomintang. The Ch'en brothers' intimate relationship with Chiang Kai-shek and their rise to powerful positions in the Kuomintang regime originated in Chiang's enormous respect and affection for Ch'en Ch'i-mei. According to one study, Chiang found in Ch'en a model for his own personality development.[4] Chiang had first met Ch'en Ch'i-mei in Japan in 1906 while pursuing his military education. In 1911 and 1912 he served as a regiment commander under Ch'en, then the military governor of Shanghai.[5] Although Ch'en was forced to relinquish this post in 1912, Chiang continued to follow him in subsequent years. When Ch'en was assassinated by agents of Yuan Shih-k'ai in 1916, Chiang lost a living revolutionary model. For several years afterward he traveled back and forth between Chekiang, Shanghai, Kwangtung, and Japan.

Ch'en Kuo-fu worked with Chiang when both served under Ch'en Ch'i-mei in Shanghai. Later, in 1920, the two joined Chang Ching-chiang and Tai Chi-t'ao to establish a stock and commodity exchange in Shanghai; Ch'en himself specialized in cotton stocks. These business operations enabled them to raise some funds for their political activities.[6] Chiang's relationship with Ch'en became significant in 1924, when Chiang was appointed president of the party's newly established Whampoa Military Academy in Kwangtung. Ch'en Kuo-fu served briefly as an instructor at the academy. Afterward, on Chiang's recommendation, he was made the party's representative in the Chekiang-Kiangsu-Anhwei region and was put in charge of recruiting cadets for the academy.[7] (Other recruiting agents were Yü Yu-jen in Shensi, Mao Tse-tung in Hunan, and Ting Wei-fen in Shantung.) Ch'en's three provinces provided over 4,000 recruits, who made up the vast majority of Whampoa's first and second classes.[8] His Shanghai residence became a center of secret recruitment and of communications with agents in central and North China. An additional 3,000 cadets from these regions passed through Shanghai for Whampoa in 1925, the year before the Northern Expedition.[*]

During the expedition itself Ch'en's importance grew. His Shanghai recruiting agency became Chiang's intelligence service. At the Second Party Congress in 1926, with strong support from Chiang, Tai Chi-t'ao, and Chang Ching-chiang (all from Chekiang), Ch'en was elected to the party's Central Supervisory Committee. Later in the same year he came to head the important Organization Department of the Kuomintang. The former head, T'an P'ing-shan, a Communist, had been ousted when the CEC passed Chiang Kai-shek's resolution to bar Communists from holding senior posts in the Kuomintang. Chiang himself replaced T'an after the CEC's vote of May 17, 1926, with Ch'en Kuo-fu as secretary of the department. Two months later Chiang relinquished the top post to Ch'en.

Meanwhile, Ch'en Li-fu, Ch'en Kuo-fu's younger brother, had re-

---

[*] Boorman, *Biographical Dictionary*, vol. 1, p. 203. Recruits from the Yangtze valley provinces had to come to Shanghai, at that time under the jurisdiction of the warlord Sun Ch'uan-fang, to board a ship for Canton. Passage was made possible through the help of underground party agents and sympathetic Chinese compradores working for foreign authorities, for example, Tu Yüeh-sheng and Huang Chin-jung of the French concession. Chang Chun-ku, p. 179.

turned from the United States, where he had been studying mining at the University of Pittsburgh, and was duly appointed a secretary at the Whampoa Academy. Later, during the military campaigns of 1926 and 1927, he served as Chiang's confidential secretary. Immediately after Ch'en Li-fu's return to China, he and his brother and several fellow compatriots laid down long-term plans to promote their political influence. In November 1926 the Ch'en brothers, together with Tseng Yang-p'u, Ch'en Chao-ying, and Chao Li-hua among others, organized the Chekiang Society of Revolutionary Comrades in Canton. Then in December Ch'en Kuo-fu made a secret trip to Nanchang in Kiangsi, where he undertook a major overhauling of the party's provincial organization, previously dominated by the Communists. The anti-Communist elements of the Kiangsi party apparatus, known as the anti-Bolshevik group and led by Tuan Hsi-p'eng and Ch'eng T'ien-fang, were then invited to join forces with the Ch'en brothers. Together they were to form most of the core of the C.C. Clique.

The C.C. Clique came into existence in June 1927, after the establishment of the Nationalist Government in Nanking. In addition to absorbing the Chekiang Society of Revolutionary Comrades and the anti-Bolshevik group, it recruited members from the so-called Stickers Clique of Kwangtung, the Western Hills Group, and the Sun Yatsenism Study Society at the Whampoa Academy.* According to a reliable Japanese source, the Ch'en brothers and 20 others made up the initial core of the clique. Later, nine other important figures were added to its top ranks.[9]

The importance of the C.C. Clique in the party became increasingly apparent. At the Third Party Congress in March 1929, the clique was represented by 40 delegates, mainly from Shanghai, Nanking, Kiangsu, and Chekiang, who organized to provide support for Chiang Kai-shek within the party's power structure. In 1931 15 percent of

---

* The Stickers Clique, so named because its members advocated the use of clubs to intimidate their Communist opponents, was an informal, right-wing political group led by Hsüeh Ying-tsou, the dean of Chungshan University Law School in Kwangtung. It apparently continued to exist until the fall of 1931, when it was absorbed by the Blue Shirt Society. See Hatano Ken'ichi, *Gendai Shina*, pp. 178–94; *Wu T'ieh-ch'eng hui-i lu* (Reminiscences of Wu T'ieh-ch'eng; n.p., n.d.), p. 67. The study group for Sun Yat-senism was founded at the Whampoa Academy by right-wing Kuomintang members and students in opposition to the existing Communist Federation of Young Soldiers.

the 72 newly elected members of the Central Executive Committee belonged to the C.C. Clique;[10] and some 50 of the 180 CEC members elected in 1935 were reportedly affiliated with the clique.[11] At the peak of its strength in the 1930's, the clique had over 10,000 members, most of whom were middle-level and lower-level party bureaucrats and cadre members. Geographically, members were heavily concentrated in the cities of Nanking and Shanghai and in the provinces of Kiangsu, Chekiang, Anhwei, and, to a lesser extent, northern Fukien. There were also a considerable number of members throughout Hupeh, Hunan, and Honan.

The primary institutional base of the clique lay in the party's Organization Department, tightly controlled by one Ch'en brother or the other throughout the decade after 1926. The department established and inspected provincial, city, and lower party organizations. It assigned high-level and middle-level personnel to various party branches in governments, the military, youth organizations, and trade-union agencies, and supervised their performance. Above all, it took charge of an intelligence network that came to function as the party's security police apparatus. Ch'en Kuo-fu headed the department from 1926 to 1932, building a strong personal following. Ch'en Li-fu served as director of the department's Investigation Division in 1928 and 1929, which enabled him to develop an internal security organization. Then, from 1929 to 1931, he was secretary-general of the party's central headquarters in Nanking. In 1932 Li-fu succeeded his brother as head of the Organization Department. From this post, which he held until 1936, he worked primarily to consolidate and strengthen Chiang Kai-shek's position in the party.[12] He also continued his activities in intelligence, investigation, and security. Later, during and after the war, the Ch'en brothers organized an elaborate secret service system called the Central Statistical Bureau.

In addition to controlling numerous positions inside the party, the C.C. Clique also gradually penetrated the administrative bureaucracy and various educational and cultural institutions. It also expanded its influence in the provinces. In 1933 Ch'en Kuo-fu took over the governorship of Kiangsu, which subsequently became the clique's main territorial base. At the provincial level the clique's tactics called for controlling the organization divisions of the party bureaus and the civil affairs departments of the governments. Wu Hsing-ya, for example, a C.C. organizer and a pivotal figure in Shanghai party politics, was dispatched to Hupeh in 1928 to take over these two organizations there; later, in 1930 and 1931, he held the same positions in Anhwei.[13] The C.C.'s energetic efforts in Hupeh provoked strong opposition from the Political Study Clique, which was trying to establish footholds in the middle Yangtze provinces.

The clique was able to recruit ambitious intellectuals, bureaucrats, and military officers to serve in the upper levels of its organization. To ensure its survival the Ch'en brothers also created the Central Political Academy to recruit and train young cadres. Though the initial purpose of the academy was to train magistrates and other administrative personnel for the national government, many graduates were sent to the provinces to consolidate the C.C. Clique's control over local administrative, educational, and cultural institutions. They also served as secret agents, penetrating unfriendly provincial governments. Chiang Kai-shek took a personal interest in directing the academy to ensure the allegiance of its graduates.[14] The impact of these young cadres was quite apparent in the war and even more so in the postwar period.

Under the leadership of Ch'en Li-fu, the C.C. machine became involved in journalistic and cultural activities, in an attempt to control the communications media. Members founded a newspaper (*Ching pao*) in Nanking, a monthly journal (*Shih-shih yüeh-pao*), a publishing company (Cheng-chung Book Company), and the National Cultural Reconstruction Association.[15] These projects, like the clique's other activities, required regular and substantial financial support; accordingly, the Ch'en brothers started planning financial enterprises in the late 1920's. Although the clique acquired its sources of revenue later than other competing bureaucratic groups, by 1937 it had developed the Kiangsu Provincial Farmers' Bank and had gained considerable influence in the National Farmers' Bank of China, organized by Chiang Kai-shek.[16] The provincial bank was organized in 1927 with land surtax revenues, previously collected by the warlord Sun Ch'uan-fang and then taken over by the victorious Kuomintang general Ho Ying-ch'in. The bank continued to rely on the land surtax for capital, and by 1935 it had accumulated some Ch $4 million.[17] Under the able directorship of Chao Li-hua, a leading C.C. member, the bank established 78 branches and agencies and more than 300

warehouses between 1933 and 1937.[18] It was the most important gov-
ernment-supported bank in the lower Yangtze delta region and employed a large number of C.C. members.

The C.C. Clique was a well-structured political group whose members shared six fundamental ideological and policy positions: (1)
they recognized Sun Yat-sen's Three People's Principles as the fundamental basis of the Nationalist revolution, and the Kuomintang as the
only party qualified to lead the revolution; (2) they regarded Chiang
Kai-shek as the supreme leader of the revolution, the party, and the
government, whose will was absolute; (3) they opposed Communism
and any other political doctrine not consistent with the Three People's
Principles, and rejected all political parties except the Kuomintang;
(4) they supported national independence and opposed foreign im-
perialism; (5) they favored the centralization of power; and (6)
they advocated the revival of traditional moral and religious teachings.[19]

In summary, the C.C. Clique is best described as a close-knit, informal group of conservative scholarly bureaucrats and politicians
who aspired to capture the party machinery and to transform the
Kuomintang into Chiang Kai-shek's effective power vehicle. They
sought control of cultural and educational media in order to spread
their conservative thinking among the people. And in fact they did
manage a great many of the Kuomintang's propaganda and educational activities; hence it is not surprising that the party seemed to be
moving steadily back to traditionalism rather than adopting new
ideas and new solutions. All in all, the C.C. Clique emerged as one of
Chiang's most effective political machines.

The Whampoa Clique

Unlike the C.C. Clique, whose power lay in its control of the party
apparatus, the so-called Whampoa Clique derived its influence from
its military and quasi-military activities. The term usually refers to
a group of men who had been affiliated with the Whampoa Military
Academy as either staff members or students. Staff members naturally gained influence much earlier than the students. In the prewar
period there were several governors, army commanders, and high-

TABLE 3

Military Men on the Central Executive Committee and the
Central Supervisory Committee, 1945

Committee	Total no. of military men	Whampoa Clique		
		Graduates	Instructors	Total
Central Executive Committee	57	23	9	32
Central Supervisory Committee	35	10	1	11
TOTAL	92	33	10	43

SOURCE: MacFarquhar, p. 173.

level party leaders who had served as instructors at the academy. Whampoa graduates were as yet relatively undistinguished in the military; their importance in this period lay in quasi-military and security activities. (The Whampoa Clique we refer to here naturally excludes any officers who joined the Communist Party.)

In the two decades after the establishment of the Nationalist Government, the Whampoa Clique's political influence grew steadily. Table 3 shows the strength of military professionals in the Central Executive Committee and the Central Supervisory Committee by 1945. Among the 43 members from the Whampoa Clique were Ho Ying-ch'in, the commander-in-chief of the army; Ch'en Ch'eng, the war minister; three war zone commanders; and eight army commanders.

Considering the limited number of people affiliated with the Whampoa Clique in the prewar period, the extent to which they developed their political and military influence is impressive. As long as the Whampoa men could be held together, Chiang had a formidable personal army in his struggle for the leadership of the party-state. The most significant aspect of the Whampoa Clique's activities, however, is often neglected. This was the development of an extraparty, quasi-secret society that proved indispensable as a power base for Chiang— the Blue Shirt Society (Lan-i She). The term Whampoa Clique essentially denotes a loose group that possessed neither an institutional framework nor an articulate ideology. In the conduct of military and political affairs, men affiliated with Whampoa achieved importance as an organized group through the Blue Shirt Society. According to a former leading member, the Blue Shirt movement was "responsible for building Chiang up as a national leader."[20]

The Blue Shirt Society

The Blue Shirt Society was an informal but well-structured political machine with definite goals. Its initial core was drawn from the right-wing segment of the Whampoa graduates and instructors. Historically, the Blue Shirts may be traced as far back as the establishment of the Sun Yat-senism Study Society on the Whampoa campus in 1924–25 by a group of anti-Communist students and their staff supporters.* The specific purpose of the group was to oppose the pro-Communist Federation of Young Soldiers.[21] The leading members of the society included Ho Chung-han, Yang Yin-chih, Feng T'i, Tseng K'uo-ch'ing, and Teng Wen-i; they drew faculty support from Wang Po-ling, Chang Chih-chung, Ku Chu-t'ung, and others. The organization's guiding principles were based on Tai Chi-t'ao's works *Sun Wen chu-i chih che-hsüeh chi-ch'u* (The philosophical foundations of Sun Yat-senism) and *Kuo-min ke-ming yü Chung-kuo Kuo-min-tang* (The national revolution and the Kuomintang of China).

By June 1926 the study society had more than 300 members. But as the Northern Expedition proceeded, it disintegrated. The Whampoa Alumni Association was founded immediately after the expedition to replace the two opposing student organizations. Chiang Kai-shek was the association's titular head, and its important officers included Tseng K'uo-ch'ing as secretary, P'an Yu-ch'iang as general manager, Yang Yin-chih as organizational head, and Yü Sa-tu, a Communist, as propaganda head. All but Yü had been core members of the right-wing Sun Yat-senism Study Society, and after the 1927 breakup of the KMT-CCP united front, the association consisted of only anti-Communist alumni. The Whampoa Alumni Association itself was dissolved in 1930. By that time the academy had been replaced by the Central Military Academy in Nanking, which subsequently created its own Alumni Information Bureau.

The most dramatic organizational development involving the

---

* Although members of the association opposed the Communists, they did not support the major policy positions of the right-wing Western Hills Group. T'ang Leang-li, p. 231.

Whampoa graduates came about in 1931 and 1932, against a backdrop of several important political events. A profound disagreement between Chiang Kai-shek and Hu Han-min over whether the party should give nominal recognition to a rising demand for constitutional government had developed into a bitter personality clash. On March 1, 1931, Chiang decided to put Hu into protective custody, a step that inevitably provoked strong opposition from leading party politicians in Kwangtung and Kwangsi, including Wang Ching-wei. Then, on September 18, the Japanese attacked Mukden, thus creating a crisis in Manchuria.[22] Hu was released following the outbreak of the crisis and subsequently formed a coalition with Wang Ching-wei. Though a rather shaky alliance based on common enmity to Chiang and his ill-defined position on Japanese aggression, it succeeded in forcing Chiang's temporary resignation from the government. These political maneuvers greatly alarmed the Whampoa faithful. The political situation was further clouded by the growing activity of the Communists in Kiangsi and bordering provinces.

The Hu-Wang coalition was short-lived. In late 1931 the fourth plenum of the CEC elected Wang president of the Executive Yuan, and he subsequently installed his chief lieutenants in important cabinet positions: Ch'en Kung-po as minister of industry, Ku Meng-yü as minister of railways, Tseng Chung-ming as vice-minister of railways, and T'ang Yu-jen as secretary-general of the Political Council. Wang's attempt to establish his own political machine while appearing to collaborate with Chiang posed an intolerable threat to Chiang's position. He apparently decided that the C.C. Clique alone could not ensure success in this competition with Wang, and that a more reliable and efficient machine was needed to consolidate his position in the fifth plenum of the CEC, scheduled for 1935. The growth of clientelism in the Kuomintang regime, then, reflected Chiang's increasing impatience with party politicians.

In the fall of 1931 Liu Chien-ch'ün, a former instructor at Whampoa, had given Chiang a patriotic essay entitled "Tui wo tang kai-ke ti chi tien i-chien" (Some suggestions for the reform of our party). In it he outlined three major threats to the republic—the deterioration of the national economy, the increasing rural poverty resulting from natural calamities and government inaction, and aggression by the Western powers and Japan—and suggested measures against them.[23]

Chiang immediately called on Liu, Chang Chih-chung, Ho Chung-han, Feng T'i, and K'ang Tse to form a secret organization based on these principles: (1) Chiang Kai-shek himself would be regarded as their supreme and permanent leader; (2) the Whampoa alumni would form the base of the organization; and (3) the members would follow the precepts of the Three People's Principles, would practice Communist organizational techniques, and would cultivate the spirit of the Japanese samurai.[24] The result was the Blue Shirt Society, which came into existence in March 1932 with its headquarters in Nanking. The core members held three general meetings during the year to lay down policy objectives and concrete plans.[25] Resolutions called on the members to strengthen their organizational control over financial, party, and military affairs throughout China, with the understanding that they would be assisted by other client groups loyal to Chiang.

Since the Blue Shirt Society was designed for clandestine operations, Chiang refused to recognize its existence publicly.[26] At first there was some disagreement about the name and structure of the organization. The founding members finally decided on a three-level structure. The nucleus of the society would be called the Power Society (Li She), and the front organization, which operated openly, the Restoration Society (Fu-hsing She). In between the two in terms of power and scope would be the Green Association (Ch'ing Hui), open only to alumni of Whampoa and later the Central Military Academy. (This name was an abbreviation of Ke-ming Ch'ing-nien T'ung-chih Hui, the Society for Young Revolutionary Comrades.) Together these three suborganizations formed what was to be known unofficially as the Blue Shirt Society.

At the top of the organization was its supreme leader, Chiang Kai-shek. A central cadre committee composed of over a dozen leaders decided policy and provided an administrative center. The organization was governed by the principle of democratic centralism. Discussion was allowed at lower levels, but decisions were made at the top; and once made, they were to be executed loyally and wholeheartedly at all levels. Absolute obedience and secrecy were the society's two fundamental principles.

The central administration consisted of a secretariat and four functional departments—organization, political training, propaganda, and security affairs. A handful of central cadres took turns directing the departments, except for security affairs, which remained under the control of Tai Li at all times.[27] There were 18 Blue Shirt branch organizations in the provinces and important cities, including ones in Nanking, Peking, Shanghai, and Hankow. The Nanking branch was divided into some 11 units. Each branch organization and each subunit was headed by a secretary. These secretaries, together with Chiang Kai-shek and the central cadres, constituted the Power Society.[28]

Members of the Green Association included the several dozen activist Whampoa alumni who were instrumental in creating the Blue Shirt Society. They constituted the upper-middle sectors of the cadre strata. At a lower level were the members of the Restoration Society, including staff members of the central headquarters and branch organizations and all of the Blue Shirts' security agents.[29] They penetrated the civilian population, the administrative bureaucracies, and various military units, serving both as watchdogs and as recruiting agents for the Blue Shirt Society.

The society initially planned for a membership of two million. But according to a confidential document released by the Bureau of Investigation of the Japanese Foreign Ministry, the total membership at the end of 1935 was slightly less than 14,000.[30] The procedure for recruiting members was very strict. The background and qualifications of each candidate were always carefully examined at local cell meetings, despite the fact that most candidates had already served as probationary members. On the recommendations of two members and the local cell unit, a candidate's name was submitted to local headquarters for approval. The prospective member had to swear absolute loyalty to the organization and its leader, and was told that he would never be allowed to quit.[31] Numerous standards for daily life were also imposed, based on the ideal of constant alertness.

In its first year the Blue Shirt Society tended to concentrate its activities in the lower Yangtze provinces and the northern coastal provinces. Major attempts were also made to develop bases in such important cities as Nanking, Shanghai, Peking, and Tientsin. Beginning in 1934 the society gradually penetrated the upper Yangtze provinces and southwestern China. Organizational efforts were concentrated in urban areas, where there were military officers, students, and intellectuals, the three groups considered the best sources of recruits. The Bureau of Investigation of the Japanese Foreign Ministry disclosed interesting membership figures for 1935 based on geographic distribution:[32]

Nanking	5,099	Shanghai	350
Peking-Tientsin-Paoting	1,173	Hunan	319
Kiangsi	946	Loyang	313
Szechwan-Sikang	817	Shansi	300
Honan	657	Anhwei	295
Hupeh	628	Fukien	183
Chekiang	593	Sian	131
Kiangsu	540	Kweichow	42
Kansu	538	Yunnan	20
Shantung	400	Inner Mongolia	13
Kwangtung	357	Sinkiang	6

Numerically, then, the strength of the society lay in Kiangsi, Szechwan, Honan, Hupeh, Chekiang, and Kiangsu—all except Honan in the Yangtze valley.*

The Blue Shirt Society had several programs, designed mainly to deal with those whom they defined as enemies of Chiang's Kuomintang regime. First of all, the Blue Shirts intended to spearhead a mass organization and indoctrination drive in provinces where the Communists were known to be active, especially the middle and lower Yangtze valley provinces. The society recognized that a security system and an intelligence network were crucial to this plan. It set up institutes to train hundreds and thousands of cadres in the areas of security, political indoctrination, and mass recruitment. Second, the Blue Shirts viewed the continued existence of regional militarists as a constant threat to Nanking's survival; they hoped to undermine the militarists' authority or make them Nanking's allies by infiltrating their armies and spreading propaganda. Finally, Chiang wanted to secure the provinces of North China before the Japanese could pacify the militarists there. Liu Chien-ch'ün's North China propaganda team had the primary responsibility for this task.

There were both military and nonmilitary cadres among the Blue

---

* Given the difficulty the central government had in penetrating Szechwan, the Blue Shirts' strength there is astonishing. A possible explanation is that most of the Blue Shirts were local recruits and members of K'ang Tse's Special Task Force, which arrived in the province in 1935.

Shirts. The professional military men—notably Chiang Chien-jen of the air force and Tu Tsung-nan, T'ang En-po, Kuan Lin-cheng, Hsü T'ing-yao, and Huang Che of the army—commanded units directly loyal to Chiang Kai-shek. Although these men held only the rank of divisional commander in the prewar years, together they represented a formidable military force. It was the nonmilitary members of the Blue Shirt Society, however, who were particularly important in the political developments of the 1930's.

Of the 25 or so key figures in this category, four were particularly important: K'ang Tse, Tai Li, Ho Chung-han, and Teng Wen-i. Each was instrumental in promoting a specific action program. K'ang Tse's Special Task Force (Pieh-tung Tui) consisted of armed security units that engaged in quasi-military activities in areas where the Kuomintang was fighting the Communists.* Tai Li's Iron-Blood Squad (T'ieh-hsüeh Tui), which was later absorbed by the more formal Military Statistical Bureau, performed a variety of functions in the areas of intelligence, sabotage, and espionage. It infiltrated garrison, police, and military police forces, focusing its activities on cities in an effort to gain covert control of China's heterogeneous urban police units. Ho Chung-han was instrumental in developing indoctrination units in in the military. His vigorous political training programs were important in helping Chiang's headquarters wage political warfare against the rural Communists. Although we lack detailed information about Teng Wen-i's career, we do know that his work was considered highly important among the Blue Shirts. From 1931 to 1934 Teng was primarily engaged in anti-Communist espionage; afterward, his interests shifted to cultural warfare and political indoctrination in the military.

K'ang Tse's Special Task Force had its origins in a special training program he created at the Central Military Academy in 1932.[33] The next year, after the fourth bandit suppression campaign in Kiangsi, a special task force under K'ang's command was officially set up at the Nanchang field headquarters. It reportedly numbered over one thousand men, the equivalent of one army regiment.[34] Meanwhile, the academy's training program continued to produce cadres, some 3,000 men in all, who were given the task of gaining control of Kuomintang

---

* The Special Task Force's normal duties involved political propaganda, indoctrination, and security maintenance. It was also trained to engage in actual combat if necessary to support military units.

organizations in important provinces and cities from party functionaries. Some units of the Special Task Force were sent to the Bandit
Suppression Provinces, where they assiduously developed programs
in rural mass mobilization and control as well as in political indoctrination. Units like this in Kweichow and Szechwan paved the way for
the penetration of central authority into these provinces. In an obvious attempt to undermine the power structure in Szechwan, K'ang
Tse's units at times defied provincial authorities and created strains
between the Kuomintang center and the Szechwan militarists.[35] In
addition to weakening Liu Hsiang's control of Szechwan, K'ang Tse's
forces were also there to broaden the Blue Shirts' territory.[36]

The Blue Shirts' most controversial activities were related to the
Iron-Blood Squad, led by Tai Li. A native of Chekiang Tai enjoyed
an extraordinarily intimate relationship with Chiang Kai-shek, who
came from the same county. After graduating from Whampoa's fourth
class, Tai rose swiftly in Chiang's power structure. When the Blue
Shirt Society was created in 1932, Tai did not receive immediate recognition in the political circle; but he was appointed a department
head in the Bureau of Investigation and Statistics of the Military
Council. Within two years he was placed in charge of military investigation in both the Military Council and Chiang's Nanchang
headquarters. The coming years saw Tai make vigorous efforts to
create an intelligence and security apparatus. When he replaced
Teng Wen-i as chief of military investigation in 1934, his staff increased from 145 to 1,722 overnight.[37] The number undoubtedly grew
even larger afterward. Several programs were set up to train security
agents, the best known being the police officer schools in Nanking
and Chekiang.[38] With the help of his protégé and assistant Sun
Ch'ang-chun, Tai Li also designed short-term institutions to train
cadre forces to infiltrate provincial police and military police units.[39]
A police chief of Wuhan in the 1930's claimed recently that by 1933
police personnel matters in the major cities of the nation were at
Tai's disposal, though this account seems to be somewhat exaggerated.[40]

In a political world of severe conflicts and ambiguous rules, Tai
Li's organization and its activities became virtually indispensable to
Chiang's survival as the party's leading political figure. But though
such clandestine operations might help eliminate formidable enemies,

they could also have devastating repercussions. One newspaper printed an instruction from the Blue Shirts' central authority dated June 14, 1933, advocating the assassination of 56 of Chiang's influential opponents, who were listed by name.[41] Chiang's rivals leveled numerous charges against Tai Li's "assassination" activities, charges whose effectiveness as propaganda was not negated by the fact that they were never proved. Still, Tai's painstaking effort to integrate China's police and military forces was a significant step that should be recognized, even though an integrated civilian and military police system under his control was not necessarily beneficial to the Chinese people.

The Blue Shirt Society was strongest in military organizations, and its operations were centered in the Military Council, which, having been given extraordinary powers to deal with Communist activities, was the most important institution in the Nanking regime. The Blue Shirts' control over central military organizations was obviously a result of Chiang Kai-shek's strategic position as chairman of the Military Council. Virtually every administrative bureau of the council was headed by a Blue Shirt. From these bureaus a control network extended to 11 provincial branch offices. In addition, all of the Nanking-oriented military schools and training camps and most of the party organizations in the army units on Nanking's payroll were controlled by Blue Shirts.[42] Many graduates of the schools were assigned duties in local and provincial military units, where they served as agents of Chiang Kai-shek's central military establishment. Ultimately, through them the society hoped to create an integrated military system under its control.

Chiang Kai-shek's major political asset was the military; unless he had widespread allegiance in the army units, his personal political power and his dream to unite China through military means would fall apart. Maintaining control of the army and ensuring its loyalty required the development of propaganda and indoctrination programs. Much of this task fell to the Political Training Bureau of the Military Council, which was headed by Ho Chung-han. Ho's contribution to the Blue Shirt Society, as well as to Chiang's military apparatus, was enormous. Although standard histories of the Kuomintang do not give him much importance, the available evidence suggests that he was one of the pivotal figures in Chiang's political and military enterprises of the 1930's. Through his efforts an extensive network of political propaganda and control was established throughout the central government's military units; and in the mid-1930's the network extended to the units of semiautonomous regional militarists.

The Political Training Bureau set up branches in Sian, Chungking, Foochow, Ichang, and the major military schools.[43] The Peking branch of the Military Council also had a training bureau, which worked closely with the Nanchang field headquarters. During the anti-Communist campaigns of the early 1930's, Ho was the chief coordinator of political activities in the Bandit Suppression Zones; political control of the military units, administrative offices, and schools in these areas was pursued according to programs he initiated and directed.[44]

To integrate separatist provincial armies into Nanking's command structure, Ho, K'ang, Liu Chien-ch'ün, and other leading Blue Shirts ordered their units into Kwangtung, Kwangsi, Kweichow, Yunnan, Szechwan, and North China. In North China, where the Japanese threat was real, militarists were in the precarious position of having to deal with both the Japanese and the Kuomintang. Chiang was suspicious of the northern militarists who had yet to show him unreserved allegiance. Thus, in June 1933, a North China propaganda team was created in the Military Council, with the explicit goal of spreading the Kuomintang's influence among regional troops in the north. Led by Liu Chien-ch'ün, one of Ho's close associates, the team carried on a wide range of political activities, especially in General Sung Che-yuan's units.[45] As the war with Japan approached, Ho and others helped Chiang establish camps in Lushan (Kiangsi) and later in O-mei-shan (Szechwan) in order to train and reorient China's heterogeneous military units.

In provinces where the Communists were reported to be active, Chiang and his Whampoa supporters promoted military education and the organization of militias. Such training programs appeared to be fairly successful in Chekiang, Kiangsu, Kiangsi, Honan, and Hupeh, where the Blue Shirt Society had established strong bases.[46] Military training for college students was carried out with relative success in the same provinces. In provinces where the Blue Shirts' influence was weak, however, local authorities were able to block this development on college campuses.

Overall, the Blue Shirt Society was most active in Chekiang, Kiangsi, and, after 1935, Szechwan. Its widespread activities in Kiangsi were facilitated by the establishment of Chiang's field headquarters at Nanchang, the capital, and were prompted in part by Communist activities there. To some degree the Blue Shirts' penetration into Szechwan can also be considered a response to local Communist activities, especially during the course of the Long March. But a survey of the origins of 39 leading Blue Shirts reveals that 13 were from Chekiang and seven from Szechwan.* Thus there was a close relationship between the location of the society's activities and the provincial origins of its leaders.

Despite the fact that the Blue Shirts' programs were military in orientation, the society did not lose sight of cultural and educational activities. Here their primary goal was to gain monopolistic control of the mass communications media. The society published some 30 newspapers and magazines and established the Chinese Cultural Association at Nanchang.[47] Under the leadership of Teng Wen-i, Ho Chung-han, and others, the Blue Shirts published numerous works on fascist ideas and practices in Germany and Italy.[48] Their growing cultural activism inevitably led to serious conflicts of interest with the C.C. Clique. By the mid-1930's there had been many direct confrontations between the two groups, mostly at the cadre level. These factional struggles soon spread into intelligence and party activities as well, culminating in the notorious intelligence rivalry between the Blue Shirts' Military Statistical Bureau and the C.C.'s Central Statistical Bureau after 1936.

The Blue Shirt Society's extensive activities were financed by Chiang Kai-shek himself; its budget was never sanctioned or regulated by the legitimate procedures set forth in the constitution of the republic. Funds came either from Chiang's personal financial sources or from institutions that he directly controlled. Thus the Military Council, its branch offices, and most military schools connected with Nanking allocated money for Blue Shirt activities.[49] Income from these institutions amounted to an estimated Ch $54,000 a month; and Chiang reportedly furnished Ch $200,000 a month to the society.†

---

* *Ran-i-sha ni kansuru chosa*, pp. 247–58. Of the remaining 19 leaders, Hunan supplied five and Kiangsu and Kwangtung two each.

† *Ran-i-sha ni kansuru chosa*, p. 69. This investigation record also notes that funds resulting from the confiscation of opium may have been appropriated for the Blue Shirts' activities.

Because of the scope of the Blue Shirts' activities, however, their expenses were well above this income. One writer reported in 1934 that the monthly budget of the society was fixed at Ch $1.2 million.[50] And this figure did not include whatever expenditures members made in their official capacities in formal institutions to promote the society's programs.

The Blue Shirts' activities reflected their ultranationalism. The society adopted an ideology of national socialism that glorified the state as supreme and divine, the Kuomintang as the only revolutionary party and the savior of China, the Three People's Principles as the highest principles of the Chinese revolution, and Chiang Kai-shek as the supreme leader, whose will was to be obeyed absolutely. Those who opposed the state, the party, the Three People's Principles, and the leader were to be eliminated. The leader's dictatorship and the Kuomintang's monopoly of power were to be supported at all times, and a persistent campaign was to be waged in the party against disloyalty to the supreme leader.

The society favored abolishing all of China's unequal treaties, recovering Chinese territory held as foreign concessions, confiscating all foreign interests, and refusing to pay back loans from foreign powers. In the area of economics it advocated "national socialism," government ownership and control of industry, and the implementation of Sun Yat-sen's Outline of Economic Planning. In order to mobilize the people behind the party, the society advocated programs to educate them about the need to defend the nation against foreign invasion and about the Kuomintang and its mission. Finally, in the area of military policy, the society demanded absolute unity of administration, command, and training; a system of universal military service; and the establishment of an air force with 3,000 planes and a defense force with 2.4 million regular soldiers, 5 million reserves, and 12 million volunteers.[51]

The ideological principles guiding the Blue Shirts bear a strong resemblance to those of the fascist movements in Germany and Italy in the 1930's. The body politic envisioned by the Blue Shirts was a kind of totalitarian state, a goal that many of their activities reflected. They employed vicious techniques, including terrorizing those broadly and arbitrarily defined as "enemies." Although Kuomintang China did not come close to adopting a totalitarian system, there were symptoms to suggest that forces driving for such a goal did exist. One might well wonder what kind of political system China would have developed after 1937 if there had been no war with Japan.

Political Study Clique

The third powerful clique in the Kuomintang regime was the Political Study Clique, an elitist group with no rank and file membership. Ch'ien Tuan-sheng portrays its members as opportunistic and practical, and states that "they interested themselves in increasing their hold on the provincial administration and also on the larger financial and business concerns of the country, whether private or government."[52] In the first decade of the Nanking Government, the clique became a political club of party politicians, bureaucrats, industrialists, bankers, and military men who had client relationships with Chiang Kai-shek, but who were alienated from the C.C. and Whampoa cliques.

The Political Study Clique did not suddenly emerge in the Nanking period. To find its origins one must go back as far as the August 1916–June 1917 parliament in Peking. On November 19, 1916, a group of parliamentary politicians under the leadership of Ku Chung-hsiu and Chang Yao-ts'eng organized the Political Study Society, which was considered to be more conservative than any of the four Kuomintang factions in the parliament.[53] After Premier Tuan Ch'i-jui dissolved the parliament, most members of the society left for South China to join the new Kuomintang military government, founded in September 1917 in opposition to Chang Hsün's monarchy. Under the new leadership of Yang Yung-t'ai and Li Ken-yuan, they allied themselves with the Yunnan-Kwangsi militarists against the Kwangtung-based Kuomintang faction of Sun Yat-sen, and became deeply involved in the politics of the rump parliament in Canton. During this time they backed Ts'en Ch'un-hsüan, a well-known political figure, against Sun. They scored a series of victories, blocking Sun's attempt to become grand marshal (*ta-yuan-shuai*) of the military government and replacing that office with a committee of seven, of which Ts'en Ch'un-hsüan later became executive chairman.[54] Yang Yung-t'ai served as governor of Kwangtung from May to October 1920, until he and his followers were expelled from the province by Li Lieh-chün, Sun Yat-sen's T'ung-meng Hui associate. In the next few years they became active in the warlord intrigues in North China. With a nucleus comprised of the old Political Study Society members, Ku Chung-hsiu and Yang Yung-t'ai organized the Society for Constitutional Government (Hsien-cheng Hui) as a parliamentary political party. The group shifted its allegiance from one warlord to another.

The connection between the Political Study Clique and Chiang Kai-shek came about through the intermediary efforts of Chang Ch'ün. Chang, once a staff member under Ts'en Ch'un-hsüan and Huang Fu, was an old acquaintance of Chiang's; the two had attended military school together in Japan and had become sworn-brothers while serving under Ch'en Ch'i-mei in Shanghai in 1911 and 1912.[55] In 1926 Chang joined Chiang's military staff at the Nanchang headquarters and immediately became a trusted lieutenant. As such he brought Yang Yung-t'ai and other members of the clique to Chiang's attention at a time when he badly needed experienced assistants to help build his power and to replace civilian leaders allied with Wang Ching-wei. Chiang was more than happy to use the talents of the Political Study Clique against the Western Hills Group, Hu Han-min, and Wang Ching-wei's left-wing Kuomintang.

The backgrounds and careers of the clique's veteran members varied. There were intellectuals (Wang Ch'ung-hui, Chang Chün-mai, Chiang Meng-lin, and Chiang T'ing-fu), graduates of Japanese military schools (Chiang Pai-li, Ch'en I, Huang Fu, Hsiung Shih-hui, Chang Ch'ün, and Hsiung Pin), and the bankers and industrialists of the Chekiang-Kiangsu financial clique (Ch'ien Yung-ming, Chang Chia-ao, Ch'en Kuang-fu, Wu Ting-ch'ang, and Yu Ch'ia-ch'ing). This last group had dominated the finances and commerce of Shanghai for decades, owning or controlling most of the leading banks, industries, and pawnshops in the city.[56] In alliance with bureaucrats, politicians, and military professionals in the Political Study Clique, they attempted to control China's economic life. A Japanese source reveals that the domination of financial and industrial activities in Shanghai, Peking, Tientsin, and Hankow was probably one of their major goals.[57]

Though poorly organized and urban-oriented, the Political Study Clique gradually expanded to include various military men and politicians not affiliated with any of the other political factions. Men like

Liu Chen-hua, Huang Shao-hung, Hsiung K'e-wu, Ch'en I, and Shen Hung-lieh—who found political cooperation necessary for political survival—joined the clique.[58] The *Ta-kung pao*, an influential newspaper published in Tientsin and Shanghai, served as the group's mouthpiece.

Clique members did well under Chiang Kai-shek. In the cabinet of the Executive Yuan in late 1935, for example, Chang Ch'ün was minister of foreign affairs; Wu Ting-ch'ang, minister of industry; Chang Chia-ao, minister of railways; Wong Wen-hao, secretary-general; and Chiang T'ing-fu, head of the Political Affairs Bureau. Provincial administration is generally referred to as the base of the clique's strength. As far as we know, these members served as provincial governors: Hsiung Shih-hui (Kiangsi, 1931–42), Chang Ch'ün (Hupeh, 1933–35), Yang Yung-t'ai (Hupeh, 1936), Huang Shao-hung (Chekiang, 1934–36, and Hupeh, 1937), Ch'en I (Fukien, 1934–37), Liu Chen-hua (Anhwei, 1933–37), and Wu Ting-ch'ang (Kweichow, 1937–?).

From these lists one may infer that the Political Study Clique had considerable influence in the administrative bureaucracy, especially in the provinces. The holding of governorships was not necessarily an accurate indication of the clique's influence, however. The clique had no definite political platform and no definite organizational structure at either the local or national level. Indeed, the question occasionally arises as to whether a factional organization called the Political Study Clique existed at all. Throughout the 1930's there was no evidence that the group was trying to establish a grass-roots structure, as were the C.C. Clique and the Blue Shirts. Still, it is undeniable that there were strong personal ties among individuals who were identified as members of the clique. As long as Chiang needed their talent and experience to maintain his position in the party, he tolerated their close contacts. It is possible that Chiang even encouraged such a factional association, especially since the clique showed no interest in developing a mass following.

Clique members were particularly important in assisting Chiang against the Communists and several northern militarists. They provided expertise and acted as intermediaries; in return, they received political and financial rewards. Huang Fu's contribution to Chiang's political enterprise is a good example. His service lay precisely in the liaison functions he performed, first between Chiang and the banker-industrialists, then between the Kuomintang center and the northern militarists. All natives of Chekiang, Huang, Chiang, and Ch'en Ch'i-mei were sworn-brothers in the early days of the republic.[59] Huang led a remarkable political career in Peking in the early 1920's and served as acting premier in October and November 1924. He developed wide contacts with influential militarists, bankers, and industrialists in North China and the lower Yangtze valley provinces. During the Northern Expedition he helped Chiang secure a huge amount of money for military payrolls from the Bank of China in Hankow and from various individuals in Shanghai.[60] His acquaintance with Shanghai's financial world made him Chiang's logical choice for mayor of Shanghai in 1927.

Six years later Huang was sent to chair the Political Affairs Council in Peking, a branch office of the Executive Yuan. The political situation in North China had deteriorated after the Japanese invasion of Jehol in February 1933; it was further complicated by the Mongols' demands for autonomy. Together with Ho Ying-ch'in, T. V. Soong, and Huang Shao-hung, Huang concluded the Tangku Truce with the Japanese in May 1933.[61] Huang Shao-hung, identified with both the Kwangsi clique and the Political Study Clique, also successfully arranged an agreement with the Mongols. Huang Fu, acting as a representative of the Kuomintang central government, tried to bring about a rapprochement with the major militarists in North China. Throughout his term as chairman of the Peking branch council (1933–35), he served as a link between Chiang and the generals in the five northern provinces under the council's official jurisdiction—Hopei, Shantung, Shansi, Chahar, and Suiyuan.[62] All in all, the efforts of Huang Fu and Huang Shao-hung in North China stabilized the political situation there, at least temporarily.

Huang Fu never joined the Kuomintang, which raises the question of how strong his ties were with the leading Kuomintang members of the Political Study Clique.[63] The evidence clearly shows that he had an intimate relationship with both Chang Ch'ün and Yang Yung-t'ai.[64] Further, the C.C. Clique, which had been antagonized by Huang's activities, somewhat sarcastically gave him the title of leader of the Political Study Clique.[65] There is no question that even if the clique did not have an actual organization, it had a significant effect on

Kuomintang politics at this time, and that Huang played an important part in this development.

The clique made a determined effort to capture party and administrative posts in several provinces during the first half of the 1930's. Here Yang Yung-t'ai, who served as secretary-general at Chiang Kai-shek's various field headquarters, was instrumental. Yang held this post from 1932 until his death in 1936, moving with the headquarters from Hankow (1932) to Nanchang (1933–35) and then to Wuchang and Chungking (1935–36). As Chiang's headquarters became the center of authority for all political, administrative, party, and military affairs in the ten Bandit Suppression Provinces, Yang's power reached its peak.* His enormous ability and the authority derived from his position as secretary-general made him perhaps the most powerful civilian leader in China during the years 1931–36.

The secretary-general took charge of a secretariat that performed a wide range of functions. At Hankow Yang's official responsibilities included correspondence, financial accounting, the investigation of emergency cases, and intelligence activities regarding the Communists and other anti-Chiang groups.[66] Later, in Nanchang and Wuchang, his jurisdiction extended even further. Occupying such a strategic position, he was closer than anyone to the center of power— Chiang. Indeed, communications for Chiang usually had to go through him. Chiang respected his intelligent and thoughtful advice, and Yang was able to use his influence to make changes in personnel and in administrative procedure. While Yang built himself up as the second most powerful man in the Bandit Suppression Provinces, an associate in the Political Study Clique, Hsiung Shih-hui, emerged as the Generalissimo's right-hand man in military affairs. During his term as governor of Kiangsi (1931–42), Hsiung held various other posts, including chief of staff and director of the administrative office at Chiang's field headquarters. Yang and Hsiung were the two pillars of Chiang's anti-Communist operations in the 1930's.

During these years Yang Yung-t'ai was instrumental in promoting what could be described as political warfare against the Communists. It was he who advocated and carried out a program whereby

---

* These ten provinces were Kiangsu, Kiangsi, Chekiang, Anhwei, Hupeh, Hunan, Honan, Fukien, Shensi, and Kansu. Szechwan and Kweichow were added to the category after 1935.

provincial administrative elites, including both the newly created administrative inspectors and the normally civilian-oriented county magistrates, were given military and security duties. In 1934 Yang called conferences of administrative leaders from the ten provinces under Nanchang's jurisdiction, one step in developing close contacts with provincial leaders. Through them he tried to institute programs of administrative reform and mass political mobilization all the way down to the village level. Most important of all, he made vigorous efforts on behalf of the New Life Movement, which was an attempt to promote military ideals and discipline among the people in order to mobilize them behind Chiang. Despite the fact that Yang's methods were ruthless, he apparently had cordial relations with the provincial militarists. When the central government was attempting to penetrate Szechwan in 1935, for example, it was he who won the friendship and respect of Liu Hsiang, the province's leading militarist.[67] By 1936 Yang and his close associates had made headway in controlling the provincial administrative and party apparatus that fell under the field headquarters' jurisdiction.

As long as the Political Study Clique had strong political ambitions, direct confrontations with the C.C. Clique were inevitable. In 1934, for example, Ch'en Kuo-fu, acting in his capacity as governor of Kiangsu, submitted a list of proposed provincial department heads to Nanchang for Chiang's approval. After seeing the list Yang suggested a change in the nomination for the most important department, civil affairs. The headquarters subsequently urged that Ku Jen-fa, who was attached to the Political Study Clique, replace the designated Ch'eng T'ien-fang. (Ku was fired soon after taking office on grounds unrelated to his public duties.)[68]

Another such clash was precipitated by Huang Shao-hung of the Political Study Clique. As minister of the interior in early 1935, Huang received an order from Chiang Kai-shek to make the collection of land taxes more efficient. In a report to Chiang, Huang cited Ch'en Kuo-fu as a good example of how a politically privileged person could own large amounts of land without paying a penny of land tax.[69] To make such a charge against the leader of the C.C. Clique required remarkable self-confidence. In fact, Huang was quoted by a Kwangsi associate as saying in the 1930's that he considered himself one of Chiang's four chief lieutenants, the others being Chang Ch'ün, Yang Yung-t'ai, and Hsiung Shih-hui.[70] All were members of the Political Study Clique.

Conclusion

The story of Chiang Kai-shek's rise to power cannot be fully told without a careful examination of the Kuomintang files. Unfortunately, these are still unavailable. Thus many of our previous conclusions must be taken as tentative. Still, on the basis of available evidence, we can assert the following propositions.

The C.C. Clique, the Whampoa Clique (especially its outgrowth, the Blue Shirt Society), and the Political Study Clique together had immeasurable influence in various party organizations and propaganda machines, in Chiang's army and intelligence network, and in the administrative bureaucracies. All of these cliques were basically conservative in terms of membership, ideological outlook, and political goals. Their increasing domination of the party-state suggests that the Kuomintang was becoming more conservative and less interested in progressive social and economic reforms. Thus it gradually shifted from a revolutionary party to a party of the status quo, narrowly preoccupied with military and ultranationalistic goals. Its organization and membership continued to be regionally based, but its conservative ideology prevented it from building on these bases and attracting the wider territorial and social support needed for national integration.

The pattern of clique politics reflects the factionalism and particularism prevailing in the leading circles of the Kuomintang. As Eisenstadt has observed, each faction tried to confine the others to their traditional limits and to isolate them from each other and from the centers of power.[71] Chiang's relations with the various factions originated in, and were maintained on the basis of, such factors as local affinity (with, for example, the C.C. leaders), school ties (with the Whampoa graduates and instructors), and oaths of brotherhood (with Chang Ch'ün and Huang Fu of the Political Study Clique). Marriage ties also helped Chiang secure political allegiance from certain important individuals, such as T. V. Soong and H. H. K'ung, who rendered valuable service to Chiang by instituting progressive reforms in finance and banking. Naturally, all these ties tended to reinforce each other in the working process of the patron-client relationship.

In general, the political machines divided along functional lines. The members of the Political Study Clique—pragmatic, capable, and experienced in administration—helped Chiang secure important administrative posts. Together with the K'ung-Soong elites, they also strengthened the financial base of Chiang's power. The programs of these urban-oriented groups in the fields of banking, public finance, private enterprise, and railway development gave Chiang's Kuomintang regime a modernizing image. But the better organized political machines on which Chiang relied the most, the Blue Shirts and the C.C. Clique, were strongly traditionalistic and nationalistic. In terms of fundamental orientation and political taste, Chiang had more in common with these two groups. His tie with the Political Study Clique was based on mutual convenience.

The Blue Shirts and the C.C.'s who were active in provincial party, propaganda, and military programs sometimes saw eye-to-eye with the members of the Political Study Clique who planned the administration of the Bandit Suppression Zones or sat in the governors' chairs. But despite the fact that all the machines shared the immediate goal of upholding Chiang's power, there were occasional conflicts of interest. Personality clashes and ambiguous or overlapping functional divisions accounted for most of these disputes. Competition over patronage and over control of local party machinery led to some violent exchanges between cadres of the Blue Shirt and C.C. cliques; two such conflicts occurred in Chinkiang and Hankow.[72] Overall, however, the consensus among clique leaders on the goal of supporting Chiang, combined with Chiang's skillful manipulation of the machines, enabled these factions to transform the Kuomintang and destroy its revolutionary legacy.

FOUR

Government Revenues and Expenditures

THE CHINESE GOVERNMENT traditionally paid little attention to the general welfare of the population. The imperial government did provide a high degree of stability and order in a vast, diversified political community. And when stability and order prevailed, the lower levels of the government bureaucracy managed to offer some social services to the people. Officials might mediate local disputes and promote religious activities, education, and bridge and road construction. One should not, however, overemphasize the significance of these efforts. Most officials were self-serving and rarely displayed benevolence. The fact that bureaucratic officials were mainly concerned with revenue extraction indicates clearly the relationship between the government and the people. The traditional Chinese government seldom took steps to promote the people's welfare.

In the early republican period provincial and regional warlords, struggling for survival in a world of political intrigues and factions, likewise had little concern for the people. In fact, their ruthless methods of obtaining resources for their military machines inflicted further hardship. The so-called central government in Peking lost control over revenues in the decade before the Nanking Government was established. Thus the Kuomintang leaders, who fully understood the significance of finances in their struggle to build a nation, had inherited a difficult situation.

From the start the various administrative branches of the party-government tended to emphasize finances. As Ch'ien Tuan-sheng has stated, financial difficulties "compelled the regime to appreciate the advantage of strict budgeting, in addition to discovering new sources of taxation and modernizing the methods of collection."[1] Institutional development in public finance was crucial; the scope and depth of the regime's activities depended on its ability to extract revenues.

The traditional Chinese financial system had no legal divisions among central, provincial, and local sources of revenue. It had adopted the principle of centralization, under which revenues collected by the local governments were regarded as central revenues. Expenditures at all levels of government were defrayed by these revenues. The national government, although it did establish some local taxation agencies under its direct supervision, by and large relied on the local governments to collect its taxes. Such a system could guarantee a regular income only when the central authorities could effectively reach the provinces. In times of political distress, when local authorities ignored or defied the central authorities, the financial basis of national government was severely weakened. During the decade 1917–27, "little or no revenue other than that under foreign control ever found its way from the provinces to the capital."[2]

Although the Nanking Government intended to develop a more orderly and realistic policy of raising revenues, the formal legal basis of its taxation powers was ill-defined. Neither the Organic Law of the Nationalist Government, promulgated on October 3, 1928, nor the Constitution of the Republic of China provided an explicit statement regarding the central government's ability to tax. The legal problem was discussed at the National Economic Conference of June 20–30, 1928, and at the National Conference on Finance of July 1–10. These two groups developed explicit, if informal, definitions of the government's taxation powers and drew clear divisions between central and provincial revenues.

At the National Economic Conference in Shanghai, T. V. Soong, the minister of finance, brought together the men whose support and talent he needed to launch his program of economic development. The conference was attended by leading merchants, industrialists, economists, and financial experts, who discussed and passed resolutions on a wide range of economic problems facing the Nanking Government. The major resolutions dealt with currency and banking, taxation, the national debt, the promotion of commerce, and expenditures for the military, national reconstruction, and industrial development.[3] Regarding taxation and expenditures, the conference called for a clear division between the authority and rights of the central government and those of the provincial governments. Under the formula it recommended, Nanking would draw its revenues primarily from customs duties and the salt tax; the land tax, the most lucrative source of revenue, was reserved for the provincial governments.

It is curious that the Nanking Government accepted provincial jurisdiction over the land tax. There are two possible reasons. First, collecting land taxes required preparatory work, such as land registration and assessment, that had not been done for decades. Considering the confusion over land ownership and the general breakdown of collection mechanisms, Nanking could not hope to administer an efficient system of land taxation in rural China. Second, since land taxes were the principal source of revenue for the provincial warlords, Nanking's insistence on jurisdiction over them would have created a solid front of opposition; and Nanking was powerless to enforce its will on the militarists at this time. Thus the Kuomintang leaders, though anxious to create an economic system that would be both national and modern, found it difficult to tap the agricultural sector. Once central and provincial jurisdictions were legally established, events revealed how hard it was for Nanking to initiate land registration and to reform the administration of its own taxes collected at the provincial level. As a result the Kuomintang regime derived its revenues mainly from the rather small modernized sector of the economy. And in the end the government's large military expenditures so dominated its small budget that rural social and economic reforms were virtually impossible.

As soon as the Economic Conference was over, T. V. Soong called another conference in Nanking to consider its proposals. Attended by various financial and taxation officials of the Nanking Government, the National Conference on Finance met to outline a general program for administering the collection and allocation of revenues. Within three years of the conference, Nanking tried to institute modern banking, budgetary, and monetary systems and to consolidate the administration of taxes that proved to be reliable sources of national revenue. In each of these areas results were mixed. The government achieved limited success in provinces where its military forces gradually established footholds.*

At the center, largely due to T. V. Soong's efforts, a system of budgetary controls was introduced. In February 1930 the government announced a set of regulations to apply to its first relatively comprehensive budget, which would run from July 1930 to June 1931 and would be prepared by the Ministry of Finance.† Budgetary techniques and procedures were specified in great detail. The regulations also recommended the division of China's fiscal policy into two parts, central and provincial, a principle that did become the working guideline of budgetary authorities. Administrative procedures aimed at establishing a system of checks and balances were set up by legislation of November 2, 1931. Under this system the Central Political Council, the Legislative Yuan, and the newly created Directorate-General of Budgets, Accounts, and Statistics were all to play important roles in planning and administering budgets. In actual practice, however, the process was dominated by the Ministry of Finance and the Political Council, which often ignored proposed budgets. Thus groups that held a majority of votes in the Political Council—most often Chiang's political machines—controlled public finance; budgetary control was never structured and was subordinated to the personal wishes of party leaders.

The Kuomintang government inherited a financial system on the verge of bankruptcy. During the first decade of its rule, it did not substantially alter the situation, continuously operating at a deficit. The fiscal year 1927–28 saw a 46.4 percent deficit.[4] However, this was an exceptional year: internal party struggles were severe, and government revenues were virtually suspended. The situation improved, at least on the surface, in subsequent years. The deficit for 1930–31

---

* The Central Financial Reorganization Committee was created in September 1928 to assist the Ministry of Finance in carrying out the program of administrative unification. It divided China into seven territorial districts. The first three districts were composed of the ten provinces later classified as the Bandit Suppression Zones, plus Kwangtung, Kwangsi, and Shantung. Nanking had only nominal jurisdiction in the last three provinces. See the *China Year Book*, 1929–30, p. 636.

† Before that, the Chinese government had had budgets only in 1914, 1915, and 1919, and all were poorly prepared. The Comptroller's Office came into existence in 1931; and it managed to produce a national budget for each following fiscal year except 1932, when the proposed budget was not approved by the Political Council.

dropped to 30.4 percent.[5] By 1935 financial deficits still existed, but they were partially compensated for by borrowing; domestic loans for this purpose, for example, increased from Ch $147 million in 1933 to Ch $170 million in 1935.[6] After that year a considerable part of the deficits was made up by issuing paper currency.

One of the most difficult problems of public finance facing Nanking involved the national debt that had accumulated since the early days of the republic. Previous governments had supported themselves by floating foreign and domestic loans. As one Japanese writer explained in 1931, "Due to the absence or unreliability of security, the number of unliquidated domestic and foreign loans has been steadily increasing."[7] In July 1928 the Committee on National Indebtedness, appointed by the National Economic Conference, placed the outstanding foreign and domestic debts of the Ministry of Finance at approximately Ch $1.6 billion and those of the Ministry of Communications at about Ch $597 million.[8] These figures naturally do not include the debts of the provinces, which perhaps amounted to large sums as well. Douglas Paauw estimates the total national debt as of 1927–28 to be two and a quarter billion Chinese dollars.[9] (This figure would seem to exclude provincial debts, although Paauw does not specifically say so.) The burden of an inherited debt of this size was incredibly heavy for a new government whose total revenues in 1928–29 amounted to only about Ch $333 million. Of the total inherited indebtedness, 83.3 percent resulted from unpaid foreign loans and 16.7 percent from domestic loans.[10]

The government considered repudiating the inherited debt, but since the need for future borrowing seemed inevitable, it apparently decided not to further jeopardize China's ability to obtain foreign loans. Some foreign loans were even paid off; for example, the salt loans were repaid for the first time in the history of modern China, and four railway loans were settled in 1936. Internal debts were repaid with more regularity but nevertheless increased sevenfold in the prewar decade. A realistic interpretation of the Nationalist policy on indebtedness reveals an acceptance of responsibility for only those loans that, in the judgment of the Kuomintang elites, were politically sensitive or affected the party-state's international credit.

Despite the already large and partially defaulted national debt, the Kuomintang elites themselves engaged in heavy borrowing. During the prewar decade the total national debt increased by approximately Ch $2 billion. On the average, 25 percent of the annual expenditures was reportedly financed by borrowing.[11] This raises the question of how the borrowed funds were actually used. Except during a brief period of reconstruction in the early part of the decade, proceeds from borrowed funds were largely allocated for military and general administrative expenses. We shall examine these expenditures in more detail later.

Revenues

Political insecurity turned the Nationalists' attention from tax reforms to immediate financial needs.[12] Throughout the prewar decade the most easily collected taxes—the customs duties, the salt tax, and the consolidated taxes (*t'ung-shui*) — constituted the government's three major sources of revenue.* Customs duties were apparently the most important source of revenue in Kuomintang China, as in many other underdeveloped nations. According to a commission of financial experts appointed by the Nationalist Government to study revenue policy: "Perhaps because of its relative freedom from political uncertainties, the customs service has developed and maintained a higher level of administrative efficiency than is to be found generally in internal revenue administration in China."[13]

During the years 1928–37 customs revenues accounted for 48.5 percent of the Nationalist Government's total income; the highest percentage was 58.4 percent in 1931 and the lowest was 36.5 percent in 1936. Salt tax revenues varied from 8.8 percent of the government's income in 1928 to 27 percent in 1930, accounting for 22 percent of all revenues during the decade. The consolidated taxes varied from 8.8 percent in 1928 to 17.5 percent in 1937, accounting for 12.6 percent of all revenues.[14] (Borrowed funds are excluded from the government's income in computing all these percentages.) During this period customs revenues as a percentage of total income declined steadily year by year. The consolidated taxes did just the opposite. Their continuous increase may be related to the gradual extension of Nanking's authority over the provinces and to general improve-

---

* Consolidated taxes were excise duties imposed on cigarettes, cigars, cotton yarn, wheat flour, matches, cement, beer, and foreign wine and liquor.

ment in their administration. At any rate, customs duties, the salt tax, and the consolidated taxes together accounted for 83.1 percent of the government's income during the decade. Some 46 percent of all national revenues came from the three provinces of Chekiang, Kiangsu, and Anhwei.[15]

Abuses in tax collection had previously been a major target of public criticism and a reflection of general political decline. Two able finance ministers of the Nationalist Government, T. V. Soong and H. H. K'ung, realized that abuses could be prevented to some extent by centralizing the system. In order to simplify tax administration, the Nationalist Government decided to reduce the number of both taxable items and tax offices, as advised by the commission of financial experts.[16] Until that time there were many overlapping taxes, each with its own collection agency. For instance, Shanghai alone had some 130 national and local tax offices in 1928. The Ministry of Finance itself maintained ten tax agencies, each with a loosely connected chain of national, provincial, and local branches.

At the beginning of the 1930's, efforts were made to unify the administrative agencies of the consolidated taxes and taxes of a similar nature.[17] In 1931 the previously separate administrations for wine, tobacco, and stamp taxes were merged into one system. Also in 1931 the Consolidated Tax Administration, established three years earlier, extended its jurisdiction to the new excise taxes on cotton yarn, matches, and cement; these taxes were introduced to compensate for the loss of the traditional likin tax, which was abolished in 1931.[18] In 1933 the Internal Revenue Administration was established, incorporating both the administration for the wine, tobacco, and stamp taxes and the administration for the consolidated taxes. Soon afterwards the Internal Revenue Administration also took over the mining tax, which had been administered by the General Revenue Department of the Ministry of Finance.*

In spite of this administrative integration, the wine, tobacco, and stamp taxes and the consolidated taxes were still collected separately. The wine, tobacco, and stamp taxes were collected by traditional tax

---

* Since many industries in the so-called Kuomintang-controlled territory were located in Shanghai's foreign settlements, the government found it impossible to collect excise taxes without the close cooperation of Western authorities. Diplomatic as well as administrative skills were thus required.

farming and quota methods; that is, local officials and contractors collected them in exchange for part of the revenue. They were usually collected at the point where goods were distributed to retailers. Each province and each major city normally had one branch office in charge of these items.

The collection of the consolidated taxes was more centralized and apparently more efficient. It was not divided along provincial lines; instead one bureau was usually responsible for taxes in several provinces. These bureaus had suboffices and inspection stations at every major point where goods were produced or distributed. The central government was to set a uniform rate for each commodity, and provincial and local authorities had no legal power to change the rates for any party. In order to prevent smuggling and tax evasion, each provincial police force maintained a special inspection squad, which worked closely with the Internal Revenue Administration. The actual implementation of this administrative plan naturally varied in effectiveness from province to province. In general, it was more effective in Kiangsu, Chekiang, Anhwei, Hupeh, Kiangsi, Honan, Hunan, and Fukien, especially in the first three. Elsewhere implementation was random and ineffective.

The Ministry of Finance recognized the need to reform the collection of the wine, tobacco, and stamp taxes along the lines of the consolidated tax system. In July 1936 it tried to integrate the collection of these taxes with that of the consolidated taxes, under the supervision of regional bureaus. This attempt failed, however; and throughout the prewar decade separate collection agencies for the two kinds of taxes continued to exist side by side.

The general tendency to centralize various agencies definitely improved administrative efficiency. At the beginning of the Nanking period, there were several thousand provincial and national tax offices. By the end of the decade nearly all the collection agencies for national revenues had been integrated into three major administrative structures: the Customs Administration, the Salt Administration, and the Internal Revenue Administration.[19] Still, in spite of these improvements, actual operations fell short of expectations. Nanking's ability to collect the taxes to which it was legally entitled often depended on its military strength in the contributing areas; provincial governments, because of either their own financial difficulties or a lack of respect for Nanking's authority, sometimes retained central government revenues collected in their provinces. Even provinces that were functionally integrated into the administrative systems, such as Hupeh, Hunan, Kwangtung, Fukien, Shantung, and Chekiang, were occasionally guilty of this. Hunan, for example, reportedly kept Ch $14 million annually in salt revenues.[20] Furthermore, the consolidated tax levy, first introduced in Kiangsu, Chekiang, Anhwei, Fukien, and Kiangsi in early 1928, was only partially in effect in 15 provinces by the end of 1936.*

Although the Nationalist Government did attempt to centralize the administration of traditional sources of revenue, it did little to find new sources or to spread the tax burden more evenly. The reforms to which the Kuomintang pointed with great pride were essentially devices to promote central control of existing tax sources in the coastal provinces and to increase immediate yields by imposing higher rates. The entire system was geared to the mounting costs of military operations. Between 1931 and 1934 import tariff rates were increased five times. The salt levies, which were severely regressive, were raised until they were 30 to 70 times greater than production costs.[21] Taxes on consumer goods were increased, which put a heavy burden on ordinary citizens.

A very large share of the tax burden fell on an extremely small sector of the economy. It is estimated that approximately 48 percent of the central government's revenues came from import duties; yet in no year did the value of imports equal more than 5 percent of the gross national product.[22] Modern industry accounted for a small percentage of the national income; yet it contributed all the consolidated taxes, which from 1928 through 1935 accounted for 12 percent of the government's revenues.[23] Agriculture, which contributed between 60 and 70 percent of the annual gross national product between 1931 and 1936, was apparently untapped as a major tax source by the Nanking Government.[24] This sector was taxed heavily by provincial governments, however.

Geographically, Nanking's revenues came primarily from eastern

---

* Hsien-ding Fong, pp. 48–49. In addition to the original five provinces, Hupeh, Hunan, Shantung, and Hopei adopted the taxes in fiscal 1928–29; Honan, Kwangtung, and Kwangsi in 1929–30; and Shansi, Chahar, and Suiyuan in 1931–32.

central China and North China, especially the lower Yangtze valley provinces and the coastal provinces. All the Bandit Suppression Provinces except Kansu and Shensi supplied revenues to the central government, as Chiang Kai-shek's military headquarters converted them into political units. Even in these provinces, however, Nanking's ability to tax was largely limited to the urban areas—the industrial, commercial, and administrative centers. Most of the rural population was outside its jurisdiction. As one writer points out:

As the distance from the center increases, variable costs are liable to rise since communications will be less good and the people, probably receiving few administrative favors, will be less amenable to paying taxes than those nearer the center. Furthermore, in these inaccessible areas banditry on an extensive scale appears to have been a serious problem, and the necessity of preventing bandits from acquiring revenue from the more productive localities near to the center is likely to incur heavy administrative costs under the category of "public safety."[25]

The Bandit Suppression Provinces, along with Kwangtung, Shantung, and Hopei, provided almost all the capital for national investment in the modern sectors of the economy. In 1928 three provinces, Kiangsu, Shantung, and Hopei, provided 61.5 percent.[26] Outside the Bandit Suppression Provinces Nanking's orders for reforms in financial administration were ignored, and salt tax revenues were not remitted to the central government.[27]

In summary, it appears that the Kuomintang's efforts toward improving tax administration primarily involved old taxes. The government showed no sign of instituting fundamental changes that might substantially alter tax distribution and promote progressive economic development. A comment from the commission of financial experts illustrates the state of Nanking's tax policy. According to the commission political and military instability "has turned financial thought from questions of tax reform to questions of immediate revenue yield, and has at the same time upset the financial relationship between central and local governments and with it the administrative control on which all sound revenue reform must rest."[28]

Expenditures

The patterns of the Nationalist Government's expenditures reveal much about the nature and direction of political development in the

TABLE 4

Military and Debt Expenditures, 1928–37

(*in millions of Chinese dollars*)

Fiscal year[a]	Military expenditures		Debt service		Total military and debt expenditures	
	Amount	Pct. of total expenditures	Amount	Pct. of total expenditures	Amount	Pct. of total expenditures
1928–29	210	50.8%	158	38.3%	368	89.1%
1929–30	245	45.5	200	37.2	445	82.7
1930–31	312	43.6	290	40.5	602	84.1
1931–32	304	44.5	270	39.5	574	84.0
1932–33	321	49.7	210	32.6	531	82.3
1933–34	373	48.5	244	31.8	617	80.3
1934–35	368	34.4	356	33.2	724	67.6
1935–36	220	21.6	275	26.9	495	48.5
1936–37	322	32.5	239	24.1	561	56.6

SOURCE: The 1928–35 figures are calculated from the annual reports of the Ministry of Finance, *China Year Book*, 1938, p. 471. The figures for 1935–36 and 1936–37 are my own calculations.

[a] The fiscal year begins on July 1.

Nanking decade. As a percentage of the gross national product, government expenditures seem small, varying from a low of 2.1 percent in 1931 to a high of 4.8 percent in 1934.[29] In terms of the government's actual financial resources, however, the expenditures were quite large; in fact the government incurred heavy deficits during this period.

Table 4 shows that Nanking's expenditures were dominated by military expenses and debt service. These priorities undoubtedly set limits on the public funds available for civil expenditures and capital investment in modernization programs. According to the Finance Ministry's own figures, military expenditures constituted from one-third to one-half of the government's total expenditures from 1928 to 1935. And some military costs were omitted from the official reports or were listed under a variety of other items. One study claims that military expenditures constituted over 40 percent of the total expenditures for every fiscal year in which an annual report was issued, averaging 46 percent a year.[30] Moreover, the Nationalist Government was running a deficit; thus if the percentages were based on actual revenues, they would be still higher.* It should be noted that pro-

* As T. V. Soong pointed out in his budget proposal to the Military Reorganization and Disbandment Conference in 1929, when expenses such as the

vincial allocations for defense and security were for the most part excluded from these figures.

Debt-service payments averaged about 34 percent of the government's annual expenditures in the years 1928–37. Payments on foreign debts resulted in a net reduction of the national income, further undermining the party-government's financial ability to meet the mounting need for administrative and economic reforms. Military expenses and debt-service payments together averaged some 75 percent of Nanking's annual expenditures. Official figures do reveal a favorable trend in civil expenditures, from 6 percent of the total expenditures in 1928–29 to about 26 percent in 1934–35. Much of the increase, however, was absorbed by the growing central administrative bureaucracy. Financial resources devoted to economic development continued to be extremely limited. The relatively small budget of the Nationalist Government was due, in part, to its failure to effect tax reforms and to its continued reliance on limited taxable sources. Sir Arthur Salter, an observer of the Chinese situation in the 1930's, further attributed Nanking's financial weakness to poverty, administrative disabilities, the government's regional rather than national nature, and its limited authority over many provinces.[31]

In view of the government's limited resources, its military expenditures were truly astonishing. Significant increases in military spending after 1930—the year Chiang Kai-shek started his military campaigns against the Communists—created unrest among leading party figures who had supported him. Some of the modernizing elites favored progressive social and economic change; but Chiang set his military needs above everything, which left very little for programs involving transportation, education, water conservation, and industrial development.

T. V. Soong, a leading supporter of modernization, was especially concerned over the urgent need to promote economic development and new methods of public finance.[32] Since Chiang insisted on the necessity of building political order through military means alone, a conflict between the two was inevitable. Increases in military spend-

---

sinking-fund charges for loans and the costs of tax collection were deducted from revenues, military expenditures (fixed at Ch $192 million) represented 78 percent of the government's net revenues. See the *China Year Book*, 1929–30, p. 639.

ing—from Ch $304 million (44.5 percent of the total expenditures) in 1931–32 to Ch $321 million (49.7 percent) in 1932–33 to a projected Ch $373 million (48.5 percent) in 1933–34—apparently constituted an important reason for Soong's resignation from his posts as vice-president of the Executive Yuan, minister of finance, and governor of the Central Bank of China in October 1933.[33]

In short, the evidence indicates that some Kuomintang leaders were genuinely concerned with the fundamental reform of China's system of public finance, perhaps with an eye toward building the regime's financial ability to deal with socioeconomic problems. Given the precarious political situation, such reforms might never have achieved their intended objectives. Yet military priorities and the heavy financial burden they entailed seriously undermined the potential for reform. The failure of attempts to create a sound financial system meant that Nanking was not able to widen its tax base in response to mounting financial needs. There was little revenue for the party's civil administrative sectors, and nonmilitary allocations were insignificant when compared with nonmilitary needs. Political development required Nanking to build adequate institutions and to initiate reconstruction programs, but the regime had no resources left to do so.

Unfortunately, continued high military spending did not bring peace, and the prospect for improving social and economic conditions was destroyed altogether. In the end, this thoughtful advice by the Commission of Financial Experts went unheeded:

The realization that taxes are in fact a contribution to collective purposes, not a mere "one-sided" compulsory exaction of wealth by the government (or it may be, by officials, largely for their private and personal benefit), must be gradually built up through the devotion of public funds to useful public purposes: to schools, public health, roads, suppression of banditry and of other forms of lawlessness; not to civil warfare, or to improvements of limited importance to the public, or to salaries of a multiplicity of officials.[34]

PART TWO

The Provinces

FIVE

Provincial and County Government: An Overview

THE DIVISION OF CHINA into provinces originated in the thirteenth century during the Yuan dynasty. Later centuries saw an increasing dependence on the province as a key administrative unit in China's centralized bureaucratic system. Throughout the Ch'ing dynasty, from 1644 to 1911, provincial divisions and boundaries survived with little revision. Natural boundaries and distinct economic character-istics encouraged regional separatism, especially when the central authority was weak and communications broke down. The revival of provincialism in the early republican period seriously hindered national integration.

The Nationalist Government in Nanking officially divided China into 28 provinces, excluding Tibet and Outer Mongolia, which were classified as territories (ti-fang).* Twenty-two of these provinces had basically the same boundaries as they had had during the Ch'ing dynasty and 15 dated back to the Yuan dynasty.[1] Six new provinces— Jehol, Chahar, Suiyuan, Ningsia, Tsinghai, and Sikang — officially came into existence in late 1928.[2] Sikang, however, had no provincial administration until 1935. Also, it should be noted that Jehol and the three provinces in Manchuria, Liaoning, Heilungkiang, and Kirin, were lost to the Japanese by 1932.

China's provinces differ greatly in size and population. In the 1930's the areas of the 28 provinces varied from about 39,000 square

---

* The Territory of Mongolia did not include southern, or Inner, Mongolia; it was divided into four new provinces. The Territory of Tibet included most of historic Tibet, but one part was added to the new provinces of Sikang. Despite these Chinese claims, Mongolia had been an independent state since 1921, and Nanking was too weak to assert control over Tibet.

miles to over 633,000 square miles; and their populations ranged from about 400,000 to over 50,700,000.[3] There were also significant differences in the number of counties each province had.[4] The total number of counties in the 28 provinces in 1935 was estimated to be 1,964. Szechwan had the most, 148 counties, and Ningsia the least, 11. At the county level, too, variations in size and population were considerable. Counties ranged from 28 square miles to over 225,300 square miles and had from 234 to 1,568,492 residents.[5] The size and population of some counties actually exceeded those of some provinces. Thus, when speaking of a province or a country, we must be constantly aware of the great range of individual differences.

The Nanking Government realized from the outset that concentrating administrative functions at the provincial level could perpetuate regional separatism. Although there were attempts in the 1920's to obtain constitutional and legal recognition of the existing system of regional autonomy, the Kuomintang leaders by and large favored centralized political control over the provinces. Thus, according to the official definition, provincial administrations were to perform intermediary functions between the central government and the county governments. In theory at least, the province was not comparable to a state in a federal system, such as that of the United States of America. The 1931 Organizational Law of Provincial Government clearly specified that the province was a territorial unit defined only for the purpose of administrative control by the central government; the Kuomintang had ruled this as early as 1925.[6] The principle, reformulated several times, remained fundamental. It is imperative, therefore, to consider bureaucratic development in the provinces in relation to the Kuomintang's attempts to develop a centralized administration.

The Kuomintang adopted the traditional administrative hierarchy consisting of three levels—national, provincial, and county. The party first promulgated the Organizational Law of Provincial Government in Canton on July 1, 1925. This law was intended to regulate the practices and procedures of provincial governments. After six official revisions a final form was reached on March 22, 1931. The revision of November 10, 1926, the first, created a committee of from seven to 11 members as the highest decision-making body in each province. In 1931 the maximum number of members was reduced to nine. In order to assert central control over provincial authorities, a revision in October 1927 stated that the members and the chairman of each committee would be appointed by the Nationalist Government in Nanking. The 1930 revision disqualified active military professionals from serving on these committees, but in practice the Kuomintang ignored this restriction.[7] The Organizational Law stipulated that the governor, the secretary-general, and the heads of the four administrative departments of the provincial government were ex officio members of the committee; the governor was to be its chairman. Decisions were to be reached by a simple majority of the members present. The governor was given one vote, but in practice his opinion often carried the meeting.[8]

The provincial decision-making structure was apparently intended to promote collective leadership and to prevent the concentration of power in the hands of one man. The eventual goal of the system was undoubtedly to provide institutional checks against regionalism, the assumption being that the concentration of power in the hands of a few men facilitated regional autonomy. In fact, however, the committee system did not prevent the development of personal and regional power, and it proved to be a serious handicap to administrative efficiency.

Provincial governments generally consisted of four administrative departments: civil affairs, finance, education, and reconstruction. Many provinces also had a bureau of public security (police), and some had a department of industry. The fact that most provinces had the same institutional arrangement is not necessarily an indication that Nanking was able to develop an integrated system of provincial government. As we shall see later, this arrangement was superficial and was mainly adopted for the sake of convenience.

In the early period of the Nanking Government, all administrative departments in the provinces maintained separate offices. Each department tended to develop its own functional and procedural chain of command linking it to similar administrative bodies in the central and county governments. Thus, although one may think of the provincial government as a combination of departments and bureaus, in practice the activities of these departments and bureaus were uncoordinated. There were no centralized systems of command and communication in the bureaucracy. Communications usually bypassed the secretariat, and each department knew very little of what the others were doing. Whenever a county wanted to communicate with the province about finances, for example, it usually went directly to the provincial department of finance. Likewise, the provincial department communicated directly with the Ministry of Finance in Nanking. Channels of communication were strictly vertical, between organizations performing the same function at different levels.

Under different circumstances such procedures might not have been an obstacle to administrative efficiency. But in China at this time most offices were uncertain of their specific functions; many problems could be solved only by crossing departmental lines, especially in the previously autonomous provincial administrations. The tendency for each department to develop its own rules of conduct, its own channels of communication, and its own operating procedures posed great difficulties; instead of indicating development, this differentiation and diffusion reflected China's political decay.

By the early 1930's it had become clear to many that the existing system needed to be reformed substantially. Attempts at collective decision making through the committee system had only added to the chaos. Committee members often clashed because of conflicting interests, particularly in the absence of an undisputed provincial leader. If anything was accomplished everyone claimed the credit, but if something went wrong no one would accept the responsibility. Further, under the committee system each member maintained his own separate administrative office and a considerable staff, which hindered coordination and increased expenditures. Between 1930 and 1937 the Kuomintang authorities introduced a series of reforms in the Bandit Suppression Zones to put an end to this highly inefficient system.

The Kuomintang's concept of provincial government stressed the administrative bureaucracy at the expense of legislative and judicial systems. Theoretically, the regime was establishing a nationwide judicial system with uniform structures and procedures. Court judges and clerks were largely appointed from above, even in some provinces hostile to Nanking. In most provinces, however, justice was actually determined by political and military power. The concept of rule by law was an ideal that bore little resemblance to reality. Under the circumstances the courts could handle only trivial cases at best. The centrally appointed judges could maintain their offices and exercise judicial authority only with the consent of local and provincial political rulers.

The legislative system had even less substance than the judicial system. There were no legislative bodies at the provincial level, except in Kwangtung, where an elective council had been established by law when the Nationalist Government still had its seat at Canton. The functions of that provincial council were mainly advisory, however, and it had little effect on the political process. Popular participation in provincial politics was ruled out as premature, if not entirely impossible. At the county and city levels legislative bodies were created in only three provinces.[9] Most counties in Yunnan reportedly established councils after the election of 1934. Kweiyang county in Kweichow set up a county assembly in 1934, but it never assumed its proper functions. Forty counties in Chekiang, as well as the city of Hangchow, elected councillors in early 1935, but they were never installed in office or summoned to meet. The Nanking decade, then, saw few efforts to accommodate the growing need for participatory politics. Sun Yat-sen's ideal of a democratic China based on local self-government was a remote dream at this time.

The Organizational Law of the County, promulgated in 1929, did provide for a council to be elected by the citizens of each county.[10] The Kuomintang officially declared that 1935 was the deadline for the establishment of county self-government. On January 8, 1934, the Ministry of the Interior, which was responsible for this task, sent a communication to all provinces instructing them to set up county councils as soon as possible, and in any case not later than the end of the year.[11] Immediately after it had dispatched this communication, however, the ministry reassessed the situation and decided to revise the 1929 Organizational Law. It then submitted a proposal to the Executive Yuan entitled Principles for Remodeling the System of Local Self-Government, which called for a delay in setting up councils and did not specify a new deadline. In the spring of 1934 the proposal reached the Central Political Council, which duly accepted it.[12]

The ministry's decision to invalidate the 1935 deadline was an admission of defeat; any real prospect for local self-government had died long before that. Shen Nai-cheng, a scholar of Chinese local government, cites several reasons for the failure, including the distrust of provincial and district administrators toward popular elections, the indifference of the common people toward local self-government, and the vicissitudes of the central government's policies.[13] All these factors did weigh heavily against the initiation of local self-government. The traditional Chinese belief systems had not fostered political consciousness among the common people, who at any rate were engaged in a struggle for subsistence and had little concern for political participation. For its part the Kuomintang regime continued to mouth the rhetoric of political tutelage, with very little thought to developing a constitutional democracy. In the first three years of the Nanking Government, some rudimentary efforts toward self-government were made in the lower Yangtze valley provinces, but the situation had changed completely by 1931.

What Shen fails to recognize in his assessment is that the Kuomintang power elites, namely Chiang Kai-shek and his associates, deliberately decided to stop all preparations for self-government. There were undoubtedly several party leaders, military men and civilians alike, who viewed the notion of self-government with deep suspicion. And the realities of political life in China gave Chiang and his associates a good excuse to drop efforts at political reform. Thus, as the Japanese threat became obvious and Communist activities increased, Chiang decided to emphasize rural control and security over democracy. The provinces already taking initial steps toward self-government were instructed to discard their plans—by order of Chiang's headquarters, not the Nanking Government. In 1931, for example, his local military headquarters told officials in Kiangsi to revive the *pao-chia* control system and to stop preparations for popular democracy.[14] Throughout the 1930's the Kuomintang authority continued to suppress participatory democracy at the county level and below.

Thus the concept of provincial, county, and local government clearly must be identified with administration. The county had always been the lowest unit in China's formal bureaucratic hierarchy. It was at this level that administrative bureaucrats interacted with local political elites, upon whom effective county administration often depended. The drastic sociopolitical decay and the prevalence of desperados (*t'u-fei*) in rural areas brought the counties to the edge of bankruptcy. Security was guaranteed, if at all, only in the walled garrison towns where county governments were located. The local gentry, mainly in defense of their own property rights and personal safety, did manage to keep an administrative apparatus in operation, but it was of the most rudimentary nature. Under such circumstances the Kuomintang regarded a program involving local self-government and elective bodies as totally unrealistic. Administrative offices, therefore, continued to be the only channels for policy decision and implementation and political participation.

During the Nanking decade provincial and county governments across China varied tremendously in their structures and functions. In the outlying provinces where militarism continued to exist, each provincial government served the needs of its rulers. Although administrative changes did take place in these provinces, patterns of change were far from uniform and certainly not in line with Nanking's official guidelines. Since the Kuomintang's authority reached to only ten provinces by 1936, administrative changes in these provinces alone can provide a basis for assessing the regime's success in promoting local political development. The next chapter will deal with this topic, focusing on such questions as what accounted for Nanking's ability to penetrate these provinces, what were the means and degree of penetration, and what changes did Nanking promote in these provinces.

SIX

The Administration of
the Bandit Suppression Zones

In LATE 1930 Chiang summoned the governors of Hupeh, Hunan, and Kiangsi to Lushan for instructions in planning a military campaign against the Communists. With Lu Ti-p'ing, the governor of Kiangsi, commanding a force of 100,000 men, the first campaign began in December. Since this force was basically composed of provincial, not central-government, troops, it was suspected that Chiang actually wanted the Red Army to destroy it.[1] At any rate, the campaign ended in military disaster, with two divisions lost. The second campaign, under the command of Ho Ying-ch'in, took place in February 1931, likewise with no military success. Nanking was shocked by the result. The third campaign was launched on July 1, and the fourth, with Chiang's trusted lieutenant Ch'en Ch'eng in command, in April 1932. Neither campaign produced the decisive military victory Chiang had hoped for. In fact, the Communists appeared to have increased their strength.

A fifth campaign, to be the decisive one, was very carefully planned for 1933. A government army of 700,000 men was dispatched to attack the main Communist force, some 150,000 strong, which was concentrated in the Kiangsi-Fukien border area.[2] Chiang reportedly adopted a new strategy of encirclement and economic blockade, recommended by his German advisers; the plan emphasized "superior resources, technical equipment, access to unlimited supplies from the outside world, mechanized warfare, and a modern air force."[3] With maximum effort the Kuomintang's strategy bore fruit. The Communists fought long and hard, but in the end they were forced to break out of the trap. In October 1934 they began their historic Long

March, reaching their destination in Shensi some 12 months later, after a 6,000-mile journey.

The spread of Communism in rural China during the Kiangsi Soviet period (1931–34) aroused serious concern in the Kuomintang over its strategy and tactics. The Communists had established Soviet districts in the Kiangsi-Fukien, Hupeh-Hunan, Hunan-Kiangsi, northeastern Kiangsi, Honan-Hupeh-Anhwei, and Hupeh-Hunan-Kiangsi border areas.[4] Although there is considerable disagreement about how much territory and how many people were under Communist influence, one study estimates 300 counties and 30 million people.[5] In Kiangsi alone the Communists may have had influence in 70 of the province's 81 counties; and the Central Soviet District in the Kiangsi-Fukien border area had a total population of three million.[6]

As the Kuomintang's anti-Communist campaigns proceeded, leaders at the Nanchang headquarters gradually realized that military escalation alone could not solve the problem. They eventually made two major decisions affecting policy. First, Chiang Kai-shek declared that the Nationalists' resources must be divided according to the formula "30 percent for military affairs, 70 percent for politics." Second, in order to maximize efficiency, the structure of provincial and local administrative agencies was to be reformed and changes in personnel were to be made. Chiang himself took a great interest in both matters. Writing in 1933 George Taylor observed:

The most impressive thing in Kiangsi today is the personality of Chiang Kai-shek. His driving force permeates every branch of administration and encourages definite tendencies which are apparent in the military organization of the provincial government, in the loyalty of its members to Chiang himself, in the civic training of Nanch'ang citizens.[7]

In a general report on political activities prepared by the Nanchang military headquarters in 1934, Chiang outlined three major goals in waging political warfare against the Communists: bureaucratic efficiency, the political indoctrination of the local population in the Bandit Suppression Zones, and the development of a new spirit among administrative officials.[8] For each goal he specified detailed programs. Regarding the first item, for example, Nanchang announced a series of administrative reforms to be carried out in the Bandit Suppression Provinces. These reforms were aimed at establishing uniform procedures and at coordinating activities among various provincial departments and between provincial and county governments. The ultimate goal was to create an administrative apparatus that would strengthen Nanchang's ability to control the population. Regarding the second and third goals Chiang launched the New Life Movement, which was to promote traditional moral virtues and to mobilize the civilian population according to disciplinary norms and procedures.[9]

Chiang Kai-shek's interest in the problems of administrative efficiency, political education (indoctrination), and political mobilization grew out of his fundamental concern with military matters and came rather belatedly. There had been considerable opposition in the party's ruling circles to his heavy reliance on military solutions. Wang Ching-wei, Hu Han-min, and T. V. Soong, Chiang's brother-in-law, had at different times expressed their disagreement. But in 1931 Chiang was able to gain the support of the Political Council and the CEC; both passed resolutions giving his military headquarters authority over party and administrative affairs in the Bandit Suppression Provinces.[10] Meanwhile, provincial militarists who were incapable of fighting the Communists in their own provinces were forced to accept Chiang's military authority for their own survival. The Communist menace, therefore, did as much to increase Chiang's influence in the regions previously outside his control as to threaten it. In order to extend central authority over these provinces, the Kuomintang's legitimate policy organs gave Chiang a mandate that concentrated military, administrative, and party powers in his hands. As a result the actual center of the Kuomintang regime shifted from Nanking to Nanchang in the course of the anti-Communist campaigns.

Administrative Reforms in Kiangsi

Kiangsi was the most crucial province in Chiang's efforts to effect changes and promote reforms. It was a major base of the Communist forces under Mao Tse-tung and Chu Teh; and Nanchang, its provincial capital, was the headquarters for Chiang's military operations during most of the 1927–35 period. Kiangsi was the testing ground for all kinds of political measures. While directing campaigns there in the summer of 1931, Chiang appointed the Committee for Restructuring Kiangsi and gave it control over military, administrative, and party affairs. Under the leadership of Ho Ying-ch'in, then director of the Administrative Office at Chiang's field headquarters, the committee made dramatic efforts to consolidate Chiang's control over the province. In the following year, after the committee's three-month appointment had run out, Chiang created the Party and Administrative Committee at his military headquarters. Through this body he was able to extend his jurisdiction over party and administrative affairs in the provinces that came to be classified as the Bandit Suppression Zones.

In early 1932 the Communists were reportedly active in 44 counties in Kiangsi.[11] Chiang divided these counties into nine districts and set up a branch of the Party and Administrative Committee in each to rule on behalf of the military headquarters. In effect, the provincial government lost control of these 44 counties to Chiang, who overruled its authority on the grounds that such measures were necessary in fighting the Communists. Although members of provincial administrative elites were allowed to join the branch committees, major decisions were made at Chiang's headquarters.

Following the same basic idea Hsiung Shih-hui, the governor of Kiangsi, further decentralized the system by dividing the province into 13 areas in June 1932. Each area had a special commissioner who controlled political and military affairs, and who also served as magistrate in the county where his office was located. The commissioner was required to make inspection tours of county and municipal governments in his jurisdiction, to supervise administrative activities, and to submit regular reports to Nanchang. As this system gradually became institutionalized, it was adopted as a working model for the other Bandit Suppression Provinces.

During Hsiung Shih-hui's term as governor (1931–41), Kiangsi made extensive administrative reforms based on Chiang's guidelines. Commonly identified as a leading figure of the Political Study Clique, Hsiung enjoyed the strong backing of Yang Yung-t'ai, who was the secretary-general of Chiang's military headquarters and the most active advocate of administrative change in the provinces. Hsiung's energetic efforts partially reflected the clique's desire to control Kiangsi for its own interests. In addition to introducing the administrative inspectorate system, Hsiung also implemented structural

changes right down to the subcounty (*ch'ü*) level. In an attempt to
reform personnel practices, Kiangsi was among the first provinces to
initiate training programs for local administrative officials. Between
1932 and 1937 about 1,700 officials received training, including some
500 magistrates and 860 subcounty administrative heads.[12] During the
same period some 340 magistrate positions changed hands; the turnover was particularly great between 1932 and 1934, reflecting the demand for high-level performance during the anti-Communist campaigns.[13]

It was also in Kiangsi that Chiang Kai-shek launched his New
Life Movement in 1934. Chiang's public lectures during the year
idealized traditional moral virtues and had an air of ritualism about
them.[14] He repeatedly emphasized that the Chinese people should
learn new habits and new attitudes about daily living from the ancient
moral teachings, as well as from men of moral fortitude. Undoubtedly, the whole movement was colored by the growing conservatism
in the Kuomintang's leadership, and Chiang might simply have crys-
tallized this thinking into an action-oriented movement. Still, it is
hard to believe that Chiang and his associates actually looked exclusively to these antecedents for solutions to contemporary problems. Chiang's conservatism in this case was not so much a supersti-
tious faith in the past as a conscious effort to restore confidence in
Chinese tradition, on which cultural nationalism could then be built.
As one writer has observed Chiang was in search of "a tightly dis-
ciplined nation in which each component would respond quickly
and unquestioningly to the wishes of the national leader."[15] Given
the Kuomintang's tendency to move toward fascist thinking and practice in the 1930's, as well as its programs of rural control, it seems
likely that the whole movement was intended to provide a traditionalistic ideological rationale for a militaristic system at the service of the
leader and the nation.

Despite the measures taken to overhaul Kiangsi's local administration, the actual results were inconsequential, since most available
resources were committed to military priorities. Land registration
was completed only in Nanchang County by 1934; only eight counties had instituted land administration bureaus by 1936.[16] The training programs sponsored by the provincial government had produced
188 financial clerks, 427 agricultural directors, and 346 policemen

by 1936—hardly sufficient to meet the administrative needs of a province with 81 counties.[17]

The provincial rulers, like their counterparts in the central government, gave major emphasis to military affairs and rural control, building up their armed forces and reviving the *pao-chia* system. Before 1932 military units and local militia were scattered throughout the province with no system of coordination. Between 1932 and 1934 there were attempts to link units at the county, subcounty, and village levels in a unified structure of command and administration. Chiang's headquarters appropriated funds for this purpose, though they were cut off in 1935.[18] During the anti-Communist campaigns every administrative unit—from the *pao-chia* unit to the administrative inspectorate district—organized defense forces (*pao-wei*). All administrative heads were ordered to serve simultaneously as leaders of local military or quasi-military units. Beginning in 1932 males aged 20 to 40 were recruited for the Communist Extermination Squad (Ch'an-kung I-yung Tui); the ages were changed to 18 to 45 the following year. The squad's total membership between 1935 and 1937 was over two million.[19] The so-called Peace Preservation Division (Pao-an T'uan) conscripted an additional 14,000 men in the 1932–37 period.[20] Recruits received six months' military and political training, after which they were given combat duties and assisted regular troops in field operations against the Communists.

Thus in Kiangsi during the 1930's there was an increasing government effort to militarize civilian life, a development that involved both administrative officials and common people alike. A major purpose of the mass organizations that resulted was to cultivate potential support for the regime, but to what degree this was successful cannot be measured. What we do know is that the Kuomintang's attempts to militarize civilian life wasted considerable human and material resources on programs that had nothing to do with improving socio-economic conditions. Annual costs for maintaining the militia and peace preservation units alone, for example, ranged from Ch $4 million to Ch $7 million in the years 1933–36.[21] And these figures do not include the sums necessary to maintain nonmilitary officials whose duties involved rural control and security. What happened in Kiangsi at this time was not exceptional; programs of this sort were simply pursued with more vigor and in more depth there. Judging from the changes that were introduced in the province, Chiang and the Kuomintang authority had minimum opposition. Regional power structures were practically nonexistent in Kiangsi in the 1930's.

Administrative Reforms in the Bandit Suppression Zones

The failure to extend bureaucratic control over the provinces resulted mostly from the usurpation of political power by military leaders. When Chiang Kai-shek succeeded in seizing administrative power in the provinces, the central administrative authority lost its jurisdiction. It is not surprising, therefore, that the party-government's blueprint for administrative change in the provinces was never realized. Administrative changes were enacted only in the service of military priorities forced on the party by Chiang and his associates. Most provincial resources were mobilized to fuel the military machines. By the end of the Nanking decade, the Kuomintang had managed to secure eight provinces as functionally integrated areas—Anhwei, Chekiang, Fukien, Honan, Hunan, Hupeh, Kiangsi, and Kiangsu.* But whether it could eventually transform them into politically integrated units loyal to the party-government remained uncertain.

During the first half of the Nanking decade, there were few changes in provincial and county administration, and no effort was made to establish administrative structures below the county level. Even in the provinces of greatest activity against the Communists—Kiangsi, Hupeh, Anhwei, and Honan—no fundamental administrative changes were undertaken until the second half of 1931. Prior to that time the Kuomintang authorities relied exclusively on military measures against the Communists. Beginning in 1932 Chiang and his close associates became convinced that the extermination campaigns needed to be accompanied by political mobilization of the population and increased efficiency in civil administration. The man who mapped out the plan for these political and administrative changes and subsequently supervised its execution was Yang Yung-t'ai. His essential goal was to create functionally integrated areas, including provinces, within which the Kuomintang could assert au-

* Although Shensi, Kansu, Szechwan, and Kweichow were officially included in the Bandit Suppression Zones by 1936, the Kuomintang's control there was still superficial in 1937, especially in Szechwan.

thority. In particular, he hoped to eliminate provincial and local forces that stood in the way of Nanking's nation-building.

The reforms had four major components. First, there were attempts to integrate the separate provincial executive departments. Each department communicated routinely with offices performing the same functions in the central government and the county governments, but there was no horizontal coordination among provincial departments. It was accordingly difficult for a provincial government to function as an administrative unit. Second, there was an effort to centralize local administration in the hands of county magistrates.[22] County government had not been functioning as a center of political authority for decades, and as a result many problems simply went unsolved, especially in the many counties with over a million people. Third, there was a movement to establish administrative structures below the county level, especially in rural areas. There was some initial thought of setting up administrative subdivisions (*ch'ü* and *hsiang*), but the major effort was to revive the ancient *pao-chia* system of collective responsibility in the villages.

Finally, an administrative inspectorate system was created to provide a link between the provincial capital and the province's county seats, many of them far from the capital. Standing between the provincial government and the county government, the administrative inspector was to exercise authority at the subprovincial level, particularly in the supervision of county officials' administrative performance. This innovation seems also to have undermined the authority of the provincial government to the advantage of Chiang Kai-shek's military headquarters. The administrative inspector, for example, was authorized to direct public security (military or quasi-military) operations within his own district, in which capacity he reported directly to Nanchang and later Wuchang, bypassing the provincial governor. In addition to these four major components of Yang's reform plan, there were several other measures, most of them designed to cut spending and increase revenues.

On July 1, 1934, the Nanchang headquarters issued its General Principles for the Consolidation of Departmental Offices of the Provincial Government, a measure attributed to Chang Ch'ün, the governor of Hupeh, where the plan was first introduced. Basically the idea was to consolidate all executive departments at one central location with a single secretariat, which would handle incoming and out-going documents, maintain the files, and take charge of purchasing, disbursing, accounting, and related duties. Department heads retained such discretionary power as was compatible with provincial as well as national laws and regulations; however, all their orders would have to be countersigned by the provincial governor. In addition to improving cooperation the new system was expected to reduce administrative staffs and expenses substantially.

The new arrangement went into effect as soon as the General Principles were distributed. But only five provinces—Hupeh, Honan, Anhwei, Kiangsi, and Fukien—had actually made the proposed changes in whole or in part by October 1934.[23] A year later, Chekiang, Kiangsu, Kansu, Shensi, Hunan, and Szechwan reportedly had not complied with the new regulations, being apparently reluctant to adopt changes that might result in increasing the central control of Nanchang and the Political Study Clique.[24] Significantly, the governors of four of the five complying provinces were members of the Political Study Clique.* The fifth province, Honan, whose governor was closer to the Whampoa Clique, made only partial changes. Its secretariat was merged with the departments of Civil Affairs and Education and the Commission on Public Security, but the departments of Finance and Reconstruction continued to maintain separate offices. The new system seemed to work best in Hupeh, where Chang Ch'ün had initiated such reforms much earlier.

The initial plan obviously did not succeed as reformers had hoped. The designation of the secretariat as a center of communication and control actually compounded administrative confusion rather than relieving it. As one dissenting governor argued, because of inadequate organization and a lack of modern technological facilities, the secretariat was unable to handle the large amount of information channeled into it, which led to interminable delays.[25] Most departments continued to send their communications directly to their counterparts in the central government, preferring an established routine to an innovation that was likely to consume additional time and energy.

The attempt to reorganize provincial governments reflects Nanchang's desire to reduce the autonomous power of provincial rulers. To this end it also tried to oversee a significant reallocation of rev-

* The four were Chang Ch'ün (Hupeh), Liu Chen-hua (Anhwei), Hsiung Shih-hui (Kiangsi), and Ch'en I (Fukien).

TABLE 5

Provincial and County Administrative Expenditures
in Selected Provinces, 1933

Province	Provincial expenditures	County expenditures	No. of counties	Annual avg. per county	Monthly avg. per county
Hupeh	Ch $1,119,000	Ch $ 880,000	70	Ch $12,600	Ch $1,050
Anhwei	1,010,000	957,000	61	15,700	1,310
Honan	911,000	1,091,000	111	9,800	820
Kiangsi	813,000	1,132,000	81	14,000	1,170

SOURCES: *Chün-shih wei-yuan-hui pao-kao*, p. 4; Ch'en Chih-mai, "Sheng-fu ho-shu pan-kung," pp. 14–17.
NOTE: The administrative expenditures included here are officials' salaries, building maintenance costs, and other expenses resulting from the normal conduct of administrative duties. Together these are called *pan-kung-fei*. The administrative affairs expenditures listed in Table D.4 of Appendix D include both provincial and county *pan-kung-fei* and many other expenses, such as pensions and the costs of running state-owned enterprises. Hence they are much larger than the figures here.

enues between provincial and county governments, as well as a redistribution of actual administrative power. Nanchang's increasing emphasis on county government was apparently related to its desire to strengthen administrative control over the population in order to exterminate the Communists. The early 1930's had already witnessed the creation of administrative or quasi-administrative units below the county level. The county government's jurisdiction thus became gradually extended. The order to increase county budgets must be seen as part of this overall tendency.

Previously, provincial governments had a substantially larger share of financial resources than county governments. As Table 5 indicates, county administrative expenditures in 1933 were incredibly low. If these figures, which date from before the reorganization of provincial administrative offices, are accurate, county governments did not have enough money even to pay the salaries of their administrative personnel. To finance their operations and to satisfy the greed of their officials, these governments had developed numerous surcharges as additional sources of revenue. The Nanchang headquarters apparently intended to reduce this practice. But in order to make county government an active, vital administrative unit, a substantial increase in official revenues was necessary.

In 1935, after the plan to reorganize provincial governments had been put into effect, the Nanchang headquarters claimed that provin-

TABLE 6

*Changes in Provincial and County Administrative Expenditures
in Selected Provinces Between 1933 and 1935*

Province	Reduction in provincial expenditures	Increase in county expenditures
Anhwei	Ch $309,164	Ch $200,000
Hupeh	293,872	275,874
Honan	237,085	236,160
Fukien	121,681	340,000
Kiangsi	72,885	480,000

SOURCES: Same as Table 5.

cial administrative expenditures were cut significantly, while county administrative expenditures increased. According to figures released by the headquarters, which are shown in Table 6, expenditures in five provinces ranged from Ch $72,885 to Ch $309,164 below those in 1933. These savings were channeled down to the county level. In two cases, Kiangsi and Fukien, increases in county budgets substantially exceeded the provincial reductions. The additional funds must have been provided by Nanchang in response to widespread Communist activities there.* In most of the Bandit Suppression Provinces, at least two-thirds of the increases in county funds did not result from the retrenchment in provincial administration. Whatever the means by which it was achieved, however, the reallocation of revenues between provincial and county governments in the Bandit Suppression Provinces was significant, especially in comparison with the situation in provinces where the Kuomintang had no influence. Provincial expenditures in Shantung, for instance, actually increased after the new administrative reforms were put into effect by Nanchang.[26]

Nanchang's efforts to strengthen administrative units at the county level and below were apparently based on three objectives. First, administrative efficiency at the local level would help the government gain control over the rural population, which had been lost as a result of drastic social upheavals. Second, local administrative efficiency

---

* An official report of the Kiangsi government indicates that provincial administrative expenditures in 1935 were down Ch $132,621. Even if we accept this figure, the increase in county expenditures was still more than three times as high. The report estimates that the reduction of expenditures strictly due to the combination of offices was about Ch $16,703. *Chiang-hsi sheng-cheng-fu ho-shih pan-kung*, pp. 21–22.

would have promoted the regular flow of revenues to the center, which was particularly crucial considering the Kuomintang's severely limited financial resources. Third, Nanchang was attempting to build an administrative command structure that would minimize the power of the provincial governments in the Bandit Suppression Zones. In addition to strengthening local units, this last effort entailed the creation of an administrative unit between the provincial and county levels, the administrative inspectorate district.

Such a division was not without historical precedent. During the Ming and Ch'ing dynasties intermediate administrative units called *fu* (prefectures) and *tao* (circuits) were established to perform two important functions. As one writer points out:

In the first place they reduced the administrative distance between provincial and *hsien* capitals, which in pre-modern China was considerable. At the end of the Ch'ing dynasty in Kuang-tung, for example, it required 4.4 days by express messenger and 12.7 days by ordinary messenger for messages to be relayed from Canton to the extremities of the province. . . . The intermediate areas also performed another valuable function . . . that of coordinating activities between *hsien* governments in order to solve military, policing, and water conservancy problems that overlapped the boundaries of these smaller units.[27]

Tao continued to exist until 1927; in fact 79 were created in 1913.[28] Kiangsu, Chekiang, Anhwei, and Kiangsi reinstituted the traditional intermediate administrative divisions in 1931.

The Nationalists probably had the same purposes in mind as the imperial government when they created intermediate districts in the Bandit Suppression Zones, that is, to coordinate intercounty activities in areas where local officials could not handle emergency problems and to reduce administrative distance. The distance to be reduced in this case, however, was between local units and the Nanchang headquarters. Since transportation systems were generally poor and inspection tours from Nanchang and the provincial capitals were often impossible, there was a danger that administrative decisions might be made at the top without adequate knowledge of the diverse conditions and special needs at the county and village levels.

The intermediate districts were first set up in Kiangsi, where the Red Army had already consolidated bases in the beginning of 1930. The Military Council wanted to integrate civilian and military power under district and local administrative chiefs, in a plan emphasizing local control rather than local self-government. On the basis of the Kiangsi experience, the Nanchang headquarters drew up the Organizational Regulations for the Administrative Inspectorate Office in the Bandit Suppression Zones, which were immediately implemented in the provinces of Honan, Anhwei, and Hupeh. (At the second conference on interior administration in Nanking in 1932, Chiang Kai-shek introduced a resolution changing the title of the new officials in Kiangsi from special commissioner to administrative inspector; their basic duties remained the same.) The system was extended to provinces outside the Bandit Suppression Zones by the Temporary Regulations for Administrative Inspectors, passed by the Executive Yuan. In March 1936 the Yuan drew up new uniform regulations to be applied in all provinces, superseding both previous sets of guidelines. Thus, before the war with Japan was declared, a nationwide system for adopting intermediate administrative units existed on paper.

It would be a mistake to believe that all the provinces actually observed the regulations, however. These administrative changes were adopted only in Kwangsi and the 12 provinces classified as Bandit Suppression Zones by 1936 (including Szechwan and Kweichow). Kwangsi's leaders accepted the system out of a determination to mobilize people and resources for survival in a new political context. Elsewhere outside the Bandit Suppression Zones, however, the system was ignored. In Shansi, for example, often called China's model province in the 1930's, Yen Hsi-shan promoted some administrative changes at the county and village levels; but he did not contemplate the creation of intermediate administrative echelons.[29]

Altogether, some 190 administrative inspectorate districts were established in China.[30] The pattern of administrative reorganization seems clear enough. Changes were intended mainly to serve the immediate military and political needs of the Nanking party-government, and they were adopted only in areas where Nanking had some military strength. Thus any unqualified statement attributing Chiang's shortcomings in national integration to Communist opposition does not ring true, because Nanking's administrative authority was extended primarily through its military efforts against the Communists. The provincial elites, for their own survival, were generally anti-Communist; Chiang and his supporters understood this very well and took advantage of it.

One should not exaggerate the extent of administrative change even in the Bandit Suppression Zones. Five of the provinces—Hunan, Szechwan, Kweichow, Shensi, and Kansu—responded very slowly. Hunan, which was included in the Bandit Suppression Zones before Communist activities were widespread there, was noted for its autonomy; the fact that Ho Chien, a native Hunanese, was governor between 1929 and 1937 clearly indicates Nanking's caution in exerting authority in that province. Szechwan and Kweichow were not opened up to central military and political influence until 1935, when Chiang seized on the Communists' Long March as a justification for sending troops and agents there. His maneuvers took advantage of the fact that the local militarists in Kweichow were weak and those in Szechwan badly divided. Still, the Kuomintang's control in these areas was minimal before 1937.

Shensi and Kansu had long been under the influence of the warlords Feng Yü-hsiang and Yen Hsi-shan. Although they were gradually penetrated by Nanking's forces, the results were quite superficial, especially in the lower units of the administrative structure. Feng had been appointed military governor of Shensi by the Peking government in August 1921, and within a year he had smashed some of the local warlords and established partial administrative control.[31] The situation deteriorated again after Feng received an appointment in the central government in late 1922. When the Kuomintang penetrated the province in the early 1930's, no local administrative networks had been created outside the vicinity of Sian, the capital.

Feng assumed control of Kansu in 1925. He contemplated undertaking administrative reforms there, primarily for the purpose of collecting revenues in order to feed his soldiers. According to James Sheridan:

Feng Yü-hsiang's officers in 1925 and 1926 had squeezed from the people every possible dollar, every available ounce of grain, to take care of the Kuominchün [Feng's army] during the struggle with Chang Tso-lin and the subsequent retreat through Kansu into Shensi. By the beginning of 1927, all of Kansu's reserves were exhausted. Drought conditions began in that year, but did not become critical until 1928. At that time, the people faced high and "almost innumerable" taxes; harvests were poor or, in some areas, nonexistent; and there were no reserves to fall back upon. On top of all this came the frightening ravages of the Muslim revolt, which left fields smoking and peasants dead or fleeing.[32]

These conditions raise serious doubts about the extent of Feng's administrative efficiency and authority. The Kuomintang was able to do little better when it replaced him as ruler of the province; its authority did not extend beyond the walled cities. Thus the creation of the Shensi-Kansu administrative inspectorate was real only on paper.

The organization of the administrative inspectorate was simple: according to the regulations put forward by the Nanchang headquarters in 1932, the office was composed of the administrative inspector, 15 to 19 administrative functionaries, one vice-commissioner of pacification (a military man), and three other military staff officers.[33] The inspector himself was also the commissioner of pacification in the district, a military title, and magistrate of the county where his office was located. The monthly budget at his disposal was slightly over Ch $4,000.[34] In theory, he was subject to supervision by the provincial government; in fact, he was responsible only to the Nanchang headquarters. The inspector had two basic administrative functions.[35] First, he had full responsibility for the government of the county where he was stationed. Second, regarding the other counties and cities in his inspection district, he was required to review the performance of their officials once every three months and to make semiannual reports to Nanchang. His supervisory power extended to budgets and expenditures throughout the district. Further, all official documents from county governments to the provincial government had to go through his office.

As well as having these administrative duties, the inspector also held the position of pacification commissioner, which was equivalent to regional military commander. All the police forces and quasi-military forces (such as militias) in the district were under his command. Regular army units stationed there, usually for the purpose of military campaigns against the Communists were also temporarily responsible to him. If there were local disturbances in areas where army troops were not available, the pacification commissioner was authorized to request troops from nearby districts. As a result of these powers, district administration took on a strong military character.

One of Nanchang's purposes in establishing the inspectorate system was to provide a single command hierarchy for various local military units. By the mid-1930's all the Bandit Suppression Provinces except

Kansu and Shensi had established public security forces. These forces were like regular army troops except that they were paid less and were not so well armed. The Peace Preservation Divisions (Pao-an T'uan) were under the direct command of a provincial public security commissioner; the County Peace Preservation Corps (Hsien Pao-an Tui) were under the jurisdiction of the county governments.[36] These forces existed side by side with militias, police units, and regular army troops; the result was often total confusion, especially in the face of organized disturbances. Hunan, where all units were under the command of the public security commissioner, was probably the only province with a centralized command system. Elsewhere, each local administrative unit (*ch'ü* or *hsiang*) and village normally organized and controlled its own forces.

In addition to establishing the inspectorate system, the Nanchang headquarters tried to impose some order on this chaos by urging the provinces to set up short-term training centers for officers and low-level cadets. In several instances two or three provinces did join together to establish such centers; but owing to their limited facilities, financial resources, and staffs, these temporary camps were not able to produce enough cadres to ensure rural control and security. Thus the Nationalists had to fall back on the centuries-old *pao-chia* system, built on the principles of mutual guarantee and collective responsibility.

Under this system every ten households constituted a *chia*, headed by a *chia-chang*; 100 households constituted a *pao*, headed by a *pao-chang*. Assisted by a handful of administrative clerks, the *chia-chang* and *pao-chang* served as local agents of the formal authority. An important part of their duties involved local security. They were to keep the peace in their jurisidictions, for example, and if they failed they were held responsible by the county magistrates. Most often, school principals, teachers, and officials of the agricultural cooperatives were ordered to help *pao-chang* in maintaining local order.[37] The heads of *chia* and *pao* were also instructed to organize or reform local militia. Through them Nanchang hoped to bring various local military units under the uniform command structure of the County Peace Preservation Corps. In some counties, however, magistrates continued to have enormous problems in dealing with militia leaders. Some units apparently remained under the control of "local bullies and rotten gentry" (*t'u-lei*).[38] Then, too, newly appointed magistrates often scared local forces away by imposing effective reform requirements; as a result whole units had to be reorganized.[39]

The *pao-chia* system provided an excellent means of mobilizing the people to meet specific village goals. In situations of rural distress the Nanchang headquarters naturally wanted to impose additional duties on the system in order to relieve both provincial and local authorities. On orders from the magistrate, *pao-chang* and *chia-chang* recruited quotas of unpaid laborers for work projects and security functions. Most jobs involved rural rehabilitation—the building of roads, bridges, schools, temples, and so on. Labor recruits also served as night patrolmen.

Yang Yung-t'ai was responsible for reviving the *pao-chia* system in the Bandit Suppression Zones.[40] His initial goals—the total mobilization and militarization of the civilian population—were closely related to the anti-Communist campaigns and were intended to reduce the burden on the regular army. Also, the *pao-chia* organization was to establish tight control over potential Communist sources of recruits. Any villager expressing sympathy with the Communists was automatically viewed as a disrupter of the peace; and the *pao-chang* or *chia-chang* in his district was obliged to report him or be held personally responsible for the consequences. By reviving the *pao-chia* system the Kuomintang allied itself with rural elites oriented toward the status quo. As one writer remarked in the 1930's, "Heads of Chia and Pao must be local rich peasants or landlords, no outsiders being eligible."[41] Such a development inevitably closed off the option to pursue fundamental socioeconomic change. The party's earlier revolutionary goals of progressive reform were sacrificed to the goal of security in rural China.

The reorganization and maintenance of public security forces produced acute financial problems. Monthly expenses of public security forces in seven Bandit Suppression Provinces in 1934 were reported as follows:[42]

Chekiang	Ch $510,000	Hupeh	Ch $400,000
Kiangsu	480,000	Fukien	360,000
Hunan	460,000	Anhwei	300,000
Kiangsi	450,000		

High as they are, these figures could represent a deliberate under-estimation of actual military costs by the Nanchang headquarters. Commissioner Fan of Hupeh frankly admitted that, taking both government and nongovernment sources together, total annual expenditures for public security in his province amounted to some Ch $15 million, or Ch $1.25 million a month.[43] At any rate, maintaining security and order created a heavy financial burden on the people. As we shall see later, it was one of the major items toward which provincial resources were allocated.

In the final analysis, one must realize that Nanchang's administrative reforms were not supported by all provincial governors. There was, quite understandably, a widespread feeling that the administrative inspectorate system was designed to undercut the powers of provincial rulers. Administrative inspectorate offices were often set up in locations that had not previously served as prefectural capitals, and that minimized the influence of existing local elites.[44] Several provincial leaders responded to this kind of challenge with passive resistance. On the question of whether or not an administrative inspector should also serve as a county magistrate, for example, even the relatively friendly governors of Kiangsu and Kiangsi insisted that the decision should be made by each individual province, based on its own particular circumstances and needs. Of the eight administrative inspectors in Kiangsi in 1933, half did not hold the position of magistrate.[45] According to one scholar Nanchang's administrative reform regulations were not seriously observed by provincial authorities:

It has often been the practice of the provincial government to ignore the [inspector] and issue direct orders to the counties. Similarly, the counties bypassed the intermediary agent to reach the provincial government directly. Consequently, the office of the administrative inspectors at times became a pure nuisance to both the provincial and county governments.[46]

Evidence suggests that the acceptance of reforms in the provinces was dictated primarily by security considerations. Many leaders were forced to adopt the administrative changes and militarization programs proposed by the Kuomintang because of the presence of Communists in their provinces. Fear and uncertainty compelled them to acquiesce to the inflow of central troops and finances into their regions. The Kuomintang too was essentially preoccupied with military considerations. In short, although there were some administrative changes, it is highly doubtful that administrative offices were able to deal with major social and economic problems. Efforts to establish systems of administrative control were, of course, more successful in some provinces than in others. Everywhere, however, the state of provincial administration remained precarious; it was the Kuomintang's military and quasi-military wings, rather than its administrative and party institutions, that imposed whatever national integration there was.

SEVEN

The Educational Background of Provincial Elites

THE ROAD to bureaucratic status in China during the 1927–37 period was unmarked and irregular, given the almost total lack of institutionalized standards. The traditional examination system had been eliminated, and the newly created recruitment system provided only a small number of the bureaucrats needed. Many obtained positions through social relationships and political intrigues. Above all, after the collapse of the Ch'ing dynasty political power had steadily shifted from the literati and land-based gentry to military men. Regional militarists became the key to bureaucratic success in the provinces, and they continued to exercise provincial and local power during the decade after 1927. There was a growing number of intellectual elites who had received modern college or graduate training in China or abroad. Some of them had influence at the Kuomintang center as well as in the provinces. But as a group their impact on China's political development at this time was highly limited.

In this chapter we shall consider the various schools attended by provincial elites. Most of the middle-level and upper-level military officers in the 1920's and 1930's came from the Japanese Cadet Military Academy (Shikan Gakko), the Whampoa Military Academy, the Paoting Military Academy, the Military Staff College, and various provincial schools. Each will be discussed in turn, followed by a consideration of nonmilitary administrative training schools. The material here provides a background for the next chapter, which will examine the social composition of various provincial elites and the changes in these groups during the Nanking decade.

The Japanese Cadet Military Academy

Following the Sino-Japanese War (1894-95), the Ch'ing government decided to send able young men to Japan to study military affairs. It instructed the provincial military governors to select promising candidates, many of whom were subsequently sent to the Japanese Cadet Military Academy at public expense. According to an agreement made with the Japanese, only students sent by the Chinese government would be allowed to enroll at the academy.[1] Generally, those selected first attended military preparatory schools in Japan, after which they took the entrance examination for the academy. If successful, they received 12 to 18 months of training there, plus three to six months of field service. Most of the first cadets at the academy came from the provinces of Hunan, Hupeh, Chekiang, and Kiangsi.[2] On returning to China the vast majority of graduates immediately became involved in military and political intrigues, affiliating themselves with the Peking government, Liang Ch'i-ch'ao's Progressive Party, or Sun Yat-sen's revolutionary movement centered in the south.

As a select group with high-quality training, graduates played an important role in Chinese politics, particularly in the 1911–27 period.[*] After the 1911 revolution academy-trained officers controlled seven provinces: Shansi (Yen Hsi-shan), Shensi (Chang Feng-hui), Fukien (Sun Tao-jen), Hupeh (Li Yuan-hung), Kiangsi (Li Lieh-chün), Kweichow (T'ang Chi-yao), and Yunnan (Ts'ai O).[3] Some of them later formed the main opposition to Yuan Shih-k'ai's imperial ambitions. One study estimates that of the 1,300 officers of brigadier rank or above in the years 1912 to 1928, 117 were trained in Japan; 61 were graduates of the Paoting Military Academy.[4] It is likely that most of those trained in Japan were graduates of the Cadet Military Academy. Many of the students sent to Japan by the government became revolutionaries and were later influential in the new provincial armies and military schools.[5]

The so-called Shih-Kuan Clique (Shikan Clique), a term referring to graduates of the Japanese academy, gradually declined in impor-

---

[*] Among the well-known alumni of the academy were Chiang Kai-shek, Chang Ch'ün, Chen Ch'i-ts'ai, Chang Shao-ch'eng, Chiang Pai-li, Ts'ai O, Li Lieh-chün, Hsü Ch'ung-chih, Sun Ch'uan-fang, Yen Hsi-shan, Li Ken-yuan, Hsü Shih-cheng, T'ang Chi-yao, Huang Fu, Ch'eng Ch'ien and Ho Ch'eng-chün.

tance after the establishment of the Nanking Government. Yen Hsi-shan did retain independent power as a provincial overlord; and a few graduates held high-level military positions at the time of the Northern Expedition, for example, Li Lieh-chün and Hsü Ch'ung-chih. Most of these men disappeared from the military and political scene immediately afterward, however. The only ones remaining were those closely associated with Chiang Kai-shek, notably Chang Ch'ün, Huang Fu, Ch'en I, Ho Ch'eng-chün, Ch'eng Ch'ien, and Ho Ying-ch'in.

The Whampoa Military Academy

The Whampoa Military Academy was founded in May 1924 to train revolutionary military cadres for the Kuomintang. It was created at a time when Sun Yat-sen had decided to turn to the Soviets for assistance. Chiang Kai-shek was sent to the Soviet Union in 1923 to study the Red Army's training system, and initial planning for the academy was carried out jointly by the Chinese and the Soviets. Despite the fact that many of Whampoa's administrators and instructors had been trained in Japan or in schools modeled on the Japanese system, the Soviet influence over the academy continued to be enormous. In addition to providing ideological guidelines and advice on organizational matters, the Russians supplied a large quantity of arms to the academy—some 3,000 rifles in May 1924 and 8,000 more (with 500 rounds of ammunition for each) in October.[6] Later 15,000 rifles, machine guns, and pieces of artillery were reportedly "obtained from the Soviets through cash purchase or other transactions."[7] It is difficult to imagine how the academy could have survived without this assistance, considering that it initially had only 30 rifles at its disposal.

The presence of Russian advisers and military instructors at the academy before the Northern Expedition helped ensure the influence of the Communists, particularly in the area of political education. Since the academy aimed at producing a professional revolutionary army, ideological indoctrination was an essential aspect of the training program. The Soviet system of party control over the military was adopted, and various educational methods were used to foster political consciousness in the students, most of whom came from rural communities and had a strong sense of patriotism.[8] Although Sun

Yat-sen's doctrines formed the academy's official ideology, there was a substantial number of Communist followers in both the faculty and the student body. Administrative staff members in charge of political education were either Communists or Communist sympathizers, for example, Teng Yen-ta and Chou En-lai. Since the academy was trying to produce a party army in a short period of time, its educational program failed to include subjects that would promote the intellectual development as well as the military proficiency of future officers.[9] Such an education limited the students' views on social, economic, and political change, which is significant considering that some of them came to occupy positions of great importance.

The history of the Whampoa Military Academy after the Northern Expedition is rather complicated. Although the Whampoa campus itself was not formally closed until 1930, the Central Military Academy that replaced it was set up in Nanking soon after Chiang Kai-shek's forces reached the city in 1927. During the Nanking period the Central Academy turned out 11,950 cadets.[10] In addition to the main campus in Nanking, there were branches in these cities before the war: Wuhan (1927–32 and 1936–41), Changsha (1926–27), Nanchang (1928–29), Loyang (1933–38), and Chengtu (1935–37). The branch campuses alone trained over 50,000 cadets, many of whom were recruited from outlying provinces and from the ranks of provincial army units.[11] The impact of the branch campuses was not significant, however, in prewar years. During the war additional campuses were set up in Kwangsi and Kweichow and in the cities of Suichin, Kwangfeng (Kiangsi), and Canton.

The importance of the Whampoa graduates as a group has already been described in Chapter Three. Their unique position in modern China's political history is essentially due to their role during the Northern Expedition and their close association with Chiang Kai-shek. Some 3,000 Whampoa graduates joined the Northern Expedition under Chiang's command.[12] Of course, not all the academy's graduates and instructors came to support the Kuomintang. There were many who had been Communists from the beginning, or who, like Lin Piao, had later joined the Communist cause; and although these men fall outside of our discussion of the Whampoa Clique, it is important to remember the critical roles they played in the Red Army. The Whampoa men who did choose to stay with the Kuomintang formed a cohesive, well-organized, formidable military clique, with a commitment to Chiang and the party-state that amounted almost to a crusade.*

A considerable number of the Whampoa instructors held key positions in both the central government and the provincial governments in the 1930's. The students as a group occupied military positions of secondary importance. Only four of them reached the position of division commander in the prewar period: Kuan Lin-cheng, Huang Chieh, Hu Tsung-nan, and Hsü T'ing-yao. The rest of the Whampoa graduates held middle-level officer positions. None became a governor, the head of a provincial civil affairs department, or a provincial party chairman. All in all, the graduates of the Whampoa Military Academy are not very important in a study of provincial administrative elites.

The Paoting Military Academy

The one school that did become exceptionally important in provincial politics between 1927 and 1937 is the Paoting Military Academy. A high percentage of military professionals throughout the 1920's and 1930's were alumni of this academy. Formally established in 1912, it was not designed to be an independent academy like the others; it was the highest institute in a military educational system.

The origins of this system go back to 1903, when the Ch'ing government established the Commission for Army Reorganization. In 1904 the commission adopted an officer-training system with three levels—primary schools at each provincial capital, four regional middle schools (at Peking, Sian, Wuchang, and Nanking), and the Paoting Military Academy in Hopei. All graduates of the three-year primary schools could automatically enter the middle schools, if they so desired. Then, after two more years of training and one year of regular military service, they could automatically attend the academy.

---

* Regarding Chiang's relationship with the Whampoa cadets, MacFarquhar has observed: "In a successful military organization the men obey their leader. To the Whampoa cadets, Chiang was that leader, the man who introduced them to the army, the man with whom they lived, worked, and fought; and thus they followed him as soldiers. But Chiang was also the confidant of Sun Yat-sen and the protagonist of his revolution, the leader of the new movement that was to save China; and thus they followed him as revolutionaries. . . . To the cadets, Chiang had come to personify the revolution." MacFarquhar, p. 163.

Although the primary schools recruited students through open competitive examinations, and although there were no fees throughout the system, most recruits came from families of "landlords, rich peasants, and prosperous merchants."[13] They were not drawn from the areas immediately around the schools, as was intended.

Academic standards in the army's schools were as good, if not better, than those in regular primary and middle schools. The primary school was more or less the equivalent of a regular junior high school, and most beginning students were 14 or 15 years old. The basic entrance requirements were physical fitness and a certain proficiency in the Chinese language. In both the primary and middle schools, the curriculum was generally modern, including such courses as geometry, algebra, the basic physical sciences, world history and geography, and physical education.[14] Unfortunately, the primary schools graduated only five classes and the middle schools only two.

The Paoting Military Academy did not come into existence until the Ch'ing government was overthrown in 1911. Its first seven classes were composed exclusively of graduates of the army's primary and middle schools; many of these men had served in various regional armies before entering the academy, civil wars having delayed their formal military education. The eighth and ninth classes, the last two, were opened up to graduates of regular high schools and candidates recommended by regional military officers. These men were almost as successful in their future careers as the men who had passed through the lower-level military schools. In all, the Paoting Military Academy produced some 9,000 cadets between 1911 and 1919.[15]

Some Kuomintang leaders considered recruiting the Paoting graduates for their revolutionary activities. In 1916 Sun Yat-sen himself apparently urged a Paoting graduate to set up an alumni association to promote involvement in the Kuomintang movement.[16] The Four Army Schools Alumni Association was subsequently established in 1918 in Shanghai with over two hundred members.* Although the Shanghai association lasted until 1926, most of its members moved to Canton, where they founded a similar association in 1923. Between

---

* The Paoting Military Academy was one of the four schools. The other three were in fact groups of military schools: the preparatory schools at Tsingho and Wuchang, the middle schools, and the primary schools. Graduates of, and even one-time students of, these schools were generally considered Paoting alumni.

1923 and 1926 many Paoting alumni held important positions at Sun Yat-sen's headquarters in Kwangtung, at the Whampoa Military Academy, and in provincial army units.[17] During the Northern Expedition Paoting alumni controlled the First, Second, Seventh, and Eighth armies.* The growing number of Paoting alumni in the National Revolutionary Army apparently alarmed Chiang Kai-shek, and in 1929, one year after the alumni association moved its headquarters to Nanking, it was dissolved under pressure from the highest military authority.[18] After that, the alumni had no nationwide organizational ties, but Paoting cliques continued to operate in many provinces. They were particularly influential in Kwangtung, Kwangsi, Hunan, and Szechwan during the Nanking decade. Although leaders in the first three provinces occasionally joined forces against Chiang, local affinity, political expediency, and ideological differences usually disrupted these attempts. Still, the impact of the Paoting graduates on Chinese politics, especially at the provincial level, was crucial.

Paoting alumni held key military positions in Kwangtung between 1923 and 1929 through the influence of Teng Yen-ta, Ch'en Ming-shu, Chang Fa-k'uei, and Li Chi-shen (who, although not a Paoting man himself, nevertheless had close career ties with graduates in Kwangsi and Kwangtung). During the Northern Expedition Li Chi-shen's Fourth Army, the Kwangtung Army, drew most of its ranking commanders from Paoting alumni. After arriving at Wuhan this army was reorganized and expanded into the Fourth and Eleventh armies, with Chang Fa-k'uei and Ch'en Ming-shu as the respective commanders. Ch'en later joined Chiang Kai-shek to oppose the left-wing Wuhan Government. The remnants of his Eleventh Army became the core of the Nineteenth Route Army, with two Paoting men, Chiang Kuang-nai and Huang Ch'i-hsiang, as division commanders.[19]

Meanwhile, portions of the original Fourth Army in Kwangtung were regrouped and expanded under the command of Ch'en Chi-t'ang. Although Ch'en never graduated from a school in the Paoting system, below him were three alumni: Yü Han-mou (later governor of Kwangtung), Hsiang Han-p'ing, and Li Yung-ching. Under Ch'en Chi-t'ang's leadership they made up a ruling clique that consolidated

---

* Li Tsung-huang, "Pao-ting hsüeh-hsiao," p. 25. Although most of the middle-level and lower-level officers in the First Army had been students in Whampoa's first and second classes, most of the upper-level officers were from Paoting.

Kwangtung and maintained it as a semiautonomous province until 1936, when Chiang's political maneuvers finally brought it under Nanking's authority.

School ties and group cohesion were also strong in the Kwangsi and Hunan armies. From the mid-1920's on, the Kwangsi Army was controlled by Paoting students, notably Li Tsung-jen, Pai Ch'ung-hsi, and Huang Shao-hung (who joined the Nanking Government in 1930).* Under Li's command during the Northern Expedition, the army showed considerable ability in brief military encounters with the Hunan Army and then with Chiang Kai-shek's forces. Although the eventual result was retreat and isolation in Kwangsi, for a while the army held Peking and threatened to control the entire lower Yangtze valley region, plus Kwangtung and Kwangsi. During the Nanking decade Kwangsi's ruling oligarchy was almost entirely composed of Paoting men.

Hunan was under the jurisdiction of the warlord Wu P'ei-fu before it was taken over by forces of the Northern Expedition. Wu's lieutenant Chao Heng-t'i was governor, and T'ang Sheng-chih, a Paoting graduate, was a division commander. Shortly before the Northern Expedition began, T'ang allied himself with the Kuomintang and defeated Chao Heng-t'i. Between 1926 and 1928 he virtually controlled Hunan, Hupeh, and Anhwei, becoming the quasi-military dictator on whom the short-lived Wuhan Government depended during its struggle with Chiang Kai-shek. T'ang drew his chief military lieutenants almost entirely from his classmates at Paoting.[20]

In 1928 T'ang was defeated by the joint forces of Li Tsung-jen and Ch'eng Ch'ien. Three of T'ang's important subordinates, all Paoting graduates—Li P'in-hsien, Yeh Ch'i, and Ho Chien—immediately changed their allegiance. Li and Yeh sided with Li Tsung-jen, who replaced T'ang. Ho Chien pledged his loyalty to Chiang Kai-shek's Nanking Government and was rewarded with the governorship of Hunan. A direct confrontation between the forces of Li Tsung-jen

---

* Although Li Tsung-jen never attended the Paoting Military Academy, he did graduate from one of the primary schools in Kwangsi affiliated with the Paoting system. Among his classmates were Pai Ch'ung-hsi, Huang Shao-hung, Hsia Wei, Huang Hsü-ch'u, Li P'in-hsien, and Yeh Ch'i. See Boorman, *Biographical Dictionary*, vol. 2, pp. 336–37. All of them except Huang Hsü-ch'u later entered the Paoting Military Academy; Huang went to the Military Staff College in Peking.

and Chiang Kai-shek soon followed. Li was driven out of Hunan in 1929, and he and his close associates withdrew to their native Kwangsi, which like Kwangtung remained an autonomous province for almost a decade. Ho Chien served as governor of Hunan for nearly a decade.

The cases of Kwangtung, Kwangsi, and Hunan demonstrate that Paoting graduates were powerful, and that their common school ties could sometimes provide a basis for concerted political and military action. In Szechwan, although the Paoting alumni did not form a cohesive group, several contending warlords had Paoting backgrounds—for example, Teng Hsi-hou, Liu Wen-hui, and Tien Sung-yao.

In conclusion, it should be noted that the Paoting alumni with significant provincial power during the Nanking decade controlled territories along the Yangtze River and in the south, notably Hupeh, Hunan, Szechwan, Kwangsi, and Kwangtung. Political and military developments in Szechwan were largely unrelated to national events. In the other four provinces the emergence of Paoting forces was related to the rise of the Kuomintang's political fortunes. Paoting military men in Kwangsi and Kwangtung had developed formidable strength even before they joined the Kuomintang's military expedition against the warlords in 1926. But the rise of Paoting influence in Hupeh and Hunan came after the Kuomintang's successful military effort against Wu P'ei-fu. The defeat of the warlords Wu P'ei-fu and Sun Ch'uan-fang in central and eastern China created a military and political vacuum, which was quickly filled by Paoting men and other Kuomintang-affiliated figures. The same thing cannot be said of the northern provinces, where Feng Yü-hsiang and Yen Hsi-shan maintained a continuing, if gradually declining, influence.

Other Military Institutions

The exact number of military institutions in the provinces is unknown, since many were created for immediate military purposes and were short-lived. At any rate, these institutions did not have a uniform training program, and their organizational and financial bases were diverse. Most important, the quality of students varied tremendously.

Historically, the Ch'ing government began to take a serious interest in developing such military schools soon after China lost the war with Japan in 1895. It subsequently sponsored army schools at Tientsin and Kaiping, which turned out many well-known warlords: Wang Shih-chen, Feng Kuo-chang, Tuan Ch'i-jui, Ts'ao K'un, Chang Hsün, Chang Huai-chih, Wu P'ei-fu, and Sung Yü-cheng. The central government also sponsored a short-term course at Paoting, which was the predecessor of the Paoting Military Academy. There were also over 200 provincial military schools of all kinds, with such divergent labels as *wu-pei, wu-t'ang, su-ch'eng, nien-chun, sui-ying,* and *chün-shu.*[21] Among the best known were those in Yunnan (founded by Ts'ai O), Manchuria (Chang Tso-lin), Shansi (Yen Hsi-shan), Nanking (Feng Kuo-chang), and the northwest (Feng Yü-hsiang).* The purpose of these schools was clearly to cultivate military officers for the armies of their warlord sponsors. For example, in Szechwan the leading warlord, Liu Hsiang, and his close associates were all graduates of the province's short-term military school.

The oldest army school in modern China is the academy founded by Tuan Ch'i-jui in 1906 in Paoting (not the same school as the Paoting Military Academy). The academy was originally called the Officers' Military Academy; the name was subsequently changed to the Military Preparatory Staff College in 1912 and then to the Military Staff College in 1913, when the school was moved to Peking.[22] When the National Revolutionary Army reached Peking in June 1928, Chiang Kai-shek immediately took over the presidency of the college. It was moved again to Nanking in late 1931, then to Changsha, and finally during the war to Chungking. Between 1906 and 1948 the college graduated 21 classes, with a total of more than 2,100 officers.[23] In addition, over 3,500 military professionals attended the college's short-term training programs for generals and upper-level staff members.[24] Two men stand out among the school's early graduates, Li Chi-shen and Huang Hsü-ch'u, who served as governors of Kwangtung and Kwangsi, respectively.[25]

The number and diversity of military elites and forces in China placed enormous obstacles in the way of Nanking's efforts to establish a centralized command system. As early as January 1929 Chiang

* The Yunnan military school was particularly important. Ts'ai O, the governor of Yunnan in 1911 and 1912 and a graduate of the Japanese Cadet Military Academy, invited his classmates from the academy to serve at the school, thus making it "a center of revolutionary and reformist ideas." Jerome Ch'en, "Defining Chinese Warlords," p. 576.

Kai-shek attempted to disband regional commands. At that time he controlled only an estimated 240,000 of the 1.6 million men under arms in China.[26] A conference on military disbandment was called in 1929; but it was a total failure because of the opposition of regional militarists like Feng Yü-hsiang, Li Tsung-jen, and Yen Hsi-shan, who quite rightly viewed the plan as an effort by Chiang to subordinate all other military commands to his own.[27] In the late 1920's and the early 1930's, Chiang Kai-shek's military power was still weak, and the foundations of the Nanking Government were still shaky. Conditions were not ripe for integration.

The situation was greatly changed by the mid-1930's. Chiang was waging military campaigns against the Communists, and he had gained control of China's commercial and industrial centers. By persistent, skillful manipulation he had divided the regional militarists. These developments, along with the pressing need for unity against Japanese aggression, all seemed to favor Chiang's plans. In 1933 he had set up a training camp in Lushan to standardize the command system and to try to eliminate regional diversity. Military officers of all ranks from various provinces were brought together to work out a common system. The training program at Lushan signified a major step in the struggle to integrate the heterogeneous military units.*

Nonmilitary Training Institutions

There were also a variety of nonmilitary institutions that trained new recruits for administrative positions and offered refresher courses for those already in service. Nanking had created several schools with short-term programs, and similar efforts were made by provincial governments. Many provincial and county administrative functionaries were summoned to training camps for short periods to learn about the new structures and procedures instituted by the regime.

One of the most important of the Nanking schools was the Central Political Academy, created especially to train cadres for the task of

---

* The training camp was moved to O-mei-shan (Szechwan), in 1935. Programs were interrupted in 1936 because of the coalition of Kwangtung and Kwangsi militarists against the Nanking Government. The camp was returned to Lushan in 1937, at which time training programs were revised in the face of the Japanese threat. High school principals and student affairs directors, members of local cadres in charge of boy scouts, and party administrative personnel were all summoned to receive military training there. See Huang Shao-hung, p. 97.

nation-building under the party's dictatorship. It was established in 1926 in Nanking under the name Central Party Affairs Academy. In 1929, after four classes had been graduated, the name was changed to the Central Political Academy, and a four-year academic program equivalent to that of a regular university was instituted. In keeping with the goal of producing loyal political cadres, the school's curriculum emphasized the social sciences, with special attention given to various branches of public administration. No engineering or science courses were offered, except for some of the pure sciences, which were deemed essential in any program of higher education. Students had to be loyal party members and lived according to strict military discipline.[28] There was no tuition.

Ch'en Kuo-fu and other C.C. members helped plan for the academy and maintained close relations with it after its establishment. As a party school it was under the control of the party's Organization Department, which the Ch'en brothers headed. In the academy's early years Ch'en Kuo-fu served as the business manager, who was responsible for raising funds for operation. Later he also served as the head of education, in which capacity he supervised the school's instructional programs and curriculum. During his term as governor of Kiangsu (1933–37), he recruited a large number of faculty and students from the academy to serve in his bureaucracy in positions ranging from administrative clerk to commissioner of provincial government.[29]

Graduates of the academy were initially intended to serve as party cadres, and most of the 252 graduates between 1926 and 1929 were dispatched to work in party branches at all levels.[30] After the academy changed to a four-year university system in 1929, however, students received a broad education in local administration. In subsequent years graduates were primarily recruited to fill local administrative posts. Some provincial rulers assigned them to the county level because, being new in an area, they were freer to deal with sensitive administrative problems and less vulnerable to pressure from the local gentry.[31] Although Kuomintang leaders wanted to place graduates of the academy in as many provinces as possible to serve as party watchdogs, there was little chance of doing so in provinces whose rulers were hostile to Nanking. Thus before the war most graduates remained in Kiangsu, Chekiang, and Anhwei. In its first decade the academy did not produce enough cadres either for the party or for local administrations. Efforts by graduates to introduce reforms— in Chiang-ling county in Kiangsu and Lan-yu county in Chekiang, for example—met with minimal success.[32] The academy was a limited source of administrative recruits; it never exerted a great influence on China's administrative bureaucracy.

The Nanking Government also made sporadic efforts to promote short-term training and orientation programs for both recruits and officeholders at lower administrative levels. Each group was given a series of courses emphasizing what Nanking considered to be the basic skills of modern administration. As early as October 1926 a joint meeting of central administrative and party representatives passed a resolution urging each provincial party-government to estab- lish a party school to train local administrative talent.[33] Little came of this resolution until after 1931, when efforts were made to set up various short-term institutes to orient recruits and local administrators to the new system. Between 1931 and 1934 these institutes trained some 3,000 people with high school backgrounds for such positions as land administrators, directors of government-sponsored cooperative societies, land-tax collectors, and the so-called local self-government cadres.[34]

In March 1936 the Ministry of the Interior established an orienta- tion school for county and city administrators in Nanking, under the supervision of Chiang Tso-pin. There were five training sessions a year, each lasting one month. An estimated 546 local administrators from three cities and 15 provinces went through the programs—401 magistrates, 29 administrative inspectors, and 116 other lower-level administrative functionaries.[35] Lectures given at the school explained the doctrines of Sun Yat-sen and suggested ways to improve local activities against the Communists. All trainees were taken on a tour to observe various administrative agencies of the central govern- ment. These visits were consistent with the assumption that strong links between central and local governments were a necessary first step in nation-building. It is difficult to assess the effects of such training programs on local efficiency. Their purpose, however, is clear. Through the programs trainees were given the opportunity to discuss their common problems and to learn about possible solutions.

In summary, like most attempts by provincial governments, Nanking's efforts to improve the quality of administrative personnel were at best marginal. Not many people received training, and few of those who did were actually appointed to administrative positions. In addition to the schools sponsored by Nanking, there were some private or quasi-public training programs—for example, those associated with rural reconstruction projects and universities. But given the size of China's population and territory and the depth of her administrative problems, efforts in this area fell far short of the needs. Thus all levels of government, from local to central, remained under the firm control of military men in the prewar decade. The lack of administrative personnel who could deal with mounting socioeconomic problems certainly did not help the decaying situation in the countryside. The military men, who had inadequate training for handling these problems, continued to devote most of their time to never-ending military and political intrigues. Without the assistance of efficient and able civilian administrators, the militarists, despite their sporadic achievements, virtually ruined whatever hope was left to save China from collapse.

EIGHT

The Social Composition and Turnover of Provincial Elites

THE KUOMINTANG'S PURSUIT of a centralized political system was from the beginning a task of enormous magnitude. It was especially difficult in China's political context, where regionalism was a primary fact of life. The social climate, the scarcity of available resources, and the exceedingly backward physical transportation network further obstructed attempts at national integration. But the party-government, inspired by a strong sense of nationalism, was not ready to settle for any kind of political federation that would recognize regional autonomy.

Centralization requires a national government to control provincial and local rulers. Was the Kuomintang regime able to impose its authority on provincial elites? How far away from the center was the party's self-proclaimed legitimacy to rule China actually accepted? Moreover, to what extent did the elites who held formal administrative positions in provincial and county governments actually rule their territorial jurisdictions? The social and political chaos following the collapse of the imperial bureaucracy made governing very difficult. Much of China, especially the countryside, had been ruled for two decades by a random assortment of bandits, military overlords, and local bullies, not to mention the regional warlords whose merciless financial squeezes put millions of peasants on the brink of starvation.

Our examination of the social characteristics and turnover of administrative elites in the provinces will help us identify more precisely what kinds of people were ruling China's provinces and counties at this time. This knowledge, in turn, will perhaps provide a fresh insight into the nature of provincial power relationships.

Magistrates

For centuries magistrates had been the leading officials at the lowest echelon of the formal administrative bureaucracy, the county (*hsien*). Their major functions in the imperial bureaucracy were to transmit local revenues to the court and to maintain security and order in their own jurisdictions. Their survival in office depended in part on their relations with informal local sociopolitical elites, usually known as the gentry. During the imperial reign magistrates acquired their position through competitive examinations. The destruction of the examination system in 1905 and of the imperial order itself in 1911 shook the foundations of the magistrates' formal careers and removed the source of their authority and power. Although magistrates continued to hold office in many provinces, they now had to live under a different set of rules, which, in the final analysis, were the personal requirements of regional warlords. There were no longer definite procedures or behavioral norms.*

When the Kuomintang regime came to power, it had every interest in creating a new administrative order to ensure its legitimate control over the magistrates. (China at this time had about 1,940 counties.) The Ministry of the Interior lost no time in announcing temporary regulations for the examination of magistrates. In accordance with the new regulations the ministry dispatched officials to the provinces to conduct examinations in 1928 and 1929. We know that three were held in Chekiang, Kiangsi, and Hunan; two in Kiangsu; one each in Anhwei, Fukien, Kwangtung, Kwangsi, Hupeh, Yunnan, Hopei, Shantung, Shansi, Chahar, and Suiyuan; and one for Honan, Shensi, and Kansu together. In all, some 1,300 candidates qualified to be magistrates through the examinations.[1] It is not clear how many of them were actually employed, but judging from the available information it was only a very small percentage. The Ministry of the Interior reported that out of a total of 2,223 magistrates in 1932, only 97 obtained their positions through central and provincial government examinations.[2]

---

* This attempt to venture into the area of county administration inevitably suffers from a general lack of reliable information. The problem is particularly acute with regard to the social characteristics of magistrates. There are no serious works that can be used as a basis of inquiry.

When the Examination Yuan was established in January 1930, it assumed official responsibility for conducting magistrate examinations. Permanent regulations were not promulgated until September 1935, however, and in the meantime the Ministry of the Interior undertook to compile lists of all candidates for the position of magistrate. After the ministry investigated these candidates, the names of those it approved were to be forwarded to provincial governments for consideration in the case of a vacancy. Such efforts were sporadic, and the criteria used for qualification were vague. The Examination Yuan itself was virtually inactive during this period. By the end of 1935 it had held no examinations. The first took place in 1936, producing only nine successful candidates. The second, given in 1937, produced 45 candidates.[3] We have no information on how many of these candidates actually served as magistrates.

At a time of such drastic social and political change, it was crucial to maintain administrative stability. The chaotic situation in the countryside had already scared away many magistrates whose revenues and survival depended on ties to regional militarists. Keeping magistrates in office became a critical test of whether the government could establish an effective administrative system. We have some data on the turnover of magistrates, thanks to Chiang Kai-shek. In February 1931, as president of the Executive Yuan, he pushed a resolution through that body requiring provincial governments to submit regular monthly reports on magistrates. The Ministry of the Interior prepared the appropriate forms, and the plan was executed immediately.[4] In 1931 14 provinces submitted reports to the ministry. The number increased to 18 the following year, after which the practice was stopped. The data from these reports is presented in Table 7.

Of the 14 provinces reporting in 1931, nine had a turnover of magistrates in over 50 percent of their counties; six of these were in the Bandit Suppression Zones. Of the 18 provinces reporting in 1932, 14 had a turnover of magistrates in over 50 percent of their counties; eight were in the Bandit Suppression Zones. Further, the three provinces with the highest percentage of counties with a turnover—Anhwei (88.5 percent in 1932), Hupeh (86.8 percent in 1931 and 89.7 in 1932), and Honan (84.7 percent in 1931 and 82.3 in 1932)—were all in the zones.

Judging from the percentages two Bandit Suppression Provinces,

Kiangsu and Chekiang, appeared to enjoy relative stability. In 1931 and 1932 an average of 38.5 percent of the counties in Kiangsu changed magistrates; the two-year average in Chekiang was 49.3 percent. Other statistics are not so encouraging, however. In Kiangsu the average term of magistrates was only slightly over one year. A survey conducted by the provincial Civil Affairs Department in 1934 reported that between April 1927 and April 1934 some 416 magistrates had been dismissed from office.[5] This represents an average of almost 60 dismissals a year, or about five every month. This dramatic reshuffling is quite possibly related to the growing power of the C.C. Clique in Kiangsu. The party's Central Political Academy, which the clique also controlled, may have been the source of replacements for magistrates whose backgrounds and political ties the clique did not find satisfactory.

TABLE 7

The Turnover of County Magistrates, 1931–32

Province and year[a]	No. of magistrate positions	No. of magistrates replaced	Total no. of magistrates	Pct. of counties with turnover of magistrates	Avg. term of magistrates (days)
*Anhwei					
1932	61	98	159	88.5%	241
Chahar					
1931	16	13	29	68.8	287
1932	16	15	31	68.7	291
*Chekiang					
1931	75	52	127	61.3	407
1932	75	29	104	37.3	486
*Fukien					
1931	64	40	104	59.4	348
1932	64	61	125	75.0	358
*Honan					
1931	111	169	280	84.7	155
1932	113	149	262	82.3	238
Hopei					
1931	120	90	210	60.8	381
*Hunan					
1931	75	50	125	58.7	414
1932	75	62	137	68.0	442
*Hupeh					
1931	68	90	158	86.8	227
1932	68	105	173	89.7	237
Jehol					
1931	15	5	20	26.7	542
1932	15	8	23	46.7	646
*Kansu					
1932	66	61	127	78.8	179
*Kiangsi					
1931	81	33	114	37.0	380
1932	81	76	157	70.3	349

TABLE 7 (continued)

Province and year[a]	No. of magistrate positions	No. of magistrates replaced	Total no. of magistrates	Pct. of counties with turnover of magistrates	Avg. term of magistrates (days)
*Kiangsu					
1931	61	44	105	55.7	384
1932	61	14	75	21.3	374
Kirin					
1931	42	12	54	26.2	710
Kwangsi					
1932	94	29	123	29.8	314
Kweichow					
1932	81	68	149	76.5	339
Shansi					
1931	105	93	198	67.6	589
1932	105	78	183	59.0	454
Shantung					
1931	108	49	157	38.0	240
1932	108	71	179	53.7	436
*Shensi					
1932	92	92	184	77.2	306
Suiyuan					
1931	17	7	24	35.3	433
1932	18	13	31	55.5	502
Tsinghai					
1932	14	10	24	71.4	571

SOURCE: *Nei-cheng nien-chien*, 1935, pp. (B)831–33.
NOTE: Asterisks (*) indicate provinces in the Bandit Suppression Zones.
 [a] There are no 1931 figures for Anhwei, Kansu, Kwangsi, Kweichow, Shensi, or Tsinghai, and no 1932 figures for Hopei or Kirin. Heilungkiang, Kwangtung, Liaoning, Ningsia, Szechwan, Sikang, Sinkiang, and Yunnan submitted no reports.

Chekiang's stability was more solid. The average term of magistrates there and in Hunan in 1931–32, some 14 to 15 months, was longer than the terms of magistrates in other Bandit Suppression Provinces. Yang Yung-t'ai's 1935 report on political work by Chiang's field headquarters confirms that magistrates in these two provinces had longer average terms; many of them reportedly had held office for several consecutive years.[6] Yang, the leading figure in efforts to bring about reforms in provincial and local government, strongly emphasized the need for administrative stability at the county level and praised Chekiang and Hunan as model provinces. But there is some evidence of instability in Chekiang. One study reveals that 22 magistrates were replaced in that province between February and August 1933 and another 14 between October 1933 and April 1934.[7]

A high percentage of turnover was not always detrimental to Nanking's interests. In some cases it reflected the changing balance of power between Chiang and the regional warlords. This is clearly illustrated in the provinces previously controlled by Feng Yü-hsiang. Four of these experienced a large turnover of magistrates in 1931 and 1932. In Kansu 78.8 percent of the counties changed magistrates in 1932, in Shensi 77.2 percent. In Honan and Chahar, for which we have figures for both years, the percentage of counties changing magistrates averaged 83.5 and 68.75 percent, respectively. This turnover resulted from Nanking's successful penetration of the area after Feng's military power had declined. Newly appointed governors had to pay more than lip service to the central government's demands, one of which was for loyal magistrates.

In two other provinces previously controlled by Feng, the percentage of counties changing magistrates was lower; Shantung averaged 45.9 percent for the two years and Suiyuan 45.4 percent. Nanking's influence in these two was not so great. Chiang Kai-shek turned Shantung over to Han Fu-chü as a reward for his defection from Feng during the military contest.[8] The subsequent years saw Shantung solidly under Han's governorship; the Kuomintang could not make any major changes there. In Suiyuan a Mongolian autonomy movement effectively blocked attempts, first by Feng and then by Chiang, to establish county administration in areas with a heavy concentration of Mongolians.[9]

The most interesting case was that of Honan, where in late 1930 Chiang appointed his trusted lieutenant Liu Chih governor. A native of Kiangsi province Liu had had a long and close association with Chiang. He had graduated from the Paoting Military Academy, had served with Chiang under Hsü Ch'ung-chih in the Second Army, and was a military instructor at the Whampoa Academy. During the Northern Expedition he was a division commander in Chiang's First Army. When Liu became governor of Honan, he was confronted with a bureaucratic machine geared to promote the interests of Feng Yü-hsiang and his associates. During his early months in office Liu moved decisively to reshape the county bureaucracy, replacing most of the magistrates. His ability to do so reflects the fact that as an outsider from the south his hands were not tied by local particularism. Liu managed to stay in office as Nanking's watchdog for six years.

Still, even though turnover sometimes represented growing central influence, frequent changes of officeholders did create insecurity, which contributed to ineffective administration. A lack of security tended to discourage elites from working to improve the bureaucracy. It also encouraged misconduct. Since officials were aware that their appointments would probably be brief, they were undoubtedly tempted to exploit their positions and get rich quickly by illegal means. Corruption, in turn, occasionally resulted in dismissal. Magistrates were isolated from rural problems and had no intention of breaking down the barriers between them and the peasants. As Yü Ching-t'ang, the head of the Civil Affairs Department in Kiangsu, commented in the mid-1930's: "Most magistrates wait for things to be done rather than do them; there are more talkers than workers among them, and more who sit in town than go out into the villages."[10]

How well did the Nanking Government understand the situation? We know that it had very little information on which to base any accurate assessment. Most magistrates, insecure and apathetic, refused to submit the regular reports demanded by the central government. Although provincial governments were required to submit lists of both magistrates in office and candidates for the position to Nanking for an examination of their qualifications, few did so. Thus the central government had a limited role in the evaluation and selection of magistrates. Table 8 summarizes its efforts along this line in the years 1930–35. Only Kiangsu, Chekiang, Hunan, Shansi, Shensi, and Honan regularly submitted magistrate lists for approval; the others did so irregularly or ignored Nanking's instructions altogether.

As Table 8 shows, the number of appointments was highest in Honan, Hunan, Kiangsu, and Chekiang. Except in Honan, however, the number of magistrates approved was far from the number needed. A separate source reveals that in 1933 the central government approved only 144 magistrate appointments out of 506 cases submitted to it; it dismissed 35 magistrates in office and disqualified 42 candidates.[11] The figures suggest that most appointees were not subjected to the central government's screening process beforehand. This reinforces our suspicion that even at the most elemental level, Nanking's ability to penetrate the provinces was minimal.

Kwangtung, Szechwan, and Yunnan submitted no information about magistrates at all. Evidently, rulers in these provinces were able to maintain relatively autonomous control over local officials. Other provinces, notably Kwangsi, Kweichow, Anhwei, Sikang, Tsinghai, Sinkiang, Kansu, Shensi, and Ningsia, occasionally submitted

TABLE 8

*The Evaluation of Magistrates and Magistrate Candidates
by the Central Government, 1930–35*

Province	Appointments	Dismissals and dis- qualifications	Qualifications under investigation	Qualification certificate demanded[a]	Total no. evaluated
Anhwei	2	1			3
Chahar	9	1	2		12
Chekiang	23	16	11	1	51
Fukien	5		21		26
Honan	127	6	33		166
Hopei	5		10		15
Hunan	41	26	26		93
Hupeh	2		7		9
Kiangsi	3	4	4		11
Kiangsu	27	13	42		82
Shansi	19	7	28		54
Shantung	3	1	21		25
Shensi	10	10	18	2	40
Suiyuan			8		8
Tsinghai	3		9		12

SOURCE: Central Statistical Bureau, "Hsien-chang ti jen-mien" (Appointment and dismissal of magistrates), *Cheng-chu ch'eng-chi t'ung-chi* (Statistics of political performance), Jan., Mar., Aug. 1933; May–July 1936.

[a] That is, a magistrate had to produce written proof of qualification to remain in office.

lists, but they were highly irregular and unsatisfactory by any normal standards. Geographic distance and inefficient communications may have been partly responsible. Anhwei is the only one of these provinces close to Nanking; the rest are quite remote.

Table 9 summarizes the available data on the age and birthplace of magistrates in 1931–32. In general, magistrates were middle-aged, averaging nearly 38. Those in Shensi, whose average age was 28, were an unusual exception. A combination of famines, Muslim revolts, and financial squeezes by warlords destroyed the social, economic, and political structures in that province and virtually eliminated the local traditional elites. The majority of magistrates were natives of the province in which they served. The percentage of nonnative magistrates was higher in the northern provinces, where some positions were filled by Manchurians fleeing from the Japanese and others by southerners who served as watchdogs for the central gov-

TABLE 9

Age and Birthplace of Magistrates, 1931–32

Province	No. of magistrates	Average age	Birthplace			
			Native		Nonnative	
			No.	Pct.	No.	Pct.
Anhwei	159	32.0	94	59.1%	63	36.9%
Chahar	60	38.5	1	1.7	57	95.0
Chekiang	231	37.5	135	58.4	93	40.3
Fukien	229	39.5	162	70.7	63	27.5
Honan	542	36.5	340	62.7	191	35.2
Hopei	210	39.0	81	39.0	129	61.0
Hunan	262	41.0	232	88.5	16	6.1
Hupeh	331	39.5	239	72.2	66	19.9
Jehol	43	47.5	17	40.0	26	60.0
Kansu	127	38.0	53	42.0	74	58.0
Kiangsi	271	37.5	186	68.6	59	21.8
Kiangsu	180	42.0	99	55.0	81	45.0
Kirin	54	45.0	11	20.0	43	80.0
Kwangsi	123	40.0	106	86.0	17	14.0
Kweichow	149	41.0	130	87.0	19	13.0
Shansi	381	38.0	284	74.5	90	23.6
Shantung	336	35.0	81	24.1	253	75.3
Shensi	184	28.0	97	52.7	43	23.4
Suiyuan	55	38.0	5	9.0	50	91.0
Tsinghai	24	40.0	6	25.0	18	75.0
TOTAL[a]	3,951	37.9	2,359	59.7%	1,451	36.7%

SOURCE: *Nei-cheng nien-chien*, 1935, pp. (B)831–33.
NOTE: There are no 1931 figures for Anhwei, Kansu, Kwangsi, Kweichow, Shensi, or Tsinghai, and no 1932 figures for Hopei or Kirin. No information is available for Heilungkiang, Kwangtung, Liaoning, Ningsia, Szechwan, Sikang, Sinkiang, or Yunnan.
[a] The number of natives and nonnatives does not add up to the total number of magistrates because the birthplace of some magistrates is unknown.

ernment. Aside from the northern provinces Kiangsu and Chekiang were the only ones with a significant number of nonnative magistrates. Very few nonnatives served in Shansi, Shensi, Kiangsi, Hupeh, Kwangsi, Kweichow, and, above all, Hunan.

As for educational background, Table 10 shows that roughly one-fourth of all the magistrates in China in 1931 and 1932 had some regular college education. Adding in those who had gone to the lower-quality academies of law and administration (*fa cheng*), we find that about half of the magistrates at this time had some modern higher

TABLE 10

Educational Background of Magistrates, 1931–32

Type of school attended	1931 (N = 1,729)		1932 (N = 2,223)	
	No.	Pct.	No.	Pct.
College	413	23.9%	557	25.1%
Law and administrative academies	638	36.9	512	23.0
Military and police academies	204	11.8	357	16.1
Other[a]	474	27.4	797	35.8

SOURCE: *Nei-cheng nien-chien*, 1935, pp. (B)831–33.

[a] Includes those who had passed the examinations sponsored by Nanking.

education in nonmilitary institutes. There were also many graduates of military and police academies, both of which provided two to four years of post-high-school education. (Although military men and police did not dominate county elites at this time, the figures are high enough to indicate there were significant security problems in the countryside.)

About two-thirds of the magistrates had received higher education of some kind in either military or nonmilitary schools, which indicates a decline in the influence of the traditional system. A majority of the ruling administrative officials in rural China had at least been exposed to the ideas and values associated with new educational institutes. The remaining one-third of the magistrates apparently had passed the examinations sponsored by Nanking or had attended traditional schools, short-term magistrate-training courses, or high schools or their equivalents. In general, this group constituted a residual traditional force. Their educational background clearly did not prepare them to accept and promote the idea of a modern administrative bureaucracy.

There was a wide range of provincial variation. With the exception of Hunan, all provinces in the Bandit Suppression Zones had a larger percentage of magistrates with education beyond high school than provinces outside the zones. Hunan's case was rather peculiar. Although Governor Ho Chien deferred politically to Nanking, the province enjoyed more autonomy than the other Bandit Suppression Provinces. This independence is reflected in the long average term of office for magistrates there and the almost exclusive employment of provincial natives as magistrates (232 out of 262 in 1931–32). Only about 30 percent of Hunan's magistrates had had higher education of any kind. The traditionalistic and particularistic character of this administration becomes even more evident when one considers that 48 of the total 75 magistrates in 1931 reportedly obtained their positions through recommendations.*

Governors and Other High Provincial Officials

A governor's status varied from province to province, depending largely on the degree of independence he had in the exercise of power. The political power of governors who were also leading military overlords approximated that of military dictators of independent states. Governors in this category were Lung Yün of Yunnan, Yen Hsi-shan of Shansi, and, to a lesser degree, Ch'en Chi-t'ang of Kwangtung. Some governors obtained semi-independent powers, subject to the nominal approval of their superiors. These included the governors in North China under Feng Yü-hsiang,† the governors in Kwangsi under Li Tsung-jen and Pai Ch'ung-hsi, and three governors under Chiang Kai-shek—Ho Chien of Hunan, Han Fu-chü of Shantung, and Ch'en Kuo-fu of Kiangsu. Chiang freely appointed governors in most of the remaining provinces. (See Appendix A for a complete list of provincial governors during the decade.) The disparity of power and status among governors is clear enough. Since there was no established institutional definition of a governor's power, much depended on the military forces under his command and his relationship with superior political forces. Although the Kuomintang government gave nominal recognition to governors, it often had no control over who acquired these positions.

A study of the educational backgrounds of governors and other leading provincial figures clearly reveals that the effects of warlordism

---

* *Hu-nan nien-chien,* 1932, p. 21. Hunan's autonomy was demonstrated in many other ways as well. In the area of economic development, for example, Ho Chien and other leading provincial figures rejected proposals from the central authorities for significant financial investments in the province. Lo Tun-wei, pp. 78–79.

† Feng negotiated with Chiang for the right to appoint governors in some northern provinces. In July 1929, for example, they reached an agreement whereby Feng could appoint his protégés as heads of the provincial governments in Shensi, Kansu, and Ningsia. Sheridan, p. 262.

TABLE 11
Education and Career Patterns of Provincial Governors, 1927–37

Province	Total no. of governors	Education						Career pattern	
		Military education			College education		Other education	Military	Civilian
		Paoting	Japanese schools	Others	China	Abroad			
Anhwei	8	2	1	1	2	—	2	*6	2
Chahar	5	1	1	3	—	1	—	4	1
Chekiang	6	1	1	—	—	1	3	*3	3
Fukien	3	1	—	2	—	—	1	3	—
Honan	4	—	—	2	—	—	1	*4	—
Hopei	5	1	1	4	—	—	—	5	—
Hunan	2	—	—	—	1	1	1	*2	—
Hupeh	6	2	1	1	1	—	1	4	2
Kansu	6	1	2	1	1	—	1	*5	1
Kiangsi	3	—	1	1	1	—	1	*3	—
Kiangsu	4	1	—	2	1	1	—	3	1
Kwangsi	5	1	—	1	—	1	2	*4	1
Kwangtung	3	1	—	1	—	—	—	2	1
Kweichow	5	1	—	2	—	—	2	*5	—
Ningsia	2	1	—	1	—	—	—	2	—
Shansi	4	—	2	2	—	—	—	*3	1
Shantung	3	1	—	—	1	—	2	*3	—
Shensi	4	—	—	3	1	—	—	3	—
Sinkiang[a]	3	—	—	—	—	—	1	—	—
Suiyuan	3	1	—	2	—	—	1	3	1
Szechwan	2	1	—	1	—	—	—	2	2
Tsinghai	3	—	—	—	—	—	3	*3	—
Yunnan	1	—	—	1	—	—	—	1	—
TOTAL[b]	75	16	10	21	7	3	17	61	13

SOURCES: (1) Nei-cheng nien-chien, 1935, pp. (B)334–43; (2) Boorman, Biographical Dictionary, vols. 1–3; (3) Biographies of Kuomintang Leaders; (4) Boorman, Man and Politics; (5) China Year Book, 1929–37; (6) Perleberg; and (7) Who's Who in China.

NOTE: See Appendix B for an explanation of the data in this table. Asterisks (*) indicate provinces where the number of governors with a military career does not equal the number with a military education. In most of these cases a man with no military education followed a military career. In Chahar and Shansi a governor with a military education followed a civilian career.

[a] The education and career of one Sinkiang governor could not be traced.

[b] The totals have been adjusted to compensate for the fact that some men held governorships in more than one province. They represent actual men, not the sums of the columns.

persisted throughout the Nanking decade. A survey of the 75 men who served as governors in 23 provinces during the decade indicates that 47 had a military education and 61 had followed a military career before becoming governor (see Table 11). Excluding Sinkiang, which remained virtually outside Chinese politics before the war with Japan, only four provinces outside the Bandit Suppression Zones (Chahar, Shansi, Kwangtung, and Kwangsi) ever had a civilian governor; and each of these served only a short term. Clearly, military men continued to dominate provinces where Nanking's authority did not reach. In the Bandit Suppression Zones there were a few more civilian governors, although the total number, nine, by no means reflected a drastic shift toward the appointment of civilians with modern educations. These nine civilian governors were close associates of Chiang Kai-shek, for example, Chu Chia-hua of Chekiang, Ch'en Kuo-fu of Kiangsu, and Yang Yung-t'ai of Hupeh. The provincial power structures they established became part of Chiang's national clientele machines. Their appointments, therefore, did not represent a major progressive change from regional warlordism, in which particularistic standards determined political relationships.

The predominantly military orientation of the governors is reflected in the limited number who had received an ordinary college education. As Table 11 shows, there were only ten in all, seven of whom served in the Bandit Suppression Zones. The 16 governors from the Paoting Military Academy constituted the largest group from a single school. Only ten governors had studied in Japanese military schools, a clear indication of the declining influence of this group. Most of these had attended the Japanese Cadet Military Academy. Of the 21 governors who graduated from various Chinese military schools other than Paoting, none attended Whampoa. (Liu Chih of Honan did serve as an instructor at Whampoa, but he was a graduate of Paoting.) This reveals how little influence the academy had in provincial politics during this period.

The percentage of military-oriented administrative officials was smaller at lower bureaucratic levels. Table 12 summarizes a 1936 survey by the Ministry of the Interior of the social characteristics of provincial leaders (including governors, the heads of departments and public security bureaus, and secretaries-general) and municipal officials (including majors, secretaries-general, and the heads of bu-

TABLE 12

Social Characteristics and Education of High-Level Provincial and Municipal Administrative Elites, 1936

Province or city	Total no.	Average age	Pct. of natives	Education					
				College education		Military education		Traditional examination	Other education
				China	Abroad	China	Abroad		
Anhwei	10	50	30%	2	4	2	1	—	1
Chahar	11	49	18	4	1	3	—	—	3
Fukien	9	47	56	2	2	2	2	—	1
Honan	11	47	18	3	4	4	—	—	—
Hopei	10	54	90	3	3	1	—	1	2
Hunan	11	47	82	3	4	2	—	2	—
Hupeh	10	46	40	2	5	2	1	2	—
Kansu	9	46	44	1	3	3	—	—	—
Kiangsi	11	46	82	—	8	1	2	—	2
Kiangsu	12	41	42	—	8	2	—	—	4
Ningsia	10	41	—	3	—	3	—	—	—
Shansi	10	49	90	4	4	1	—	1	3
Shantung	9	46	22	—	3	3	—	—	2
Shensi	11	50	27	4	2	2	—	1	2
Suiyuan	8	47	13	3	1	2	—	—	3
Tsinghai	9	41	11	3	—	2	—	1	—
Yunnan	10	47	100	2	5	3	—	—	—
Nanking	6	44	—	3	3	—	—	—	—
Peking	7	40	—	2	1	4	—	—	—
Tientsin	7	44	—	3	3	—	1	—	—
Weihaiwei	1	34	—	—	1	—	—	—	—
TOTAL	192			47	65	42	7	8	23

source: "Ti-fang kao-chi hsing-cheng kuan-li tiao-ch'a tung-chi," (Statistical survey of high-level administrative officials in some provinces and municipalities), *Nei-cheng t'ung-chi chi-k'an* (Statistics quarterly of the Interior), no. 2, 1937, pp. 101–3.

note: Provincial officials included in the survey were governors, department and public security heads, and secretaries-general; municipal officials were majors, secretaries-general, and bureau heads. Chekiang, Kwangsi, Kwangtung, Kweichow, Sinkiang, and Szechwan submitted no figures.

reaus). It shows that 25.5 percent of the 192 officials surveyed had a military education. In contrast, the percentage for governors during the 1927–37 decade was 62.7. According to the available evidence the percentage of military men serving as magistrates was even lower, 11.8 percent in 1931 and 16.1 percent in 1932. About 58.3 percent of the provincial and municipal elites in the 1936 survey had a college education. Only 13.3 percent of all governors during the decade had a college education; the comparable percentages for magistrates were 23.9 in 1931 and 25.1 in 1932.

Although these statistics are random and do not cover all ruling elites at the provincial and county levels during the Nanking decade, they do point out some significant differences among officials at various levels. The influence of the military in the provinces was greatest at the level of governor and gradually decreased in lower administrative echelons. College backgrounds were more widespread among urban administrative elites and provincial government leaders; most of those who attended college served as heads of departments. If one is to make a tentative generalization, it appears that provincial political power was largely controlled by military men, who recruited college-educated elites to assist them. A majority of the college-educated officials in the 1936 survey had received their higher education abroad.

The available information indicates that governors, intermediate officials, and magistrates belonged to the same basic age group, a vast majority being in their 40's. Very few officials were over 50; drastic sociopolitical change had disrupted the careers of older men. Magistrates appear to have been slightly younger than other officials, but we have only 1931–32 statistics for them. The most important exceptions to the age pattern were the governors of Kwangsi and Kiangsi, most of whom were under 40 years old. Political events in Kwangsi in the first half of the 1920's had produced an oligarchy of younger militarists, notably Huang Shao-hung, Li Tsung-jen, and Pai Ch'ung-hsi, who successfully eliminated the older warlords and established firm control over the province. Held together by school ties (all were Paoting men) and a strong sense of regionalism, this group asserted independent control over Kwangsi until 1936. In Kiangsi the appointment of younger governors may have been related to Chiang Kai-shek's concerted efforts against the Communists, who were particularly active there, in the first half of the 1930's.

As we have already said, the majority of magistrates were natives of the provinces in which they served, with some exceptions in North China. Provincial and municipal governments had a much weaker nativistic character, according to the 1936 survey by the Ministry of the Interior (Table 12). In only six of the 17 provinces reporting—Fukien, Hopei, Hunan, Kiangsi, Shansi, and Yunnan—did natives account for over half of the high-level administrative elites. Of the 192 officials in all, 110 had a college education, 65 in foreign schools. The percentages of magistrates with a college education are considerably lower. Thus there seems to be a strong correlation between nobility and education.*

Table 13, which shows the age and provincial origins of governors in 23 provinces during the decade, reveals a relatively small percentage of nativism. In only six provinces—Kiangsu, Kwangsi, Kwangtung, Shansi, Szechwan, and Yunnan—were over half the governors natives. Together Tables 12 and 13 reveal some interesting patterns and variations regarding nativism among governors and provincial and municipal administrative officials. Only Yunnan, Shansi, and Hunan show strong nativism in both tables. Szechwan, Kwangsi, and Kwangtung each had a very high percentage of native governors, but unfortunately they did not submit figures to the 1936 survey. Judging from their political relations with the Kuomintang regime before 1936, they might also have had a high percentage of native provincial and municipal officials. Three of Kiangsu's four governors were natives, but the percentage of natives in other administrative elite groups was only 42 percent. The province was consolidated in the 1930's by the C.C. Clique, whose leader, Ch'en Kuo-fu of Chekiang, served as governor from 1933 to 1937. The recruitment of provincial and municipal officials was no doubt influenced by the patron-client relations of the clique, which often cut across provincial boundaries. Hopei and Kiangsi each had a low percentage of native governors (one of five and one of three, respectively) but a very high percentage of natives in the other elite groups (90 and 82 percent).

* Hopei represents the most pronounced exception to the general pattern of a large percentage of native magistrates and a smaller percentage of natives in higher administrative positions. The majority of its magistrates in 1931 came from other provinces, whereas its provincial and municipal administrative elites in 1936 were 90 percent native. The high percentage of nonnative magistrates in 1931 reflects the inflow of immigrants after the Manchurian Incident.

TABLE 13

Age and Birthplace of Provincial Governors, 1927–37

Province	No. of governors	Age				Birthplace		
		40 or over	Under 40	Un-known	Avg.	Native	Non-native	Un-known
Anhwei	8	6	1	1	45.7	2	5	1
Chahar	5	3	2	–	44.8	–	5	–
Chekiang	6	4	2	–	46.1	2	4	–
Fukien	3	3	–	–	47.6	1	2	–
Honan	4	2	2	–	43.5	–	4	–
Hopei	5	3	1	1	41.3	1	4	–
Hunan	2	2	–	–	40.5	1	1	–
Hupeh	6	5	–	1	47.4	3	3	–
Kansu	6	4	–	2	46.7	1	5	–
Kiangsi	3	1	2	–	40.0	1	2	–
Kiangsu	4	3	1	–	41.5	3	1	–
Kwangsi	5	–	3	2	35.0	4	1	–
Kwangtung	3	2	1	–	43.0	2	1	–
Kweichow	5	2	2	1	41.6	1	2	2
Ningsia	2	1	1	–	39.5	–	2	–
Shansi	4	3	1	–	49.5	3	1	–
Shantung	3	2	–	1	42.0	–	2	1
Shensi	4	4	–	–	46.0	2	2	–
Sinkiang	3	1	–	2	61.0	–	2	1
Suiyuan	3	3	–	–	42.6	–	3	–
Szechwan	2	1	1	–	40.5	2	–	–
Tsinghai	3	1	1	1	44.0	–	3	–
Yunnan	1	1	–	–	40.0	1	–	–

SOURCES: Same as Table 11.
NOTE: See Appendix B for an explanation of the data in this table.

Altogether, a certain degree of nativism existed in nine provinces—Yunnan, Shansi, Szechwan, Kwangsi, Kwangtung, Hunan, Kiangsu, Hopei, and Kiangsi. In the case of Yunnan, Shansi, Szechwan, Kwangsi, and Kwangtung, nativism did coincide with political independence from Nanking. But Kiangsu, Hunan, Kiangsi, and Hopei did not enjoy the same autonomy; in fact, as Bandit Suppression Provinces, the first three were subject to considerable control from Nanking. Even within the Kuomintang's jurisdiction, then, provincialism continued to exist, despite the talk of eliminating it. At the same time, in some provinces that did enjoy varying degrees of political autonomy from Nanking—notably Kweichow, Shantung, Suiyuan, Chahar, and Ningsia—nativism was generally low. One possible explanation is that the weakness of power groups in these provinces permitted outsiders from nearby provinces to come in and establish political bases.

Provinces with the lowest percentages of native governors were Chahar, Ningsia, Suiyuan, Shantung, Honan, Hopei, Kansu, Tsinghai, Sinkiang, Kweichow, and Anhwei. The situation in the first seven reflected the decline of Feng Yü-hsiang's power in North China and the increasing degree of central penetration. At one time or another in the 1920's, all of these seven provinces were under the control of Feng or Yen Hsi-san. When Feng's military base began to crumble, some of his chief lieutenants defected to Nanking and were rewarded with governorships in provinces of which they were not natives. In other provinces previously controlled by Feng, such as Kansu and Honan, Nanking successfully installed its own men.

In Sinkiang, Tsinghai, and Kweichow separatist forces had always been weak, and power vacuums were traditionally filled by outsiders, either regional warlords or appointees of the central government. On several occasions Nanking had difficulty exerting its authority over these provinces, owing to ineffective means of communication and transportation. Anhwei also failed to develop strong native political forces, placed at it was between various contending regional forces in North China and the lower Yangtze valley.

The political changes after 1911 and the central government's inability to control provincial administration resulted in great variations in the terms of governors and department heads. Table 14 shows the average terms of governors and the heads of civil affairs departments in 23 provinces during the Nanking decade. The overall average of governors' terms was 26.6 months. In nine provinces (Anhwei, Chahar, Chekiang, Hopei, Hupeh, Kansu, Kwangsi, Kweichow, and Shensi), the average term was less than two years. In all nine the frequent turnover was apparently related to outside political influence. Only two, Kwangsi and Chekiang, had strong native militarists or political groups. The relatively short average term in Kwangsi was a result of political instability in 1928–30, when forces from both Yunnan and the central government intervened in the province. The short term in Chekiang was perhaps related to the fact that many of the leading natives held national office, thus leaving the provincial

TABLE 14

*Average Terms of Provincial Governors and Heads of
Civil Affairs Departments, 1927–37*

Province	Governors			Civil affairs dept. heads		
	Total months of service	No.	Avg. term (months)	Total months of service	No.	Avg. term (months)
*Anhwei	117	9	13.0	120	11	10.9
Chahar	105	5	21.0	105	5	21.0
Chekiang	117	6	19.5	122	6	20.3
Fukien	107	3	35.7	122	8	15.3
Honan	114	4	28.5	114	8	14.3
*Hopei	109	6	18.2	109	6	18.2
Hunan	110	2	55.0	110	4	27.5
Hupeh	115	6	19.2	115	11	10.5
Kansu	80	6	13.3	105	9	11.7
Kiangsi	116	3	38.7	116	8	14.5
Kiangsu	116	4	29.0	116	10	11.6
*Kwangsi	122	6	20.3	122	2	61.0
Kwangtung	109	3	36.3	120	7	17.1
Kweichow	97	5	19.4	120	7	17.1
Ningsia	104	2	52.0	104	4	26.0
Shansi	112	4	28.0	112	6	18.7
Shantung	110	3	36.7	110	5	22.0
Shensi	81	4	20.3	81	6	13.5
Sinkiang	104	3	34.7	104	6	17.3
Suiyuan	105	3	35.0	105	3	35.0
Szechwan	104	2	52.0	104	6	17.3
Tsinghai	106	3	35.3	106	5	21.2
Yunnan	114	1	114.0	114	3	38.0
TOTAL	2,474	93	26.6	2,556	146	17.5

SOURCES: *China Year Book*, 1928–38; *Nei-cheng nien-chien*, 1936, pp. 334–42.
NOTE: Asterisks (*) mark provinces where one of the governors served twice, nonconsecutively. Thus the actual number of governors in these provinces is less than the number in the second column. The total months of service of governors and civil affairs heads differ in some provinces because civil affairs heads were appointed to take charge of administration there before formal provincial governments were established and governors appointed.

government vulnerable to influence from outside forces. In Hunan, Ningsia, Szechwan, and Yunnan, the average term of governors exceeded four years. The unusually long terms in Yunnan, Hunan, and Szechwan reflect their semiautonomous status. To a lesser degree this was also true of Kwangtung and Shantung.

Table 14 also shows the average terms of the heads of provincial civil affairs departments, who were second in importance only to

TABLE 15

Average Terms of Provincial Department Heads,
March 1933–July 1937

Province	Total no. of dept. heads	Average term (months)	Province	Total no. of dept. heads	Average term (months)
Anhwei	10	20.8	Kwangtung	13	14.2
Chahar	14	14.9	Kweichow	11	18.9
Chekiang	14	14.9	Ningsia	11	18.9
Fukien	9	23.1	Shansi	9	23.1
Honan	8	26.0	Shantung	4	52.0
Hopei	11	18.9	Shensi	9	23.1
Hunan	7	29.7	Sinkiang	12	17.3
Hupeh	9	23.1	Suiyuan	7	29.7
Kansu	13	16.0	Szechwan	12	17.3
Kiangsi	7	29.7	Tsinghai	7	26.3
Kiangsu	8	26.0	Yunnan	6	34.7
Kwangsi	12	15.3			

SOURCES: *China Year Book*, 1934–38; *Nei-cheng nien-chien*, 1936, pp. 334–42.
NOTE: Not all provinces had the same number of departments in these years. This table considers four departments (civil affairs, reconstruction, education, and finance) for each province except Kwangsi, Kwangtung, and Tsinghai, which had only three departments for two of the four years covered. In Kwangsi, Kwangtung, and Tsinghai the total months of service from which average terms are calculated was 184. In each of the other provinces the total was 208 months.

governors, for 1927–37. Table 15 shows the average terms of major provincial department heads for 1933–37. Although there are no precise patterns in turnover rates within or across provinces, we can draw some broad conclusions from comparing these figures. In most of the provinces governors' terms were either equal to or longer than those of the other elite groups. The greater turnover of department heads gives rise to the speculation that they depended largely on their connections with governors for survival.

In general, the heads of civil affairs departments had the highest rate of turnover. It may be that this office often served as the battleground between provincial forces and the Kuomintang center; the C.C. Clique, for example, tried to install its members in this position in various provinces. This speculation is supported by a comparison of the turnover of civil affairs department heads inside and outside the Bandit Suppression Zones. The seven provinces with the highest rates of turnover were all inside the zones. On the average, governors and heads of civil affairs departments in the ten Bandit Suppression

TABLE 16

*Average Terms of Officials in the Bandit Suppression Zones
and Other Provinces, 1927–37*

	Average term (months)	
Type of official	Ten Bandit Suppression Provinces	Other thirteen provinces
Governors	22.8	30.5
Heads of civil affairs departments	13.8	22.1

Provinces (before the 1935 inclusion of Szechwan and Kweichow) had a significantly higher turnover rate than those in the other provinces. As Table 16 shows, both governors and civil affairs heads outside the Bandit Suppression Zones served some eight months longer than those inside the zones.

These statistics on the turnover of provincial elites suggests that central penetration did not have a stabilizing influence on provincial government. Although the absence of established procedures for recruiting provincial rulers was related to the instability, the fundamental causes were factionalism at the Kuomintang center and tenuous relations between the center and the provinces. Factional competition between the C.C. Clique and the Political Study Clique often affected the appointment of important provincial officials in the Bandit Suppression Zones. Each group attempted to install its own men in key provincial offices. Further, the tenuous relations between Nanking and various provincial leaders often led to bargains and compromises in the appointment of important officials.

The Kuomintang center clearly did not penetrate very far into the provinces. Nor did it institute standard rules and procedures for recruiting county and provincial rulers. Judging from the evidence presented in this chapter, Nanking was not able to control the majority of provincial and county elites who exercised power and authority at levels closer to the common people. The Examination Yuan, which was responsible for standardizing recruitment procedures, engaged in only token activities. The Executive Yuan, while claiming a constitutional right to appoint provincial governors and department heads, was in fact powerless in this area.

The central government's influence over the selection of provincial personnel was largely limited to the Bandit Suppression Zones. Time and again we have pointed out that the real power in the Kuomintang regime lay in the Military Council, controlled by Chiang Kai-shek. It was his headquarters that often determined changes of top-level provincial elites within Nanking's jurisdiction. Thus the Kuomintang government was most able to effect changes in personnel in the provinces where Chiang's anti-Communist military campaigns provided a convenient pretext for growing central political control. Even in these provinces, though, the selection of county and provincial elites was still subject to informal bargaining and competition among political factions and provincial strongmen. As a party the Kuomintang had very little authority over provincial rulers. The regime's penetration of the provinces was largely sustained by Chiang's military power.

In provinces outside the Bandit Suppression Zones, Nanking's authority was minimal. Personnel changes in these provinces were decided either by provincial overlords exclusively, as in Szechwan, Yunnan, Shansi, Kwangtung, and Kwangsi, or by compromises between the central government and regional militarists, as in the North China provinces. In the provinces outside the Bandit Suppression Zones, governorships remained in the hands of military men. Also, the traditional factors influencing the selection of magistrates did not decline so rapidly there as in the Bandit Suppression Zones.

In the final analysis a study of the social characteristics and the turnover of provincial and local elites reinforces the view that the Kuomintang, though representing an emerging integrative force, still had to operate in a political milieu not entirely within its control. It did exercise some control over personnel in the Bandit Suppression Zones, but its influence was far from stabilizing. Provincial and county rulers were slow to come to terms with the Kuomintang. There is little evidence that the party-government had gained control over most of them before the outbreak of the war with Japan.

NINE

Provincial Revenues and Expenditures

BEFORE 1927 taxes collected by provincial and local administrative offices were regarded in principle as national revenue. Officials' salaries and other local expenses were deducted from the taxes before they were transmitted to the provincial offices, which in turn subtracted their own expenses and handed the remainder over to the central government. Such a system inevitably became hopelessly confused. Since provincial and local administrations had no independent sources of revenue, they often took most of the taxes collected, leaving the central government with inadequate funds. Several sources, most notably the land tax, though technically belonging to the central government, had gone entirely for the maintenance of provincial governments ever since the 1911 revolution.

When the Nationalists came to power, a formal line was drawn between national and provincial revenues and expenditures, with the land tax and several other revenue sources reserved for the provinces. Accordingly, there were two types of financial administrative agencies in the provinces—the national taxation agencies, administering taxes to which the central government was legally entitled, and provincial taxation agencies. Among the former were agencies in charge of the customs duties, the salt tax, and the consolidated taxes. Centralized control systems were fairly well established for the customs duties and the salt tax, on which the Nationalist Government counted heavily for revenue. The customs administration was particularly effective in collecting taxes with a minimum of corruption.

The Internal Revenue Administration collected the consolidated taxes in 11 provinces.[1] The provincial offices were under the supervision of regional bureaus in Shanghai (in charge of Kiangsu, Chekiang, and Anhwei), Hankow (Hunan, Hupeh, and Kiangsi), Tsingtao (Shantung and Honan), and Canton (Kwangtung, Kwangsi, and Fukien). These offices apparently functioned quite well, except when there was political interference from provincial military leaders, as in Fukien and Kwangtung during the first half of the 1930's. One must realize, of course, that eight of the 11 provinces were more or less within reach of Nanking's authority.

The other type of financial administrative agency in the provinces was under the legal jurisdiction of the provincial governments themselves. These agencies varied considerably from one province to another; there was no uniformity at all. The number of personnel in an agency varied from a few people to two or three dozen. Generally, a staff included one to three secretaries, two or three division officers, and several clerical assistants. Some provinces had touring revenue inspectors as well.

At the beginning of the Nanking decade, one salient characteristic of financial administration in all provinces was the lack of offices in charge of accounting, statistics, and auditing. Some provinces came to realize that an adequate system of information was essential for the development of a modern taxation system. Beginning in 1929 Nanking and the provincial governments set up schools to train statisticians, accountants, and auditors. The new school system was not able to produce enough qualified technicians during this period of social and political change, however; and administrative clerks with traditional educational backgrounds did not have enough technical knowledge to do the work. To meet these urgent needs provincial governments recruited people with a high school education for several months of training. Hunan, for example, worked hard to produce accountants this way, developing an auditing department that employed more than 40 trained clerks.[2] Kwangtung created the Bureau of Statistical Investigation in 1933 and managed to staff it with 38 administrative clerks by June 1935.[3]

In June 1933 the Executive Yuan, then headed by Wang Ching-wei, took a step toward establishing a uniform structure for statistical bureaus when it issued temporary organizational guidelines to local administrations. Nearly a year later, in April 1934, the Nationalist Government published formal operational regulations for statistical bureaus. In fact, however, the first bureau based on these regulations did not come into existence until 1941, and only seven provinces (Kwangtung, Kwangsi, Kiangsu, Kweichow, Honan, Szechwan, and Chekiang) had established bureaus by the end of the war. Thus, although the Nationalist Government was obviously concerned about this matter, the development of statistical organizations was limited. Most provinces did not set up separate departments and assigned only a handful of people in existing departments to do this kind of work. With no statistical information provincial elites were ignorant of the actual situation in their own provinces.

Only the few provinces with trained clerks could turn out official publications. At least six provinces (Kiangsi, Hupeh, Hunan, Fukien, Kwangsi, and Shansi) published provincial yearbooks, and four others (Kiangsi, Anhwei, Chekiang, and Honan) were able to publish some statistical information regarding budgets, personnel, and the like. All of these publications were irregular, however, and suffered from inadequate information. This lack of information seriously crippled efforts to collect taxes, to develop other sources of revenue, and to allocate resources efficiently.

Kiangsu was the first province to institute a budgetary system, publishing its expenditures (in round figures) for the 18th fiscal year of republican China in 1930. Following this lead several other provinces released their budgets for the 19th fiscal year. In subsequent years most provinces made progress in preparing more comprehensive budgets. On February 26, 1930, the Nationalist Government had promulgated regulations governing trial budgets for the fiscal year from July 1930 to June 1931. These regulations set forth in detail the techniques and procedures involved in budget-making and specified the categories of provincial revenues and expenditures to be listed.

Revenues

An analysis of provincial revenues and expenditures during the Nanking decade is complicated by incomplete data and contradictory sources. Although it is difficult to assess the relative reliability of different sets of figures, those published by the Ministry of Finance in *Ts'ai-cheng nien-chien* (Public finance yearbook) are most safely

accepted. Arthur N. Young, former financial adviser to the Kuomintang government in Nanking, regards them as authoritative and the
best available.[4] Other important sources of statistical information for
the 1930's generally adopted figures released by the ministry. Among
these are the *China Year Book, Shen-pao nien-chien* (*Shen-pao* yearbook), compiled by the staff of *Shen-pao*, and *Ti-cheng yüeh-k'an*
(Land administration monthly), an authoritative journal devoted to
the study of land and agriculture. Although there are minor differences among these sources, their figures are basically the same. The
China Year Book provides the most complete year by year information; *Ti-cheng yüeh-k'an* offers a categorical breakdown of both revenues and expenditures that best serves our purposes here.[*]

The Ministry of Finance sources give figures on provincial revenues
for the fiscal years 1930–31 to 1935–36. A study of the data reveals
that complete revenue figures for each fiscal year are available for
eight provinces: Anhwei, Chekiang, Honan, Hopei, Hunan, Hupeh,
Kiangsu, and Shantung. In addition, complete figures for some years
are available for Kiangsi, Fukien, and Kwangtung. Eight of these 11
provinces were in the Bandit Suppression Zones. The fact that all the
Bandit Suppression Provinces but Kansu and Shensi were able to produce comprehensive budgets may reflect the extension of Nanking's
influence during the course of the anti-Communist campaigns. The
other three provinces for which we have considerable information,
Kwangtung, Shantung, and Hopei, were coastal provinces with traditionally well-administered taxation systems. They had treaty ports
open to continuous foreign trade, even in times of social and political
chaos, and the efficient customs administrations there no doubt had
an important effect on the ability of the provincial governments to
prepare annual revenue reports.

Since the reliability of available statistics is open to question, any
analysis of them must be made with caution. We can draw from them
only general patterns of financial development in the provinces. The
figures in Tables C.1 and C.2 in Appendix C indicate that Kwang-

---

[*] Aside from the Finance Ministry's data, other sets of figures are available
from the Comptroller's Office and from the Directorate General of Budgets,
Accounts, and Statistics. It is possible that the differences between these figures
and the ministry's may result from variations in accounting methods, such as the
use of different time periods for certain items. The absence of information about
how the different sets of data were compiled precludes any meaningful comparison of them in this chapter.

tung, Hopei, Shantung, Kiangsu, Chekiang, and Hupeh had the highest total revenues during the period under study. With the exception of Hupeh, where Wuhan is located, they are all coastal provinces. The figures also indicate that there was little fluctuation in terms of annual revenues in most provinces. Revenues in some Bandit Suppression Provinces even showed a tendency to decrease over the six-year period. Aside from Kwangtung the few provinces with a significant trend toward higher annual revenues were in the north and the southwest. These increases will be partially explained in light of our subsequent discussion of subsidiary loans and land taxes.

Subsidiary loans. Subsidiary loans were funds given to provinces by the Nanking Government. Most provincial governments did not have enough revenues to bear military costs or to promote reconstruction projects. Although the people's tax burden was heavy, most revenues collected at the county and local levels never reached the provincial capitals. As Chiang Kai-shek's military campaigns brought Nanking's authority to more provinces, there was an increasing demand for revenue. The central government's promotion of local administrative reorganization, the training of administrative personnel, mass military mobilization, and road building for military maneuvers all entailed costs that provincial rulers were either unwilling or unable to meet. Under the circumstances the Kuomintang had to bear a portion of the costs. Thus provincial governments, particularly those in the Bandit Suppression Zones, where Chiang's anti-Communist campaigns required greater expenditures for military purposes, received subsidies from Nanking.

The item of loans is absent in revenue lists for several provinces for all or some fiscal years between 1930 and 1936. In some instances the absence of figures on loans reflects a general lack of data for a province in a given year. When other figures are available for the province in the year, however, I have interpreted the absence to mean that no loans were received. (See Appendix C, Table C.3, for a summary of the available data on loans.) Only Kiangsu and Hupeh show loans for each year. All the Bandit Suppression Provinces except Shensi and Kansu received subsidiary loans in at least three of the six years. Shensi and Kansu apparently did not receive loans from Nanking until fiscal 1935–36, that is, not until the Communists settled in certains parts of their territory after the Long March.

An examination of the amount in loans received by each province during the period also reveals the importance of the Bandit Suppression Zones. Again Shensi and Kansu were the only two provinces in the zones that received relatively little in loans. Among the provinces outside the zones, Hopei received the largest amount, comparable to the amounts received by some Bandit Suppression Provinces. Chahar, Yunnan, and Kweichow also received substantial loans from Nanking. In the case of Kweichow these were probably related to Nanking's anti-Communist campaigns. Some Communists passed through Kweichow in 1934 during the Long March, thus providing a pretext for military and political penetration of the province by Nanking. Loans were subsequently given to the provincial government for pacification and to cooperative provincial militarists as rewards.

Under the governorship of General Sung Che-yuan, Chahar received subsidiary loans. Sung, previously an important protégé of Feng Yü-hsiang, controlled the strategic area facing Japanese troops in Jehol and Manchuria. After 1932 Nanking was exceedingly worried about the northern provinces that guarded the pathways to Peking. Although Chiang was able to buy Sung's nominal allegiance during his confrontation with Feng Yü-hsiang, relations between the two men were by no means stable. Subsidiary loans, then, became one of the main bargaining tools by which Chiang attempted to win Sung's support against possible Japanese aggression. Liu Chien-ch'ün's propaganda activities in North China, especially in the ranks of Sung's army, were a clear indication of Nanking's concern over this powerful northern warlord.

Yunnan received loans from Nanking primarily because the warlord Lung Yün never openly repudiated Nanking's authority. In the late 1920's he even supported Chiang Kai-shek by sending troops to Kwangsi, whose military leaders were engaged in a campaign against Chiang. Throughout the prewar period Lung maintained his autonomy from Nanking. His relations with Chiang, although cool, remained friendly. Thus Lung was able to obtain some support from the Nationalist Government when Yunnan was in financial need.

Loans as a percentage of total revenues show great variation from province to province. Even in the same province annual figures fluctuated widely. In calculating these percentages I have included only those fiscal years in which figures for both total revenues and loans are available from the same source. Since the information is incomplete we can only show how important loans were for each province. In the ten provinces of the Bandit Suppression Zones, percentages varied from 8.8 percent in Shensi (based on figures for one year) to 31.7 percent in Anhwei (based on figures for five years). Loan revenues as a percentage of total revenues exceeded 13 percent in all ten provinces except Shensi. In provinces outside the Bandit Suppression Zones, percentages varied from 1.4 percent in Shantung to 37.1 percent in Kweichow (both based on figures for one year). In addition to Kweichow two other provinces had high percentages: Yunnan, 30.1 percent (two-year figures), and Chahar, 19.5 percent (four-year figures).

A comparison of subsidiary loans and total revenues indicates that over half of China's provinces relied heavily on subsidies from the central government during all or at least part of the Nanking decade. The Kuomintang authorities obviously channeled large sums of money to some of the provinces, but there is no way to determine exactly how they decided to make these allocations. Most of the money is not clearly itemized in accounts of public expenditures. The four provinces that received the largest amounts in loans (over Ch $18 million each) were Kiangsu, Kiangsi, Anhwei, and Hupeh. The last three were the areas most troubled by Communist activities, which clearly suggests that military priorities influenced these appropriations. In terms of factional politics Kiangsi and Hupeh formed the territorial stronghold of the Political Study Clique, and Kiangsu and Anhwei that of the C.C. Clique. The fact that these provinces received large sums was certainly not a matter of coincidence.

In the final analysis the available figures on loans as a source of provincial revenues indicate some tentative patterns. The ten provinces in the Bandit Suppression Zones as a group apparently received far larger amounts from the Nationalist Government than provinces outside the zones. Moreover, the loans they received generally constituted a significant percentage of their total revenues, so far as we can judge from the years when figures on both loans and revenues are available. The disproportionate size of loans received by the Bandit Suppression Provinces suggests that Nanking was trying desperately to funnel more money into these areas in the hope of stopping the Communists. Indeed, the initial year in which a province reported loans tends to coincide with the date of Chiang's decision to move against the Communists there.

The party-government was also using subsidiary loans as political rewards to provincial leaders who had shown allegiance to Nanking, or at least had shown no open hostility. This included leaders in North China, which had become strategically important in the early 1930's because of Japan's military ambitions there and in Manchuria. Since these leaders were not oriented toward the Kuomintang, Chiang was worried that they might collaborate with the Japanese. As a result two important provinces in North China, Hopei and Chahar, received a considerable amount of financial aid from Nanking. Hopei received over Ch $8 million in the 1930's, the largest sum in all the provinces outside the Bandit Suppression Zones. The loans to Hopei were closely related to the establishment of the Peking Political Affairs Council after the Japanese invasion of Jehol in 1933. A branch of the Executive Yuan, this body had nominal jurisdiction over the five northern provinces—Chahar, Hopei, Ningsia, Shansi, and Shantung—until it was terminated in 1935.[5] Several important figures representing Nanking, notably Huang Fu, Ho Ying-ch'in, and Huang Shao-hung, were dispatched to Peking to watch over the increasingly troublesome situation in North China.

Still, aside from Hopei, provinces outside the Bandit Suppression Zones received relatively small subsidies from Nanking. Although loans to Chahar, Yunnan, and Kweichow constituted a fairly high percentage of total revenues, they were relatively small sums in absolute terms.*

Land taxes. Land administration has always been an important function of the Chinese bureaucracy. China is an agrarian society, with over 80 percent of the population deriving its income from agriculture. Traditionally, land taxes were a major source of government revenue. To a large degree the effectiveness of the administrative bureaucracy can be determined by its performance in the area of land administration. Rural China had experienced many socioeconomic dislocations since the early nineteenth century, and land administration had been seriously disrupted. Any attempt to re-create order

---

* One Bandit Suppression Province, Shensi, did receive a smaller amount in loans than Chahar, Yunnan, or Kweichow, mainly because the Kuomintang authorities paid little attention to it until the Communists settled there in 1935.

ran up against numerous problems: ownership disputes, unclaimed deserted lands, the uneven distribution of taxes, the evasion of land taxes by the privileged, and the overall decline of agricultural productivity.

During the period of warlordism rural administration virtually collapsed; there was no basis on which the government could assess or collect land taxes. Provincial militarists, who relied on land revenues to finance their wars, had little interest in fair administration, let alone reform. They collected taxes largely by coercion. As a result, the Nanking Government had hardly any information regarding land ownership or the size of holdings. Unfortunately, although the land tax remained a major source of revenue, little effort was made to reestablish a functioning system, and progress was much too slow.

The land tax, formally designated a provincial revenue by the Nationalist Government, was the major item of direct taxation throughout the Nanking decade. It was supposed to be paid by landowners. The last cadastral survey, a record of the boundaries, size, and nature of landholdings, had been made in 1713 and was useless for taxation purposes. The compilation of such a survey is both time-consuming and costly. Thus the party-government and the provincial administrations adopted the less expensive procedure of land registration, or the reporting of land titles by the owners themselves.

Numerous proposals regarding land administration were brought up in the party's Central Executive Committee. When the Communists shifted to their rural strategy in the late 1920's, some Kuomintang leaders favored measures to compete with them on land problems; years elapsed, however, before the party-government managed to develop a policy. The National Conference on Finance held in May 1934 finally produced a set of 35 guidelines for land survey and registration, but these were not immediately translated into action. It was not until February 1936 that the General Principles for the Organization of Land Administration Bureaus were officially promulgated by the Executive Yuan.

The Kuomintang's failure to deal with the chaotic situation in rural China was due in part to its reluctance to provoke united opposition from provincial rulers. But the failure itself had a high political cost. As one American observer in the early 1930's remarked: "The most important thing, however, that stands out in the government policy

TABLE 17

Extent of Land Survey and Registration in
Six Provinces, March 1936

Operation	No. of cities and counties surveyed or registered					
	Kiangsu	Chekiang	Anhwei	Kiangsi	Hupeh	Yunnan
Land survey	18	5	4[a]	6	9[a]	37
Land registration	14	2	1	3	2	—

SOURCE: Cheng Chen-yü.
[a] One or more units in Anhwei and Hupeh had completed a substantial portion of the work, but not all of it.

[in Kiangsi] is its neglect of the land problem. No one appears to be much concerned about the agrarian conditions which produced the very classes that made Communism possible."[6]

Before the announcement of the General Principles in 1936, there were some sporadic efforts by provincial governments to establish various kinds of land administration offices. Immediately after the announcement the Nationalist Government instructed the provinces to comply fully with the organizational procedures outlined. By mid-1936 six provinces—Kiangsu, Anhwei, Kiangsi, Tsinghai, Fukien, and Honan—had reportedly organized bureaus of land administration as independent administrative units.[7] Most of the others added sections on land administration to their civil affairs or finance departments. Szechwan, a province divided among hostile warlords, went only so far as to set up a preparatory commission on land administration. In Ningsia the task of land administration was undertaken by the General Bureau of Frontier Development.

Moreover, only six provinces—Kiangsi, Chekiang, Anhwei, Kiangsu, Yunnan, and Hupeh—had accomplished anything in the way of surveying and registering land by 1936.[8] The extent of these operations there as of March 1936 is shown in Table 17. As the table indicates Kiangsu and Yunnan were the most active, although their figures could be exaggerated. Kiangsu was the territorial base of the C.C. Clique, which strongly advocated reform in land administration. Even there, however, surveys had been completed in only 18 of 63 counties and cities, and land registration in only 14, which meant that about half of the counties and cities were unaffected.

Yunnan had completed land surveys in 37 of 110 counties and cities but had made no effort in land registration. In Chekiang, Anhwei, Kiangsi, and Hupeh, the situation was even worse. And almost all the other provinces had failed to survey or register land in a single county. Thus John Lossing Buck's estimate that 39.2 percent of the arable land in North China and 20.9 percent in South China had not been registered appears to be far too low.[9] His speculation that as much as 70 percent of the land in many counties in the south and southwest was unregistered is probably closer to the truth.[10] Almost one decade after the Kuomintang had come to power, then, one of the most fundamental conditions for a sound taxation system, not to mention an agrarian policy, was still unmet.

Table C.4 in Appendix C summarizes the available data on land tax revenues. Six provinces had complete figures for 1930–36, and another seven had figures for five years. In all, 17 provinces had figures for four or more years. Of the ten Bandit Suppression Provinces only Kansu and Shensi had figures in fewer than four years.

Among the provinces with figures for all six years, Shantung, Kiangsu, and Honan raised the largest amounts in land taxes. Their totals were Ch $91.5 million, Ch $64 million, and Ch $43 million, respectively. In the group with figures for five years, Chekiang and Shansi had the highest totals, Ch $60.5 million and Ch $33.4 million, respectively. Kwangtung collected Ch $25.3 million in the four years for which we have figures. In terms of annual income from the land tax, these six provinces were far ahead of the others. It should be noted that Shantung, Kwangtung, and Shansi were not in the Bandit Suppression Zones.

The table clearly reveals that the land tax constituted the major source of provincial revenues. In the vast majority of provinces it accounted for at least 20 percent. In Shantung, Shansi, Tsinghai, Chekiang, Honan, Ningsia, and Kiangsu, it constituted over 45 percent. Apparently, there were no characteristic differences between provinces inside the Bandit Suppression Zones and those outside regarding land tax revenues.

Some provinces for which figures are not available are known to have had high land taxes. Szechwan is the most notorious example. Throughout the 1920's and the first half of the 1930's, the province was divided among several contending warlords, each of whom collected land taxes and numerous surtaxes.[11] Between 1916 and 1935 frequent battles among them exhausted the province's financial resources.[12] Beginning in the late 1920's the warlords collected land taxes in advance. By 1932, for example, Teng Hsi-hou of the 28th Army had collected taxes 40 years in advance from some counties in his jurisdiction; Liu Wen-hui of the 24th Army, 25 years in advance; and Tien Sung-yao of the 29th Army, 28 years.[13] By 1934 the 28th Army was collecting taxes 74 years in advance, and the 29th Army 66 years; six other military units were collecting taxes at least 22 years in advance.[14] The land tax budget of the 21st Army for the fiscal year 1934–35 was reported to be as high as Ch $28.6 million.[15]

Although a complete list of official figures for all provinces is unavailable, the figures we have indicate that land taxes were exceedingly high. Local studies and surveys on taxes confirm this. Chen Han-seng's survey of Pan-yu county in Kwangtung, for example, shows that the amount of tax per *mou* of agricultural land (0.15 acre) increased from 0.44 *yuan* in 1928 to 1.39 *yuan* in 1933, five years later.[16] This represents an increase of over 200 percent. In some of the inland provinces the situation was apparently even worse. According to a study of Nan-cheng county in southern Shensi during the mid-1930's, the land tax and its surcharges had increased about 400 percent since 1929.[17] At the time of the study the tax per *mou* in Nan-cheng county stood at 2.52 *yuan*, considerably more than in Pan-yu.[18] The annual income per *mou* in the county ranged from four to slightly over ten *yuan*.[19] On the average, then, over one-third of the income from the land went for taxes. In the event of famine or military clashes among regional warlords, conditions deteriorated still further.

Excessive taxation, as well as plundering by provincial militarists and local bandits, led to land desertion. Chen Han-seng's 1932 survey of northeastern Szechwan and southern Shensi, for example, revealed a significant degree of land desertion by small landlords unable to pay taxes.[20] Peasants were even more likely to abandon their homes and lands under such circumstances. Rural distress was further compounded by a land shortage. A 1935 study of the 1873–1933 period reported that the average area of land under cultivation per family, including the holdings of landlords and rich peasants, amounted to only 30 *mou* (4.5 acres).[21] In the wheat-growing north the average was 40 *mou* (6 acres), and in central and southern China only 20 *mou*

(3 acres).[22] The problem, as Tawney puts it, was that there was insufficient land to provide the peasants with food, let alone all their other needs.*

Although the figures given in the official reports indicate that land taxes were high and constituted the largest single source of provincial revenue, these figures do not reflect the actual amounts levied and collected. Considerable sums were retained by tax collectors and corrupt local officials, and went unreported. For example, a correspondent of the Nanking paper *Chung-yang jih-pao* (Central daily) reported that the chief of a local tax collection office in Chinkiang, the capital of Kiangsu, had retained some Ch $100,000 between 1930 and 1934.[23] Further, there were numerous surtax charges, some attached to the land tax, which in themselves amounted to staggering sums. The additional burdens placed on the peasantry by collection practices and by the levying of surtaxes will be examined in the following sections.

Tax collection. Provincial revenues were primarily collected at the county level. Methods varied, but there were three general systems. Some taxes, including special consumption taxes, business taxes, and land taxes, were to be collected by regular administrative offices with county and local branches. Others, like the butchery tax and the house levy, were to be collected by tax farmers, who were either members of the local chamber of commerce or individuals licensed by the county. Finally, temporary surtaxes and miscellaneous taxes with clearly specified purposes, such as taxes for maintaining local militia units and troops in transit, were to be collected according to a quota system. Ordinarily, the provincial government set a target figure and assigned certain quotas to the counties, which in turn usually divided the quotas among districts (*ch'ü*) and villages. The village headmen, *pao-chang* and *chia-chang*, were ultimately held responsible. The pro-

---

* Tawney, p. 7. The shortage of arable land was aggravated by the widespread practice of poppy cultivation. Since opium represented a more lucrative source of revenue than other crops, peasants in many provinces (Hopei, Shantung, Kansu, Shensi, Jehol, Honan, Szechwan, Yunnan, Kweichow, Fukien, and Anhwei) were encouraged or compelled to plant poppies. Warlords in Szechwan even imposed a "laziness tax" (*lan-chuan*) on those who did not do so. As Jerome Ch'en has noted ("Historical Background," p. 32), the amount of cultivated land devoted to poppies increased from 3 percent in 1914–19 to 20 percent in 1929–33; land devoted to barley decreased from 23 to 19 percent in these years, and that to sorghum from 23 to 16 percent.

vincial government also appointed some temporary administrative officials called *p'ai-k'uan wei-yuan* to ensure the collection of these assigned taxes and fees.[24]

In actual practice the failure to develop bureaucratic structures at the county level created an even greater dependence on traditional collection methods than the above outline suggests. In the case of such an important item as the land tax, for example, county administrations continued to depend on nongovernmental collection agencies. Although in some provinces, especially in the Bandit Suppression Zones, county governments were instructed to set up offices to administer the land tax, these offices never operated adequately. Some counties had established granaries (*liang-kuei*) staffed by several clerks who were to prepare and maintain grain tax records. The clerks continued to use the traditional titles of office.[25] Their salary was either a fixed monthly payment, usually very low, or a fixed proportion of the revenues collected.

Many counties never even had a *liang-kuei*. Instead the magistrates often assigned the grain clerks' job to the headman of an administrative village, the *hsiang-chang*, who could hardly perform it without relying on families that had traditionally collected land taxes in the area. There are at least two reasons why local administrators had to rely on these people. First, local governments had no proper records of land ownership on which to base tax assessments and were making little progress in compiling them. Thus the relatively comprehensive records kept by the numerous families who had been living for decades on the collection of taxes, and who had become a semibureaucratic group, were indispensable. Second, many counties were so large that it was impossible to maintain an administrative network down to the village level, forcing the county governments to seek the cooperation of the rural gentry.

Often, the magistrates would dispatch informal representatives (*ts'ui-cheng-li*) to rural areas to supervise or execute the collection of land taxes. Many of them had previously been county clerical functionaries. A survey of Kiangsu by the Joint Commission on Rural Reconstruction disclosed in 1934 that in Ch'ang-shu county alone there were between 500 and 600 of these positions, most of which were hereditary.[26] Many *ts'ui-cheng-li* had been in communities for so long that the magistrates simply had to continue to appoint them. Acting in a quasi-official capacity they formed a privileged and unpopular class; they often associated with the landlords, whose main interest was to evade their share of the land tax.

The lack of sound administration in land-tax collection generated a lot of ill will and resentment toward the government among the peasants. Chinese tax officials traditionally had earned the reputation of being the most corrupt of bureaucrats, and corruption grew in the absence of institutional supervision. Particularism and nepotism prevailed throughout the prewar decade. Corruption and graft were widespread. The *ts'ui-cheng-li,* aware of their importance, used their exclusive knowledge of the situation in the countryside to retain a portion of the taxes they collected. Also, when payment had to be made in currency instead of in kind, they often took advantage of the peasants' ignorance of the exchange rate to collect excess taxes. At the same time, big landholders who occupied government positions or were socially influential were paying less than their fair share.* The result, of course, was an excessively heavy tax burden on the common peasants.

The harmful effects of this system of local taxation were pervasive, involving economic hardship, political terrorism, and the evasion of social responsibility. The Kuomintang's efforts to eliminate the system never went beyond the so-called model counties and the counties within the effective jurisdiction of large cities. An account of tax farming in Hopei in the 1930's reveals its extent and vividly describes its evils:

Except for two or three taxes collected directly by the county governments, such as the land tax and deed tax, most taxes are farmed out. . . . The brokerage tax and the miscellaneous tax are the most important. Most of the tax collectors are "rotten gentry"; a smaller number are merchants. . . . Those who have contracted for the right to collect taxes unfailingly and arbitrarily raise the rate at the time of collection. Because they have the armed police of the county at their disposal, they can carry on their oppression at will and the peasant can only submit meekly.

The difference between the amount collected at a specific rate and the lump sum contracted for as payment to the provincial and county treasuries is not the only source of income for the tax farmer. All sorts of traditional usages enable him to exploit his position so as to secure additional

---

* A survey of over one hundred landlords in Hopei revealed that the landlords actually owned 1,657.68 *mou* of land but reported only 883.64 *mou* to the county governments to be assessed for taxation. Many of those who made false reports held local administrative titles. Probably tax collectors were bribed to accept these false reports. Sun Hsiao-ts'un, pp. 20–22.

profits. Thus, in the grain brokerage, it is an old custom that the broker who acts as measurer has a right to what is spilled. In modern times the spilling has become a matter of considerable skill, and the amount spilled during sales transactions forms a not negligible portion of the broker's income. Although forbidden by provincial as well as *hsien* authorities, the practice persists.[27]

The writer goes on to list other abuses, including the tendency of tax farmers to take the law into their own hands in punishing alleged tax evaders and the practice of subcontracting tax collection to disreputable individuals in the various towns and villages. "In fact," he concludes, "this semiofficial occupation, by its very nature, had attracted many persons who were successful precisely because they were bullies and ruffians. If all these men were deprived of their means of livelihood they would be liable to create a great deal of trouble to the government."[28]

In summary, there were two major types of corruption: *fu-shou*, which literally means "over-extraction," and *chung-pao*, which means "squeeze" and refers to the retention of tax revenues by corrupt officials. *Fu-shou* could be a deliberate overcharge, made possible because the regulations governing taxation were not clearly expressed or popularly known. In cases involving the calculation of exchange rates between grains and currency, the lack of standard measurements was likely to result in excessive charges. A survey of the situation in Hupeh by Nanking University confirmed that this was a widespread practice.[29]

Chung-pao usually occurred in one of three ways. Often tax collectors simply recorded taxes as unpaid and then kept the money for themselves. Or they might report that the land for which they had in fact already collected taxes was deserted or damaged by natural calamity and hence untaxable. Finally, they often charged extra fees for delays in payment. Occasionally, collectors made a deal with local officials and retained a portion of the taxes under the guise of local administrative fees. For example, in the rural communities of Hopei there were thousands of unclassified, so-called administrative police, who were unemployed officials or local bullies (*tu-hao*). Less than a hundred were on any official payroll; the rest lived on embezzled taxes.[30] In Chekiang as much as 90 percent of the tax revenue collected was reportedly retained by means of *chung-pao*.[31]

Miscellaneous surcharges. In addition to regular taxes there were numerous surcharges that placed heavy financial burdens on the common people. In the absence of a coherent taxation policy and effective administrative machinery, the provinces depended on such miscellaneous surcharges for much of their revenue. Kiangsu, for example, had as many as 147 different surcharges.[32] In many provinces the surtax attached to the land tax actually exceeded the amount of the tax itself. In the years 1931–35 Kiangsu, Chekiang, Anhwei, Hunan, Honan, and Hupeh reportedly received more revenue from the surtax than from the regular land tax.[33] Increases in the surtax in these Bandit Suppression Provinces were evidently needed to keep up with the costs of campaigns against the Communists.

At the county level surtaxes were often the major source of finances. Various surtaxes accounted for 60 to 90 percent of the revenues in most of the counties that prepared budgets.[34] The 1933 budgets of Wan-nien and Shang-kao counties in Kiangsi, for example, indicate that 98.95 percent and 94.51 percent of their respective revenues came from land surtaxes alone.[35] According to a 1933 survey in Kiangsu, 29 different kinds of land surtax were imposed by the county governments.[36] A report by the Executive Yuan's Commission on Rural Reconstruction indicates that in some counties in the province the combined total of all surtaxes was 26 times more than that of all regular taxes.[37]

Thus, even though the Nationalist Government did not tax the agricultural sector directly, the burden on the peasantry was oppressive. Both the provincial and county governments created various surtaxes whenever financial need arose, and there was no institutional check against excessive local taxation. At the Second National Conference on Finance, held in 1934, the need to decrease land surtaxes and abolish miscellaneous taxes received much attention. The conference emphatically urged the Nationalist Government to prohibit or reduce the surtaxes according to four basic principles: (1) land surtaxes should not exceed the basic land tax, or in districts where the land tax was relatively small, 1 percent of the value of the land; (2) after a fiscal year had begun no provincial or county government should be allowed to increase land surtaxes under any circumstances, regardless of whether or not the surtaxes exceeded the basic land tax; (3) the apportionment of temporary taxes by local subdivisions should be strictly prohibited, and provincial authorities should formulate rules restricting the assessment of surtaxes for the purpose of local improvements; and (4) surtaxes collected for specific purposes should be discontinued when the prescribed period had elapsed or when the reason for the tax no longer existed. The government subsequently instituted some measures to reduce land surtaxes in Hopei and the middle and lower Yangtze valley provinces. However, the situation remained largely unchanged throughout the prewar period; it even tended to deteriorate in provinces where the need for revenue was especially urgent.

The headquarters of the Military Council at Nanchang was very concerned about the situation in the Bandit Suppression Zones. In a 1935 report on the political tasks of the headquarters, Chiang Kai-shek summarized the problem:

In recent years every province has experienced various kinds of rebellious disturbances. Government expenditures grow steadily higher. Whenever a program is begun, new taxes arise. Surtax charges are often attached to the regular taxes as needed, and miscellaneous taxes are also created. Occasionally, [the local authorities] collect unspecified taxes from house to house according to their wishes. As a result tax items are numerous. The people have suffered immensely under this heavy tax burden.[38]

To improve this situation, in mid-1933 the headquarters had ordered the ten provinces in the Bandit Suppression Zones to eliminate a long list of surtaxes and miscellaneous taxes. According to Chiang's report over 1,700 such tax items had been abolished by 1935, with a total reduction of some Ch $14.6 million in taxes in the zones.[39] Another source reveals that in June 1935 the Ministry of Finance approved a reduction of some Ch $8.5 million in land surtaxes in the provinces of Kiangsi, Ningsia, and Kansu.[40] Whether or not these provinces actually executed the provision is unknown. But at least the figures provide us with an idea of the surtax situation.

There were many other financial burdens on the people that were not recorded in official statistics. For example, from time to time magistrates, accompanied by some 30 to 80 official aides, toured rural areas to supervise the collection of land taxes. Wherever the magistrates went, the local residents were responsible for meeting all their expenses, including the cost of entertainment and fancy banquets. In 1931 Ch'eng-ku county in southern Shensi reportedly had over 200 official aides whose function was to assist in the collection of taxes.[41] Even the programs of land measurement and registration, which the Nanking Government often mentioned with pride, worked hardships on the people. According to one study:

> The Kiangsu provincial government sent out special land measuring squads to the different districts, but the administration and discipline of these squads has always been deplorable. . . . Demands were presented, of course, by the landowners of such villages for measurement, but according to official regulations this involved a fee of 30 cents per *mou*, and in addition the squads had to be given a feast of welcome and daily meals.[42]

The villagers, of course, had to comply with these demands to ensure the accurate measurement of their land.

Military requisitions for labor, money, and goods were the most serious burden the people had to bear. Regional militarism and the breakdown of the system of tax administration encouraged the growth of requisitions as sources of revenue for provincial warlords, local bandits, and militia units organized by gentry. In 1929 and 1930, for instance, at least 823 of China's 1,941 counties were subjected to military requisitions.[43] By the early 1930's more than half the counties had been so coerced.

Military requisitions represented one of the worst kinds of exploitation in terms of both the demands made and the methods used. One writer describes the situation this way:

> Owing to the sudden increase of troops, the deficiency of funds, squeeze amongst officers, and arrears in pay, many Chinese troops have to depend upon the requisitions they are able to make for their food, clothing, housing, and transportation. . . . Aside from money and labor, requisitions were made on nearly a hundred articles, including cosmetics and heroin. In some places the troops even went so far as to ask the community to furnish them with women.[44]

Chen Han-seng, a noted scholar of rural China, states that military requisitions were often ten to one hundred times greater than the land tax, sometimes even several hundred times greater.[45]

To take just one example, in Kansu it was common practice for local militarists and roaming bandit groups to force requisitions on the people. Even after the Kuomintang gradually gained control of the provincial administration, such methods persisted; officials dispatched from the provincial capital to rural areas often brought dozens of

soldiers with them to collect military requisitions.[46] Here and elsewhere these requisitions could not be met without the cooperation,
either voluntary or forced, of members of the local gentry. They were
frequently collected by threats and deceit, with tenants and small
landowners bearing the major burden.

In summary, there was a great discrepancy between the taxes de-
livered to the government and the sums of money actually squeezed
out of the peasants. Official taxes were levied excessively and inequi-
tably, and there were many unofficial financial demands on the peasants as well. In the case of the land tax, peasants were exploited not
only by tax collectors and corrupt officials but also by all who invested
in land and passed their taxes on to those below them. Provincial governments were interested in obtaining the greatest possible return
from the land tax; landlords were interested in extracting rent from
their tenants while evading taxes on their holdings. If both were
to be satisfied, land tax revenues could be maintained at a high level
only by increasing the levies on the smaller parcels of land held by
peasants. This forced many peasants to give up their land and become
tenants. As a result the process of rural decay and local corruption
gathered momentum. The existing administrative network failed to
reverse the trend and became increasingly dysfunctional. The heavy
reliance of the Kuomintang and the provincial governments on highly
inadequate traditional mechanisms reveals that they were unable to
develop a sound system of revenue extraction or to mobilize domestic resources effectively and equitably for any scheme of modernization.

Provincial Expenditures

Tables D.1 and D.2 in Appendix D summarize the data on total
annual provincial expenditures available in *Ti-cheng yüeh-k'an* (Land
administration monthly). During the five fiscal years 1931–32 to 1935–
36, the annual expenditures of most provinces showed some degree
of fluctuation but no marked steady increases or decreases. Only
Hupeh, Kiangsu, and Yunnan had significant increases in the last two
fiscal years. Provincial expenditures in Hunan, Kiangsi, Chahar, and
Shantung were relatively stable over the years; those in Kiangsu,

Hupeh, Fukien, Ningsia, and Yunnan tended to fluctuate wore widely. There is no noticeable difference between provinces inside the Bandit Suppression Zones and those outside in regard to total annual expenditures.

The fact that provincial expenditures did not increase significantly during the period has at least two implications. First, Nanking's military and political campaigns in the Bandit Suppression Zones apparently did not result in increases in expenditures for the provincial governments there. Second, since most provinces based their expenditures on estimated income, apparently no provincial government was able to increase its financial capabilities significantly during the decade.

Expenditures on party affairs. Provincial revenues allocated for Kuomintang party affairs were extremely small (see Appendix D, Table D.3). As a percentage of total provincial expenditures, expenditures on the party ranged from about 1 percent in Chekiang, Hupeh, Kiangsu, Kwangsi, and Kweichow to about 6 percent in Ningsia. According to the partial figures available, Shantung, Hunan, Hopei, Kwangtung, and Fukien allocated the largest amounts per year for party affairs. The data do not reflect the party's strength in the Bandit Suppression Zones or the lower Yangtze valley provinces, leading to the speculation that perhaps the central government absorbed many party expenses in these provinces. This seems especially likely in Kiangsu, Chekiang, and Hupeh. All were considered to be strongholds of the Kuomintang regime; yet their expenditures on party affairs were relatively small.

Five provinces outside the Bandit Suppression Zones spent relatively significant amounts on Kuomintang activities. The high percentage of expenditures going to party affairs in Ningsia and Tsinghai, 6 percent and 5 percent, respectively, are hard to explain. Even though these expenditures are not large in absolute terms, averaging only Ch $142,000 per year for Ningsia and Ch $41,000 for Tsinghai, they are surprising, considering the small populations of these provinces and the general lack of party organization there. The relatively high amounts spent by Shantung, Hopei, and Kwangtung are much easier to understand. Expenditures for party activities increased in Shantung after the warlord Han Fu-chü shifted his allegiance from Feng Yü-hsiang to Chiang Kai-shek. Hopei's expenditures were largely absorbed by the party organizations in Peking and Tientsin. Kwangtung, the Kuomintang's original territorial base, remained under the control of politicians and military men who, although generally unfriendly to Chiang's Nanking Government, still belonged to the party.

No expenditures on the party were reported for Yunnan, Szechwan, Suiyuan, and Sinkiang. This is a clear indication of the virtual absence of Kuomingtang activities and organizations in these provinces.

Military and public security expenditures. Provincial expenditures on military, quasi-military, rural militia, and police activities were generally combined under the heading of public security. Based on the figures available during 1931–36, Table D.3 in Appendix D shows that 11 provinces allocated over 15 percent of their expenditures for military and public security affairs. Although the lack of data prevents an extensive comparison with expenditures in the two previous decades, Arthur N. Young speculates as follows:

A compilation of provincial budgets for various dates in the twenties showed total estimated outlay of C $275 million, of which 68 per cent was for the military. . . . The greatly reduced allocations in the thirties for "public safety" [public security], as compared with military outlay, reflect the efforts of the National Government to centralize military power in its hands and get rid of warlords, the cost of whose surviving armies was either incorporated into the national budget or met to a reduced extent from provincial revenues augmented by subsidies from Nanking.[47]

Mr. Young is generally too optimistic about the Kuomintang's ability to overcome the challenge of hostile provincial forces at this time. Nevertheless, it is probably quite true that provincial expenditures for public security decreased in the 1930's. What we do not know is whether the combined expenditures of the central and provincial governments for military activities were below those of the previous years.

As a percentage of total expenditures, provincial public security expenditures ranged from 3 percent in Shansi (based on figures for two years) to 43 percent in Kansu (based on figures for three years). Kwangtung reported no outlay for public security in the only year in which its total expenditures were made available. Five of the eight provinces that spent 20 percent of their expenditures or more for public security were in the Bandit Suppression Zones. Of the ten provinces in the zones, only Kiangsu and Hunan had relatively low percentages, 14 and 11 percent, respectively. In contrast, of the provinces outside the Bandit Suppression Zones, only Shantung, Kwangsi, and Kweichow allocated a relatively high percentage of expenditures for public security. One should remember that these sums do not include subsidies received from Nanking during the course of the anti-Communist campaigns, which would raise the figures for the Bandit Suppression Zones even higher. Naturally these large expenditures for public security strained provincial resources and hindered the development of constructive programs.

Miscellaneous expenditures. Administrative affairs expenditures, which included all the administrative costs of the finance system, the judiciary, and the civil bureaucracy, were generally high (see Appendix D, Table D.4). All the provinces for which figures are available except Kwangtung allocated at least one-fifth of their total expenditures for this purpose. (In the one year for which we have figures for Kwangtung, it allocated 19 percent.) The outlying provinces of Tsinghai, Ningsia, and Kweichow devoted as much as 58, 49, and 41 percent, respectively, to administrative affairs. The cost of maintaining administrative machinery put a severe strain on their limited resources. There were no significant differences in this category between provinces inside and outside the Bandit Suppression Zones in terms of absolute amounts or percentages.

Table D.4 in Appendix D also shows local expenditures on education, cultural activities, transportation, reconstruction, public health, and industry. Since allocations for public security, administrative affairs, and Kuomintang party affairs were so high, resources for improving the general social and economic situation were limited. When socioeconomic expenditures are considered as a percentage of total expenditures, we find a great deal of provincial variation. Kiangsu and Fukien, with 44 percent and 42 percent, respectively, were clearly in the lead. At the other end of the scale were Ningsia and Shansi, with 16 percent each. No geographic pattern is discernable in these variations, however; nor do there seem to be significant differences between provinces inside and outside the Bandit Suppression Zones. It is somewhat surprising to note that Chekiang apparently placed a rather low priority on socioeconomic improvement, allocating only 19 percent of its total expenditures for that purpose.

The remaining provincial expenditures, including both itemized miscellaneous allocations and unitemized allocations, amounted to about one-fourth of the total expenditures. Among these items debt service and reserve funds whose purpose was unspecified often absorbed the largest share.

In conclusion, let us summarize several important characteristics of provincial finance during the Nanking decade. First, financial administration continued to rely heavily on traditional mechanisms. This is clearly evident in the case of the land tax. T. V. Soong's efforts to consolidate and modernize China's financial systems had only limited effect. The failure to pursue land cadastre and land registration made it virtually impossible to institute an equitable land taxation system. Only Kiangsu, Chekiang, Anhwei, Kiangsi, Hupeh, and Yunnan made any progress in land surveys and registration. All except Yunnan were major territorial bases of the Kuomintang regime. Even so, in Kiangsu, which had the best record, only about half of the counties and cities had been officially surveyed or registered.

Second, largely because of the failure to improve financial administration, provincial revenues remained fairly steady throughout the decade, and in some cases decreased. Under the circumstances provincial authorities had very little hope of improving socioeconomic conditions, even if they desired to do so. Third, subsidiary loans, land taxes, and various surcharges were the primary sources of provincial revenue. Subsidiary loans were either funds allocated to the provinces by the Kuomintang regime or central government revenues retained in the provinces. They were an especially important source of income in the Bandit Suppression Zones, in provinces of strategic value, and in provinces whose leaders had displayed political allegiance to Nanking. The land tax was the principal source of provincial revenue. But the fact that it was not assessed or collected equitably demonstrated the backwardness of public finance in the provinces.

Finally, the allocation of resources varied from one group of provinces to another. In the Bandit Suppression Zones, where it seems likely that military expenses were largely assumed by the central government's Military Council, expenditures were concentrated on public security activities and administrative affairs. A good deal of this money went to programs designed to complement Chiang's military efforts through the militarization and political indoctrination of citizens. The provinces outside the Bandit Suppression Zones were certainly not without military burdens. In fact, the limited figures available indicate that military costs and the costs of maintaining a civil administrative bureaucracy absorbed almost half of their total revenues throughout the period. It is not surprising that the vast majority of provinces at this time devoted only a small portion of their revenues to such items as education, cultural activities, transportation, rural reconstruction, public health, and industry, no matter how urgently these areas needed attention. The provincial governments had no better record in making socioeconomic improvements than the central government.

Conclusion

THERE HAS BEEN a good deal of speculation on whether or not the 1949 Communist victory in China was inevitable. Proponents of one thesis have argued that social and political change there in the first half of the twentieth century made a profound social revolution necessary and inevitable. According to them China was such a sick society that no marginal change would have been sufficient to save her. Their equally vociferous opponents attribute the Communist success to the outbreak of the Sino-Japanese War and the inept postwar China policy of the United States. They maintain that the Kuomintang would have been able to defeat the Communists and unite China had the war not intervened.

To students of modern China these arguments have become familiar themes. Although both serve to emphasize particular aspects of modern China's social and political history, the controversy remains unsettled in the eyes of this writer. Indeed, we still know very little about China in the 1920's and the 1930's; even many aspects of the war and the postwar period remain unclear. This book has not been based on any speculations or assumptions like those above. Instead its purpose is to analyze the major aspects of Chinese political development in the decade before the war. Hopefully, it will encourage other scholars to pay more attention to this tremendously important decade, about which so little has been written.

The Kuomintang, which under various names had been politically active for over a quarter of a century, emerged in 1927 as the leading political force in China. It came to power in a period of political decay. The imperial order had been destroyed, and a decentralized warlord system had grown up to replace it. The feudalization of political power and the breakdown of the centralized bureaucracy posed serious problems for the Kuomintang. The consolidation of this power and of fragmented territorial units became the most crucial task in the struggle to build a nation.

Like many modern nationalist political parties in the Afro-Asian world, the Kuomintang considered itself the only legitimate party and the only party capable of leading efforts toward national integration. The available evidence, however, indicates the party's clear limitations in developing institutional mechanisms to achieve this goal. Especially telling is its failure to build a membership and an organizational structure outside Kwangtung, its initial sanctuary, and the provinces of the middle and lower Yangtze valley. Moreover, a legitimate decision-making structure was never developed within the party itself. Several institutions initially designed to determine policy gradually evolved into bodies with more political status than power. Appointments to the Central Executive Committee, the Political Council, and their standing committees, for example, were used to reward political supporters of the regime and to appease political opponents. As a result these bodies grew in size and became increasingly ineffective. The failure to develop legitimate decision-making institutions meant that power lay with whoever had the force to back up his political ambitions. Chiang Kai-shek emerged as the man with that force.

The Kuomintang regime dominated by Chiang Kai-shek had three prominent characteristics in the 1927–37 decade. First, the central party and the government became militarized; that is, authority was largely controlled by military men and resources were allocated according to military priorities. This militarization precluded the development of both civilian leadership and an institutional base to support such leadership. It enabled Chiang to buttress his power in a military structure that was largely independent of civilian control by the party or the government. It also enabled him to ignore social, political, and international issues that he preferred not to face.

Second, the regime's authority structure came to be dominated by informal client groups connected with Chiang, namely, the Blue Shirts, the C.C. Clique, and the Political Study Clique. Relations between Chiang and the members of these groups were based on such particularistic factors as school ties and local affinity. Although the client groups consisted of both civilians and military men, civilian members believed in upholding Chiang's military power. The cliques effectively blocked other competing senior civilian leaders from exercising influence in the determination of public policy. Party leaders such as Hu Han-min and Wang Ching-wei, although they had prestige and followers, were fatally handicapped by the lack of stable, independent bases of power. The elimination of Hu, Wang, and others from the decision-making process had unfortunate repercussions for the regime, which needed a broad-based consensus on fundamental policies. In part, it tended to perpetuate regionally based power groups, since some civilian leaders who were alienated from the regime made alliances with regional or provincial forces against Nanking. Thus, in the final analysis, although Chiang's ability to replace his rivals with loyal followers may have gained him the dominant position in the regime, it also created factors that threatened to undermine his pursuit of real power.

Finally, under Chiang and his extremely conservative and ultra-nationalistic client groups, the regime moved in the direction of fascism. There was a growing emphasis on the techniques of political control and on the personification of political power in an infallible leader, Chiang Kai-shek. The activities of the Blue Shirts and the C.C. Clique clearly reflect an attempt to transform the Kuomintang into a party of a fascist nature. Chiang's supporters moved step by step to institute control mechanisms in rural areas within the regime's jurisdiction. The resulting mobilization of some members of the rural population was not intended to incorporate them into the political process in any meaningful way; instead it was part of a concentrated effort to organize a mass following for Chiang. This whole trend toward fascism was ultimately detrimental to the party and to Chiang himself. The Kuomintang had inherited a genuine revolutionary legacy, however incomplete and unsystematic its performance had been in implementing it. The new emphasis on control placed Chiang in the impossible position of affirming revolution and the status quo simultaneously. Furthermore, the party was operating in a sociopolitical environment that had been thoroughly disrupted; few viable systems existed to uphold the status quo. What China truly needed was drastic change, neither control nor maintenance of the existing order. This does not mean that the success of the Communists was inevitable. The Kuomintang had a chance to promote major changes short of revolution. Perhaps if other, more progressive, party leaders had had more power, they would have done so.

The changes and developments in the Kuomintang's power structure shaped the patterns of the party's nation-building. In 1927 China was still plagued by regional militarism. By 1935–36 the regime had extended its political influence from the two provinces that it initially controlled, Chekiang and Kiangsu, to eight other provinces: Anhwei, Kiangsi, Hupeh, Honan, Hunan, Fukien, and, to a lesser degree, Kansu and Shensi. Much of this central penetration was made possible by anti-Communist military operations. Communist activities in these provinces posed a serious threat to local rulers, who could not suppress them alone. Since Chiang Kai-shek was committed to eliminating the Communists, he was able to force his way into certain areas on the basis of this common interest. Most provincial rulers who had to deal with the Communists came to accept some degree of central authority, as exercised by Chiang's military headquarters. Chiang adopted the same strategy of central penetration in Szechwan and Kweichow in 1935–36, but the outbreak of the Sino-Japanese War in 1937 cut short these attempts.

The important questions concerning the provinces are to what extent was the Kuomintang able to effect changes there and by what means did it do so. In summary, we may draw the following conclusions regarding relations between the center and the provinces and the political developments that resulted from this interaction. First, by the end of the decade the Kuomintang had established political authority, in varying degrees, in the ten provinces classified as the Bandit Suppression Zones. It was able to introduce certain administrative changes in these provinces and to influence the selection of provincial and county-level administrative personnel. The Kuomintang authority was not free, however, to make appointments without consulting provincial rulers. In fact, compromises were often necessary to avoid provoking serious opposition. Neither was Nanking able to establish a uniform, centralized administrative system throughout the zones. Matters of provincial finance continued to remain outside central control. In short, Chiang Kai-shek and the Kuomintang regime were forced to rely on political bargaining and compromise to achieve their ends.

Second, the major instrument of central penetration was the Military Council, which was headed by Chiang Kai-shek and had field headquarters in Nanchang and later in Wuchang and Chungking. These headquarters, not party or government bodies, exercised political control in the Bandit Suppression Provinces. Nanking's resources were allocated largely by the military headquarters for purposes determined by Chiang and his followers. The limited changes effected in the provinces by the center were also closely related to military objectives. The regime's major agents were military men and members of Chiang's client factions, whose selection and activities were largely outside the control of Nanking's civilian authorities. Thus there was little chance that central penetration would result in the development of strong provincial administrative and party institutions.

Third, little was accomplished in the way of socioeconomic reform. The central government and all provincial governments continued to allocate most of their resources to military, quasi-military, and administrative purposes. The percentage of revenues allocated to improving socioeconomic conditions was relatively small. This no doubt was responsible for further socioeconomic decline, particularly in rural China. Both central and provincial authorities, although they needed much larger incomes, were slow to improve mechanisms of taxation. The financial reforms sponsored by Nanking did bring some minor improvements, but the traditional taxation system continued to prevail in most places, growing more corrupt and inequitable. This was symptomatic of a general disintegration of socioeconomic systems in most of China outside the major cities and walled towns.

Finally, outside the ten Bandit Suppression Provinces, the Kuomintang's authority was nominal or nonexistent. A high degree of provincialism continued to exist in Shansi, Kwangsi, Kwangtung, Yunnan, and Szechwan. Varying degrees of autonomy also existed in Kweichow and the outlying provinces in the north and northwest. Here provincial or regional militarists appointed their own officials and ran their own administrative and financial affairs with little or no concern for the wishes of the central authority. On the one hand, we may speculate that even if the Communists had not been active and there had been no war with Japan, it would have taken the Kuomintang a long time to bring these provinces into its domain. On the other hand, we are assessing the Kuomintang's performance over a relatively short period of ten years. This performance may compare favorably with that of many developing nations after World War II.

Still, it does not necessarily follow that if there had been enough time, the Kuomintang under Chiang Kai-shek would have managed to build an integrated nation. In fact, the evidence presented here tends to argue against that. The conclusions we draw from this study, however, must be weighed against such factors as war, the limited time span involved, and the complexity of the social, economic, and political problems that had developed in the preceding century. In the process of preparing this volume, I have become convinced that our knowledge of China during the prewar decade is not adequate to permit the formulation of any general theory at this time. Many of the generalizations that have evolved out of the partisan debate on the issue are based, in my opinion, on speculation.

Appendixes

Provincial Governors, 1927-37

ANHWEI
Ch'en Tiao-yuan
(Oct. 1927-May 1929)
Fang Chen-wu
(May-Oct. 1929)
Shih Yü-san
(Oct. 1929-Jan. 1930)
Wang Chin-yü
(Jan.-Mar. 1930)
Ma Fu-hsiang
(Mar.-Sep. 1930)
Ch'en Tiao-yuan
(Sep. 1930-Apr. 1932)
Wu Chung-hsin
(Apr. 1932-May 1933)
Liu Chen-hua
(May 1933-1936)
Liu Shang-ch'ing
(1936-1937)

陳調元
方振武
石友三
王金鈺
馬福祥
陳調元
吳忠信
劉鎮華
劉尚清

CHAHAR
Chao Tai-wen
(Oct.-Nov. 1928)
Yang Ai-yuan
(Nov. 1928-Jan. 1931)
Liu I-fei
(Jan. 1931-Aug. 1932)
Sung Che-yuan
(Aug. 1932-June 1935)
Ch'in Te-ch'un
(June 1935-1937)

趙戴文
楊愛源
劉翼飛
宋哲元
秦德純

CHEKIANG
Ho Ying-ch'in
(Oct. 1927-Nov. 1928)
Chang Jen-chieh
(Nov. 1928-Dec. 1930)
Chang Nan-hsien
(Dec. 1930-Dec. 1931)
Lu Ti-p'ing
(Dec. 1931-Dec. 1934)
Huang Shao-hung
(Dec. 1934-1936)
Chu Chia-hua
(1936-1937)

何應欽
張人傑
張難先
魯滌平
黃紹竑
朱家驊

FUKIEN
Yang Shu-chuang
(Aug. 1928-Dec. 1932)
Chiang Kuang-nai
(Dec. 1932-Dec. 1933)
Ch'en I
(Jan. 1934-1937)

楊樹莊
蔣光鼐
陳儀

*HEILUNGKIANG
Ch'ang Yin-huai
(Dec. 1928-Feb. 1929)
Wan Fu-lin
(Feb. 1929-Nov. 1931)
Ma Chan-shan
(Nov. 1931-1933)

常蔭槐
萬福麟
馬占山

HONAN
Feng Yü-hsiang
(Jan.-Dec. 1928)
Han Fu-chü
(Dec. 1928-Oct. 1930)
Liu Chih
(Oct. 1930-1935)
Shang Chen
(1936-1937)

馮玉祥
韓復榘
劉峙
商震

HOPEI
Shang Chen
(June 1928-Aug. 1929)
Hsü Yung-ch'ang
(Aug. 1929-Nov. 1930)
Wang Shu-ch'ang
(Nov. 1930-Aug. 1932)
Yü Hsüeh-chung
(Aug. 1932-June 1935)
Shang Chen
(June 1935-1936)
Feng Chih-an
(1936-1937)

商震
徐永昌
王樹常
于學忠
商震
馮治安

HUNAN
Lu Ti-p'ing
(May 1928-Mar. 1929)
Ho Chien
(Mar. 1929-1937)

魯滌平
何鍵

HUPEH
  Chang Chih-pen
    (Dec. 1927-May 1929)
  Ho Ch'eng-chün
    (May 1929-Mar. 1932)
  Hsia Tou-yin
    (Mar. 1932-July 1933)
  Chang Ch'ün
    (July 1933-1935)
  Yang Yung-t'ai
    (Jan.-Oct. 1936)
  Huang Shao-hung
    (1937)

張知本
何成濬
夏斗寅
張羣
楊永泰
黃紹竑

*JEHOL
  T'ang Yü-lin
    (Dec. 1928-1933)

湯玉麟

KANSU
  Liu Yü-fen
    (1929-Nov. 1930)
  Ma Hung-pin
    (Nov. 1930-Dec. 1931)
  Shao Li-tzu
    (Dec. 1931-May 1933)
  Chu Shao-liang
    (May 1933-Dec. 1935)
  Yü Hsüeh-chung
    (1936)
  Ho Yao-tsu
    (1937)

劉郁芬
馬鴻賓
邵力子
朱紹良
于學忠
賀耀祖

KIANGSI
  Chu P'ei-te
    (Nov. 1927-Sep. 1929)
  Lu Ti-p'ing
    (Sep. 1929-Dec. 1931)
  Hsiung Shih-hui
    (Dec. 1931-1937)

朱培德
魯滌平
熊式輝

KIANGSU
  Niu Yung-chien
    (Nov. 1927-Mar. 1930)
  Yeh Ch'u-ts'ang
    (Mar. 1930-Dec. 1931)
  Ku Chu-t'ung
    (Dec. 1931-Oct. 1933)
  Ch'en Kuo-fu
    (Oct. 1933-1937)

鈕永建
葉楚傖
顧祝同
陳果夫

*KIRIN
  Chang Tso-hsiang
    (Dec. 1928-July 1932)
  Ting Chao
    (July 1932-1933)

張作相
丁超

KWANGSI
  Huang Shao-hung
    (May 1927-May 1929)
  Wu T'ing-yang
    (May-June 1929)
  Yü Tso-po
    (June-Oct. 1929)
  Lü Fan-yen
    (Oct.-Nov. 1929)
  Huang Shao-hung
    (Nov. 1929-1932)
  Huang Hsü-ch'u
    (1932-1937)

黃紹竑
伍廷颺
俞作柏
呂煥炎
黃紹竑
黃旭初

KWANGTUNG
  Li Chi-shen
    (June 1927-Nov. 1928)
  Ch'en Ming-shu
    (Nov. 1928-1931)
  Lin Yün-kai
    (1932-1937)

李濟深
陳銘樞
林雲陔

KWEICHOW
  Chou Hsi-ch'eng
    (Apr. 1927-June 1929)
  Mao Kuang-hsiang
    (Oct. 1929-Mar. 1932)
  Wang Chia-lieh
    (Mar. 1932-1935)
  Wu Chung-hsin
    (Apr. 1935-1936)
  Hsüeh Yüeh
    (1937)

周西成
毛光翔
王家烈
吳忠信
薛岳

*LIAONING
  Chia Wen-hsüan
    (Dec. 1928-Jan. 1931)
  Ts'ang Shih-i
    (Jan. 1931-1933)

翟文選
臧式毅

NINGSIA
  Men Chih-chung
    (Nov. 1928-June 1931)
  Ma Hung-k'uei
    (June 1931-1937)

門致中
馬鴻逵

SHANSI
  Yen Hsi-shan
    (Mar. 1928-Aug. 1929)
  Shang Chen
    (Aug. 1929-Aug. 1931)
  Hsü Yung-ch'ang
    (Oct. 1931-1936)
  Chao Tai-wen
    (1936-1937)

閻錫山
商震
徐永昌
趙戴文

SHANTUNG
  Sun Liang-ch'eng
    (May 1928-May 1929)
  Ch'en Tiao-yuan
    (May 1929-Sep. 1930)
  Han Fu-chü
    (Sep. 1930-1937)

孫良誠
陳調元
韓復榘

SHENSI
  Sung Che-yuan
    (1929-Oct. 1930)
  Yang Hu-ch'eng
    (Oct. 1930-May 1933)
  Shao Li-tzu
    (May 1933-1936)
  Sun Wei-ju
    (1937)

宋哲元
楊虎城
邵力子
孫蔚如

SIKANG[a]
  Liu Wen-hui
    (1936-1937)

劉文輝

SINKIANG
  Chin Shu-jen
    (Nov. 1928-May 1933)
  Liu Wen-lung
    (Aug. 1933-Oct. 1934)
  Li Yung
    (Oct. 1934-1937)

金樹仁
劉文龍
李溶

SUIYUAN
  Hsü Yung-ch'ang
    (Oct. 1928-Aug. 1929)
  Li P'ei-chi
    (Aug. 1929-Aug. 1931)
  Fu Tso-i
    (Aug. 1931-1937)

徐永昌

李培基

傅作義

TSINGHAI
  Sun Lien-chung
    (Sep. 1928-Jan. 1931)
  Ma Ch'i
    (Jan. 1931-Mar. 1933)
  Ma Lin
    (Mar. 1933-1937)

孫連仲

馬騏

馬麟

SZECHWAN
  Liu Wen-hui
    (Nov. 1928-Dec. 1934)
  Liu Hsiang
    (Dec. 1934-1937)

劉文輝

劉湘

YUNNAN
  Lung Yün
    (Jan. 1928-1937)

龍雲

SOURCES: (1) *Nei-cheng nien-chien*, 1935, pp. (B)334–43; (2) Boorman, *Biographical Dictionary*, vols. 1–3; (3) *Biographies of Kuomintang Leaders*; (4) Boorman, *Man and Politics*; (5) *China Year Book*, 1929–37; (6) Perleberg; and (7) *Who's Who in China*.
NOTE: Asterisks (°) indicate provinces that were under Japanese occupation in 1934–37 and are accordingly not covered in this book.
  a Sikang had no provincial government in 1927–35.

Data Problems Affecting Tables 11 and 13, Chapter 8

A survey of the social characteristics and backgrounds of the governors in all 28 provinces is difficult because no single source provides a complete list of names and terms of office. The most reliable information comes from the *China Year Book, Shen-pao nien-chien* (*Shen-pao* yearbook), and *Nei-cheng nien-chien* (Yearbook of the Interior), the official publication of the Ministry of the Interior. Unfortunately, the three sources occasionally contradict each other, making arbitrary choices necessary. Biographical accounts and various provincial yearbooks, incomplete as they are, help clarify some of the confusion.

The tables examine 90 governors in 23 provinces. The five provinces of Kirin, Heilungkiang, Liaoning, Jehol, and Sikang are excluded; the first four were occupied by the Japanese in the early 1930's, and Sikang did not officially establish a government until 1936. The total number of governorships in the 23 provinces was actually 93, since Anhwei, Hopei, and Kwangsi each had a governor who served two nonconsecutive terms. Each man is counted only once under these provinces in Tables 11 and 13. (All 93 governorships are considered in Table 14, which deals with the average terms of governors.)

Each of the following men served as governor in more than one province: Ch'en Tiao-yuan (Shantung, Anhwei), Huang Shao-hung (Kwangsi, Chekiang, Hupeh), Lu Ti-p'ing (Kiangsi, Hunan, Chekiang), Han Fu-chü (Honan, Shantung), Shang Chen (Honan, Hopei, Shansi), Hsü Yung-ch'ang (Hopei, Shansi, Suiyuan), Shao Li-tzu (Kansu, Shensi), Sung Che-yuan (Chahar, Shensi), Wu Chung-hsin (Anhwei, Kweichow), Yü Hsüeh-chung (Kansu, Hopei), and Chao Tai-wen (Shansi, Chahar). In fact, then, only 75 men in all are considered in Tables 11 and 13. Each of the 11 men listed above is included under each province in which he served; a breakdown by province would otherwise be impossible. The totals in Table 11, however, have been adjusted to take multiple governorships into account, and represent actual men. (Liu Wen-hui also served in two provinces, Szechwan and Sikang, but since Sikang is not listed in the tables, this is irrelevant to our calculations here.)

Biographical information on Li Yung of Sinkiang is not available. Thus he has been excluded from the statistical compilation.

Provincial Revenues, 1930-36

The source for the tables in this Appendix is *Ti-cheng yüeh-k'an* (Land administration monthly), vol. 4, nos. 2–3 (1936), pp. 173–99.

TABLE C.1

Provincial Revenues in the Bandit Suppression Zones, 1930–36
(in millions of Chinese dollars)

Province	1930–31	1931–32	1932–33	1933–34	1934–35	1935–36	TOTAL
Anhwei	16.2	15.6	9.8	11.1	11.1	11.2	75.0
Chekiang	21.7	25.2	24.7	23.1	21.5	21.3	137.4
Fukien	—	27.5	26.2	16.9	15.3	19.9	105.9
Honan	14.5	17.8	10.1	11.3	13.6	15.4	82.8
Hunan	10.7	17.1	15.5	14.3	14.1	16.6	88.3
Hupeh	13.0	23.6	17.0	17.6	18.7	24.6	114.5
Kansu	—	—	5.2	—	7.0	4.7	16.9
Kiangsi	—	—	17.7	17.1	21.9	19.0	75.8
Kiangsu	14.3	26.2	17.1	21.9	26.9	31.6	138.0
Shensi	—	14.0	—	—	—	18.2	32.2

NOTE: The totals do not necessarily equal the sums of the annual figures because of rounding.

TABLE C.2

Provincial Revenues Outside the Bandit Suppression Zones, 1930–36
(in millions of Chinese dollars)

Province	1930–31	1931–32	1932–33	1933–34	1934–35	1935–36	TOTAL
Chahar	2.3	2.3	2.9	3.9	3.5	3.2	18.2
Hopei	15.6	38.2	23.2	25.8	22.6	26.5	151.9
Kwangsi	—	13.7	13.2	—	—	—	27.0
Kwangtung	13.0	34.2	57.2	64.7	82.1	—	251.2
Kweichow	—	2.6	2.9	2.9	4.6	4.9	18.0
Ningsia	—	1.1	2.2	1.4	1.5	4.4	10.7
Shansi	10.8	11.3	13.7	—	—	—	35.9
Shantung	21.9	24.6	24.5	23.6	23.8	25.0	143.3
Sinkiang	3.5	3.2	—	—	—	—	6.8
Tsinghai	—	2.0	0.8	0.8	0.9	1.0	5.5
Yunnan	—	3.1	3.3	3.6	5.3	—	15.4

NOTE: No figures are available for Suiyuan or Szechwan. The totals do not necessarily equal the sums of the annual figures because of rounding.

TABLE C.3

Subsidiary Loans from Nanking to the Provinces, 1930–36

Province	No. of years figures available[a]	Total revenues (Ch $ 000)	Subsidiary loans	
			Amount (Ch $ 000)	Pct. of total revenues
Kweichow	1	4,589	1,700	37.1%
*Anhwei	5	58,788	18,657	31.7
Yunnan	2	6,927	2,084	30.1
*Kiangsi	4	75,781	19,906	26.3
*Honan	4	59,042	11,780	20.0
Chahar	4	13,531	2,647	19.5
*Hunan	3	47,795	8,558	17.9
*Hupeh	6	114,501	18,096	15.8
*Chekiang	3	73,031	11,471	15.8
*Kiangsu	6	137,959	20,599	14.9
*Fukien	5	105,860	14,580	13.8
*Kansu	1	4,727	615	13.0
Tsinghai	1	1,001	122	12.2
*Shensi	1	18,205	1,607	8.8
Hopei	5	125,404	8,750	7.0
Kwangsi	1	13,243	811	6.1
Ningsia	1	4,386	186	4.2
Shansi	1	13,682	253	1.8
Shantung	1	24,970	350	1.4

NOTE: Asterisks (*) indicate provinces in the Bandit Suppression Zones. No figures are available for Kwangtung, Sinkiang, Suiyuan, or Szechwan.

[a] That is, the number of years for which figures on both subsidiary loans and total revenues are available. The following subsidiary loan figures are excluded from the table because the corresponding total revenue figures are unavailable: Kwangsi, Ch $58,000 (1934–35), and Shansi, Ch $254,000 (1934–35).

TABLE C.4

Land Tax Revenues, 1930–36

Province	No. of years figures available[a]	Total revenues (Ch $ 000)	Land taxes Amount (Ch $ 000)	Land taxes Pct. of total revenues
Shantung	6	143,343	91,547	63.9%
Shansi	3	35,863	18,980	52.8
Tsinghai	4	2,462	4,663	52.8
*Chekiang	5	115,962	60,503	52.2
*Honan	6	82,810	42,987	51.9
Ningsia	5	10,691	5,025	46.9
*Kiangsu	6	137,959	63,979	46.4
Sinkiang	2	6,754	2,869	42.5
*Anhwei	5	58,788	20,129	34.3
*Kansu	3	16,883	4,970	30.0
*Kiangsi	4	75,781	21,487	28.4
*Shensi	1	13,995	3,300	23.6
Hopei	5	125,404	27,734	22.1
Chahar	6	18,151	3,801	20.9
Kweichow	4	13,032	2,669	20.5
*Hunan	6	88,270	17,982	20.4
Kwangsi	2	26,987	5,469	20.3
Yunnan	3	10,052	1,938	19.3
*Fukien	5	105,860	14,788	14.0
Kwangtung	3	156,108	19,179	12.3
*Hupeh	6	114,501	7,798	6.8

NOTE: Asterisks (*) indicate provinces in the Bandit Suppression Zones.

[a] That is, the number of years for which figures on both land taxes and total revenues are available. The following figures on land tax revenues are excluded from the table because corresponding total revenue figures are unavailable: Shansi, Ch $6.5 million (1934–35) and 7.9 million (1935–36); Tsinghai, 1.4 million (1930–31); Kwangsi, 2.2 million (1933–34) and 2 million (1934–35); Kwangtung, 6.1 million (1935–36); Suiyuan, 1.2 million (1932–33); and Szechwan, 6.9 million (1935–36).

Provincial Expenditures, 1931-36

The source for the tables in this Appendix is *Ti-cheng yüeh-k'an* (Land administration monthly), vol. 4, nos. 2–3 (1936), pp. 173–99.

TABLE D.1

Provincial Expenditures in the Bandit Suppression Zones, 1931–36
(*in millions of Chinese dollars*)

Province	1931–32	1932–33	1933–34	1934–35	1935–36	TOTAL
Anhwei	15.6	9.8	11.1	11.1	11.2	58.8
Chekiang	25.2	24.7	23.1	—	21.3	94.3
Fukien	30.8	26.2	16.9	—	19.3	93.3
Honan	17.8	10.1	11.3	—	—	39.3
Hunan	17.2	15.4	14.3	14.1	16.6	77.6
Hupeh	28.0	17.0	17.6	18.7	24.6	105.9
Kansu	—	12.1	—	4.6	4.7	21.4
Kiangsi	—	17.7	17.1	21.9	19.0	75.8
Kiangsu	26.2	25.6	21.9	26.9	31.7	132.2
Shensi	20.8	—	—	—	18.2	39.0

NOTE: The totals do not necessarily equal the sums of the annual figures because of rounding.

TABLE D.2

Provincial Expenditures Outside the Bandit Suppression Zones, 1931–36
(*in millions of Chinese dollars*)

Province	1931–32	1932–33	1933–34	1934–35	1935–36	TOTAL
Chahar	2.3	3.1	3.9	3.5	3.1	15.9
Hopei	38.2	23.2	25.8	—	—	87.2
Kwangsi	11.0	13.2	—	—	—	24.3
Kwangtung	43.1	—	—	—	—	43.1
Kweichow	8.9	9.0	6.1	6.0	—	30.0
Ningsia	3.3	2.2	1.4	1.5	4.0	12.4
Shansi	17.8	13.7	—	—	—	31.4
Shantung	24.6	24.5	23.6	23.6	25.0	121.3
Sinkiang	8.9	—	—	—	—	8.9
Tsinghai	0.9	0.9	0.9	—	1.0	3.8
Yunnan	5.4	4.3	3.6	13.6	15.4	42.4

NOTE: No figures are available for Suiyuan or Szechwan. The totals do not necessarily equal the sums of the yearly figures because of rounding.

TABLE D.3

Expenditures on Party Affairs and
Public Security, 1931–36

Province	No. of years figures available	Total expenditures (Ch $ 000)	Amount (Ch $ 000)	Pct. of total expenditures
	PARTY AFFAIRS EXPENDITURES			
Ningsia	5	12,367	708	6%
Tsinghai	4	3,777	173	5
*Hunan	5	77,588	2,772	4
Shantung	5	121,292	4,677	4
*Honan	3	39,322	1,011	3
*Anhwei	5	58,788	1,316	2
Chahar	5	15,915	365	2
*Fukien	4	93,260	1,812	2
Hopei	3	87,151	1,505	2
*Kansu	3	21,439	480	2
*Kiangsi	4	75,781	1,323	2
Kwangtung	1	43,095	874	2
Shansi	2	31,448	511	2
*Shensi	2	38,986	946	2
*Chekiang	4	94,287	1,095	1
*Hupeh	5	105,883	1,219	1
*Kiangsu	5	132,187	951	1
Kwangsi	2	24,259	286	1
Kweichow	4	26,999	313	1
	PUBLIC SECURITY EXPENDITURES			
*Kansu	3	21,439	9,284	43%
*Shensi	2	38,986	12,949	33
*Kiangsi	4	75,781	19,347	26
Kweichow	4	26,999	6,717	25
Kwangsi	1	13,243	3,071	23
*Fukien	4	93,260	18,456	20
*Hupeh	5	105,883	21,292	20
Shantung	5	121,292	24,090	20
*Chekiang	4	94,287	17,463	19
*Anhwei	5	58,788	10,520	18
*Honan	3	39,322	6,349	16
*Kiangsu	5	132,187	18,387	14
Chahar	5	15,915	1,734	11
*Hunan	5	77,588	8,550	11
Tsinghai	4	3,777	343	9
Ningsia	4	9,106	547	6
Hopei	3	87,151	4,435	5
Shansi	2	31,448	873	3

NOTE: Asterisks (*) indicate provinces in the Bandit Suppression Zones. No figures in either category are available for Sinkiang, Suiyuan, Szechwan, or Yunnan. No public security figures are available for Kwangtung.

TABLE D.4

Expenditures on Administrative Affairs and
Socioeconomic Affairs, 1931–36

Province	No. of years figures available	Total expenditures (Ch $ 000)	Amount (Ch $ 000)	Pct. of total expenditures
ADMINISTRATIVE AFFAIRS EXPENDITURES				
Tsinghai	4	3,777	2,196	58%
Ningsia	5	12,367	6,111	49
Kweichow	4	26,999	11,158	41
Chahar	5	15,915	6,008	38
*Anhwei	5	58,788	21,082	36
Shantung	5	121,292	41,646	34
*Hunan	5	77,588	25,442	33
*Kansu	3	21,439	6,970	33
*Kiangsi	4	75,781	18,184	24
*Honan	3	39,322	12,037	31
*Hupeh	5	105,883	27,477	26
*Kiangsi	4	75,781	18,184	24
*Chekiang	4	94,287	21,956	23
*Kiangsu	5	132,187	30,868	23
Hopei	3	87,151	18,946	22
*Shensi	2	38,986	8,102	21
*Fukien	4	93,260	18,810	20
Shansi	2	31,448	6,252	20
Kwangtung	1	43,095	8,096	19
SOCIOECONOMIC AFFAIRS EXPENDITURES[a]				
*Kiangsu	5	132,187	57,561	44%
*Fukien	4	93,260	39,544	42
Kwangsi	2	24,259	8,717	36
*Hunan	5	77,588	26,298	34
*Anhwei	5	58,788	18,860	32
*Hupeh	5	105,883	31,032	29
*Shensi	2	38,986	10,105	26
*Honan	3	39,322	9,665	25
Kweichow	4	26,999	6,089	23
Tsinghai	4	3,777	881	23
Hopei	3	87,151	17,903	21
Shantung	5	121,292	25,992	21
Kwangtung	1	43,095	8,493	20
*Chekiang	4	94,287	17,506	19
Chahar	5	15,915	2,733	17
*Kansu	3	21,439	3,623	17
*Kiangsi	4	75,781	13,034	17
Ningsia	5	12,367	2,012	16
Shansi	2	31,448	5,117	16

NOTE: Asterisks (*) indicate provinces in the Bandit Suppression Zones. No figures are available for Sinkiang, Suiyuan, Szechwan, or Yunnan.

[a] Socioeconomic affairs include the areas of education, culture, transportation, reconstruction, public health, and industry.

Notes

Notes

Complete authors' names, titles, and publication data for works cited in the Notes are given in the Bibliography, pp. 211–20.

Introduction

1. Hsiao Kung-chuan, p. 501.

2. In 1840, 29 percent of the 1,949 local officials had purchased their titles; in 1895, 49 percent of the 1,975 officials had done so.

3. Some comprehensive works on the history of the Kuomintang are Hatano Ken'ichi, *Chugoku Kokuminto*; Tsou Lu; and Yü.

4. I am particularly grateful to Professor Lyman P. Van Slyke of Stanford University for his help in crystallizing these points on Chiang's use of factional politics.

Chapter One

1. Jerome Ch'en, "Defining Chinese Warlords," p. 563.

2. *Ibid.*, pp. 582–83; see also Bloch, p. 693.

3. Hsi-sheng Ch'i, pp. 405–25.

4. See Sheridan, pp. 20–21, for a discussion of the patron-client relationship. Jerome Ch'en ("Defining Chinese Warlords," pp. 576–77) notes several factors on which these relationships were based, such as educational ties, local affinity, marriage ties, brotherhood oaths, and filial sentiment.

5. Sheridan, pp. 156–57, 248, 251; Gillin, *Warlord*, pp. 154–57.

6. Bloch, pp. 697–99.

7. For the history of the KMT-CCP united front, see Van Slyke, pp. 7–20, and Isaacs, pp. 174–85.

8. T'ang Leang-li, pp. 154–60.

9. *Ibid.*, p. 163.

10. *Ibid.*

11. Shirley, p. 73.

12. T'ang Leang-li, pp. 140–45.

13. Chiang seemed very reluctant to accept the appointment at first. Payne, p. 100.

14. Loh, "Politics," p. 434.
15. T'ang Leang-li, pp. 256–57; Isaacs, pp. 174–85.
16. Jerome Ch'en, "The Left Wing Kuomintang," p. 565.
17. Tsou Lu, p. 453.
18. Sheridan, p. 241.
19. Some have called traditional China a cultural rather than a political entity. For example, see Roxby's article.
20. Whitney, p. 28.   21. Easton, p. 177.
22. *Ibid.*, p. 176.   23. *Ibid.*, p. 192.
24. *Ibid.*, p. 193.

Chapter Two

1. Sporadic examinations were held by the Peking warlord governments after 1916, but they were inconsequential.
2. Gasster, pp. 91–92.
3. Ray Chang, pp. 117–18. Officials of the first rank (T'eh Jen) received Ch $800 a month. Officials of the second rank (Chien Jen) received from Ch $430 a month in the eighth and lowest grade to Ch $680 in the first and highest. Officials in the third rank (Chien Jen) received from Ch $180 a month in the twelfth grade to Ch $400 in the first. Officials in the fourth rank (Wei Jen) received from Ch $55 a month in the sixteenth grade to Ch $200 in the first. The exchange rate between 1929 and 1937 was as follows: Ch $1 was worth U.S. $0.36 in 1929, $0.21 in 1931, $0.19 in 1932, $0.33 in 1933, and $0.29½ in 1937 (1929–33 figures from Salter, pp. 14–16; 1937 figure from *China Year Book*, 1938, p. 210).
4. Ray Chang, pp. 118–19, lists the requirements for participating in each examination.
5. *Ibid.*, p. 119.
6. Ch'en Chih-mai, "Chung-kuo ti kuan," p. 889.
7. Li Chih-t'ang, p. 72. According to the author, 10 of the 34 appointees soon lost their jobs, 15 were appointed as temporary employees, and only 9 actually had tenure by 1936. Thus the first examination, which cost over Ch $1 million, produced only 9 civil-service employees.
8. Po Fen, p. 3.
9. *Ibid.*, p. 4.
10. *K'ao-shih yuan kung-pao*, appendix, p. 35.
11. Ch'ien Tuan-sheng, *Government*, p. 241.
12. Ma Wu, *Wo-ti sheng-huo shih*, pp. 75–80.
13. Ray Chang, p. 109.   14. *Ibid.*, pp. 109–10.
15. Chang Fo-ch'üan, p. 4.   16. Lo Tun-wei, pp. 73, 76.
17. Ch'en Kung-po, p. 243.   18. Chang Fo-ch'üan, p. 4.
19. Ray Chang, p. 110.
20. Kennedy, see esp. pp. 92–228. The author's findings are based on an examination of the party's official journal, *Tang-wu yüeh k'an*.
21. Wright, "From Revolution to Restoration." This ideological trans-

formation has also been described as neo-traditionalism. See Eisenstadt, pp. 758–59.

22. T'ang Leang-li, pp. 229–30.

23. Ch'ien Tuan-sheng, *Government*, p. 98.

24. Kennedy, pp. 138–41.

25. *Ibid.*, p. 137.

26. *Ibid.*, pp. 142–43.

27. *Chung-kuo Kuo-min-tang nien-chien*, 1929, p. 789.

28. *Ibid.*, 1934, p. (A)25.   29. *Ibid.*

30. *Ibid.*, p. (B)40.   31. *Ibid.*, 1929, p. 1016.

32. *Ibid.*, 1934, p. (B)40.

33. The official source is not consistent on the number of provincial branches. *Chung-kuo Kuo-min-tang nien-chien*, 1934, p. (C)138, lists branches in ten provinces: Kiangsu, Kiangsi, Hunan, Hupeh, Kwangtung, Kwangsi, Shantung, Shansi, Hopei, and Suiyuan. In another list on pp. (C)231–32, however, the source omits the provinces of Kiangsi, Kwangtung, and Kwangsi.

34. *Ibid.*, pp. (C)231–33.

35. *Ran-i-sha ni kansuru chosa*, pp. 175–76.

36. Shirley, p. 74.   37. *Ibid.*, pp. 73–74.

38. Rush, pp. 2–3.   39. Easton, p. 299.

40. North and Pool, pp. 435–39.

41. Ch'en Chih-mai, *Chung-kuo cheng-fu*, p. 83.

42. Ch'en Chih-mai, "Kuo-min-tang," p. 623.

43. Ch'ien Tuan-sheng, *Government*, p. 122.

44. Ch'en Chih-mai, "Kuo-min-tang," p. 608.

45. Hu and Sun.

46. Ch'en Chih-mai, "Kuo-min-tang," pp. 610–11.

47. *Ibid.*, p. 616.

48. *Ibid.*, pp. 618–21.

49. Ch'ien Tuan-sheng, *Government*, p. 143.

50. *Cheng-chi hui-i kung-tso pao-kao*, p. 2.

51. Eastman, p. 9.   52. Hsü Kao-yang, p. 2.

53. F. F. Liu, p. 64.   54. *Ibid.*

55. For details see F. F. Liu, pp. 60–74, and Ch'ien Tuan-sheng, *Government*, pp. 181–84.

Chapter Three

1. Ch'ien Tuan-sheng, *Government*, pp. 96–100.

2. For example, see Loh, "Politics," p. 440, and Boorman, "Wang Ching-wei," pp. 514–15.

3. Gillin, "Problems," pp. 835–41.

4. Loh, *Early Chiang Kai-shek*, pp. 26–29.

5. *How Chinese Officials Amass Millions*, p. 1.

6. Boorman, *Biographical Dictionary*, vol. 1, p. 202.

7. Jordan, pp. 11–14.

8. *Kung-chi Ch'en Kuo-fu*, p. 8.

9. The original 20 were Hsü En-tseng, Yü Ching-t'ang, Chang Tao-fan, Chang Li-sheng, Fang Chüeh-hui, Tseng Yang-p'u, Hung Nan-yu, Fang Chu, Li Tsung-huang, Wu Hsing-ya, Ch'en Chao-ying, Chao Li-hua, Lo Chia-lun, Ch'eng T'ien-fang, P'an Kung-chan, Wu K'an-hsien, Chang Ch'ung, Hsiao T'ung-tzu, Chou Ch'i-kang, and Ting Mo-chün. The additional nine were Yeh Ch'u-ts'ang, Ting Wei-fen, Chu Chia-hua, Shih Ying, Shao Yuan-ch'ung, Ch'en Pu-lei, Miao P'ei-ch'eng, Tai K'uei-sheng, and Wang Lu-i. Hatano Ken'ichi, *Chugoku Kokuminto*, p. 461.

10. North and Pool, pp. 334–35.

11. Hatano Ken'ichi, *Chugoku Kokuminto*, p. 462. Hatano mistakenly says 1936 instead of 1935.

12. Boorman, *Biographical Dictionary*, vol. 1, p. 207.

13. Shih Pu-chih, pp. 7–8.

14. F. F. Liu, p. 79.

15. Boorman, *Biographical Dictionary*, vol. 1, p. 207.

16. *How Chinese Officials Amass Millions*, pp. 3–5.

17. *Ibid.*, p. 3.

18. *Ibid.*, p. 4.

19. Hatano Ken'ichi, *Chugoku Kokuminto*, p. 462.

20. Eastman, p. 10. The remark comes from a conversation between the former member and Mr. Eastman.

21. The pro-Communist students first organized the Sparks Society, which was changed to the Federation of Young Soldiers after most of the original members had graduated from the academy. See Ch'en Shao-hsiao, pp. 31–33.

22. Ch'ien Tuan-sheng, *Government*, pp. 98–99.

23. Hatano Ken'ichi, *Chugoku Kokuminto*, pp. 464–65.

24. *Ibid.*, p. 465.

25. For details see Hatano Ken'ichi, *Gendai Shina*, pp. 179–88.

26. After the Blue Shirt Society was formed, Chiang flatly denied its existence in an interview with reporters from *Ta-kung pao* (Tientsin). The interview is recorded in *ibid.*, pp. 188–90.

27. Ch'en Shao-hsiao, p. 14.

28. *Ran-i-sha ni kansuru chosa*, p. 47.

29. *Ibid.*

30. *Ibid.*, p. 131.

31. This summary of recruitment procedures is based on *ibid.*, p. 60.

32. *Ibid.*, pp. 112–30.

33. Ch'en Shao-hsiao, pp. 37–38. Most of the 270 graduates of this program were dispatched to Chiang's Kiangsi-Hupeh-Anhwei bandit suppression headquarters.

34. *Ibid.*, p. 48.

35. Ma Wu, *Wo-ti sheng-huo shih*, pp. 108–10. See also Ch'en Shao-hsiao, p. 51; Kapp, p. 545.

36. Ch'en Shao-hsiao, pp. 52–53.

37. *Tai Yu-nung hsien-sheng nien-p'u*, p. 25.

38. Ch'en Shao-hsiao, p. 70.

39. *Ibid.*, p. 39.

40. Ts'ai Meng-ch'ien, p. 61.

41. "Salvation by Assassination," pp. 6–7. An unidentified Chinese pamphlet printed in Hong Kong at the same time provides the same information as this article in the *China Forum*. According to the article, the document was signed by the character "hua," which apparently stood for the ruling organ of the Blue Shirt Society. The article also claimed that the document's authenticity was supported by a dispatch of the Canton Central News Agency received in Shanghai. I have been unable, however, to determine where the document originated and why it was written. At any rate, the names included Communists (Ch'en Shao-yü, Chin Pan-hsien), Kwangtung political and military leaders (Hu Han-min, Li Chi-shen), left-wing writers (T'ien Han, Mo Tien), and other minor provincial militarists and their protégés.

42. *Ran-i-sha ni kansuru chosa*, pp. 143–44.

43. *Ibid.*, pp. 152–53.

44. For an excellent account see Boorman, *Biographical Dictionary*, vol. 2, pp. 65–66.

45. Liu Chien-ch'ün, p. 64.

46. *Ran-i-sha ni kansuru chosa*, p. 158.

47. *Ibid.*, pp. 161–65. Another source claims that there were over a hundred publications directly or indirectly under the auspices of the Blue Shirts. Ch'en Shao-hsiao, p. 44.

48. Ch'en Shao-hsiao, pp. 21, 43.

49. *Ran-i-sha ni kansuru chosa*, pp. 68–70.

50. Ch'ü Wei-wen, p. 21.

51. This summary of the Blue Shirts' ideology is based on Hatano Ken'ichi, *Chugoku Kokuminto*, pp. 467–68.

52. Ch'ien Tuan-sheng, *Government*, p. 130.

53. Liu Sheng-min, pp. 3–4.

54. Li Chien-nung, pp. 346–47.

55. Liu Sheng-min, vol. 2, no. 11, p. 10; Boorman, *Biographical Dictionary*, vol. 1, p. 320.

56. For a perceptive, detailed account of the Chekiang-Kiangsu financial clique, see Ma Wu, "Chung-kuo tzu-ch'an chieh-chi," vol. 7, no. 1, pp. 26–28, and no. 2, pp. 81–85; see also Yamagami Kaneo, *Sekko zaibatsu ron* (On Chekiang financial magnates; Tokyo, 1938), pp. 114–16, for a listing of members.

57. *Ran-i-sha ni kansuru chosa*, p. 176.

58. *Ibid.*, p. 8.

59. Boorman, *Biographical Dictionary*, vol. 2, p. 188.

60. Shen I-yün, pp. 253–54, 263–64. This book by the wife of Huang Fu is one of the most reliable and informative memoirs written in Chinese in recent years.

61. Boorman, *Biographical Dictionary*, vol. 2, pp. 191, 207.

62. *Ibid.*, p. 191; see also Shen I-yün, pp. 501–25.

63. Shen I-yün, p. 292. According to Mrs. Huang, Chiang Kai-shek and Chang Ching-chiang pressured Huang to join the party, but he refused.

64. Mrs. Huang (Shen I-yün) mentions frequent associations and correspondence between Huang and both Chang and Yang, especially the former.

65. *Ibid.*, p. 451. Mrs. Huang records this without denying it.

66. *Chung-hua min-kuo fa-kuei ta-ch'üan*, p. 1466.

67. Ma Wu, *Wo-ti sheng-huo shih*, pp. 104–10.

68. Ch'en Kuo-fu, p. 123.

69. *Ibid.*, p. 47. Ch'en denied the accusation that he did not pay land taxes.

70. Huang Hsü-ch'u, p. 5. The author, like Huang Shao-hung, was a member of the Kwangsi military oligarchy; he served as governor of the province from 1932 to 1937 and now lives in Hong Kong.

71. Eisenstadt, p. 757.

72. *Ran-i-sha ni kansuru chosa*, pp. 175–76.

Chapter Four

1. Ch'ien Tuan-sheng, *Government*, p. 206.

2. *China Year Book*, 1929–30, p. 628.

3. *Ibid.*, pp. 628–32.

4. Paauw, "Chinese Public Finance," p. 297. This chapter makes numerous references to Douglas Paauw's study, and I wish to acknowledge his contribution especially.

5. *Ibid.*

6. Hsien-ding Fong, p. 50.

7. Masutaro, p. 10.

8. *China Year Book*, 1929–30, p. 657.

9. Paauw, "Chinese Public Finance," p. 383.

10. *Ibid.*

11. Paauw, "Kuomintang," p. 217.

12. *Report on Revenue Policy*, p. 3.

13. *Ibid.*, p. 8. The commission was composed of ten American financial experts and three secretaries: E. W. Kemmerer (president), O. C. Lockhart, Arthur N. Young, B. B. Wallace, William Watson, W. B. Poland, F. A. Cleveland, John P. Young, F. B. Lynch, R. W. Bonnevalle, Edward F. Feeley, F. W. Fetter, and J. McGregor Gibb.

14. These figures are cited in Paauw, "Chinese Public Finance," p. 131.

The original source is Ming-chung Tay, *Das Finanz und Steuerwesen Chinas* (Jena, 1940), p. 24.

15. Whitney, p. 66.
16. *Report on Revenue Policy*, pp. 3–4.
17. For a good discussion of this, see Hsien-ding Fong, p. 48.
18. *Ibid.*   19. *Ibid.*
20. P'eng Jui-fu, p. 53.   21. Ma Yin-ch'u, p. 59.
22. Paauw, "Chinese Public Finance," p. 164.
23. Shun-hsin Chou, p. 41.
24. For percentages of the gross national product resulting from agriculture for the years 1931–36, see Ta-chung Liu, pp. 10–13.
25. Whitney, p. 109.
26. *Ibid.*, p. 65. Figures for Manchuria are excluded. Kiangsu accounted for 31.9 percent, Shantung for 10.3, and Hopei for 19.3.
27. *Ibid.*, p. 66.
28. *Report on Revenue Policy*, p. 3.
29. Paauw, "Chinese Public Finance," p. 250.
30. *Ibid.*, p. 380.
31. Salter, p. 55.
32. For details see Yi C. Wang, pp. 440–42.
33. Boorman, *Biographical Dictionary*, vol. 3, p. 151.
34. *Report on Revenue Policy*, p. 1.

Chapter Five

1. *Nei-cheng nien-chien*, 1937, pp. (B)7–8; Shen Nai-cheng, p. 165.
2. For details on the creation of these six new provinces, see Lu Wei-chen's article. Formerly special administrative areas, they became provinces with only minor changes in their boundaries.
3. Shen Nai-cheng, pp. 164–65. There are different ways to measure the size of the provinces. For a detailed comparison of the various methods, see Tseng Shih-ying, pp. 54–59.
4. For listings of subprovincial administrative divisions, see *Nei-cheng nien-chien*, 1937, pp. (B)8–9.
5. *Nei-cheng kung-pao*, vol. 9, no. 1 (1936), p. 236. The official unit of measurement adopted here is the "square market li" (*p'ing-fang kung-li*), which equals 0.0961 square mile.
6. *Chung-hua nien-chien*, vol. 2, p. 378.
7. Shih Yang-ch'eng, p. 69.
8. Ch'ien Tuan-sheng, *Min-kuo cheng-chu shih*, p. 423.
9. Shen Nai-cheng, pp. 191–92.
10. *Hsien tsu-chih fa*, art. 29.
11. *Nei-cheng kung-pao*, vol. 7, no. 2 (1936), p. 29.
12. For details see Shen Nai-cheng, pp. 185–88.
13. *Ibid.*, pp. 183, 190–91.
14. Wang Tz'u-p'u, p. 2.

Chapter Six

1. Wang Ching-wei et al., p. 41.
2. Clubb, p. 201. Edgar Snow (p. 191) cites a different figure for the government force, 900,000, which is probably slightly exaggerated.
3. Snow, p. 191.
4. Lyman P. Van Slyke, ed., *The Chinese Communist Movement* (Stanford, Calif., 1968), p. 29.
5. Ilpyong J. Kim, "Mass Mobilization Policies and Techniques Developed in the Period of the Chinese Soviet Republic," in A. Doak Barnett, ed., *Chinese Communist Politics in Action* (Seattle, 1969), p. 79.
6. Lyman P. Van Slyke, ed., *The Chinese Communist Movement* (Stanford, Calif., 1968), p. 29.
7. Taylor, p. 303.
8. *Kuo-min cheng-fu chün-shih wei-yuan-hui pao-kao*, p. 1.
9. Chiang Chieh-shih, p. 52.   10. Ni Wei-ch'ing, p. 128.
11. *Ibid.*, p. 133.   12. Wang Tz'u-p'u, pp. 19–20.
13. *Ibid.*, pp. 9–10.   14. Chiang Chieh-shih, p. 52.
15. Eastman, p. 13.
16. Hsiung Shu-ping, "Shih-nien lai chih Chiang-hsi ti-cheng" (Land administration in Kiangsi in the last decade), in *Kan-cheng shih-nien*, pp. 2–8.
17. Cheng Han-ch'ing, "Shih-nien lai chih Chiang-hsi kan-pu hsün-lien" (Cadre training in Kiangsi in the last decade), in *Kan-cheng shih-nien*, pp. 3–4.
18. Liao Shih-ch'iao, "Shih-nien lai chih Chiang-hsi ho-p'ing pao-wei" (Peace preservation in Kiangsi in the last decade), in *Kan-cheng shih-nien*, pp. 1–2.
19. Wang Tz'u-p'u, p. 22.
20. Liao Shih-ch'iao, "Shih-nien lai chih Chiang-hsi ho-p'ing pao-wei," in *Kan-cheng shih-nien*, pp. 3–5.
21. *Ibid.*, pp. 11–12.
22. Yang Yung-t'ai, *Yen-lun chi*, p. 74.
23. *Chün-shih wei-yuan-hui pao-kao*, pp. 3–4.
24. *Ibid.*
25. Huang Shao-hung, p. 320. Huang served as governor of Kwangsi, Chekiang, and Hupeh during the decade.
26. Ch'en Chih-mai, "Sheng-fu ho-shu pan-kung," p. 16.
27. Whitney, p. 131.   28. *Ibid.*, p. 82.
29. Gillin, *Warlord*, pp. 30–58.   30. Whitney, p. 83.
31. Sheridan, pp. 103–5.   32. *Ibid.*, p. 251.
33. Arts. 4, 5, 8–10 of the Organizational Regulations, in *Kuo-min cheng-fu chün-shih wei-yuan-hui pao-kao*, pp. 8–9.
34. Yang Yung-t'ai, "Nan-ch'ang hsing-ying tsung-p'ing," p. 30. Yang

cites a figure of over Ch $5,000, but part of this was for administrative expenses in the county where the inspector's office was located.

35. Arts. 9, 13, 15 of the Organizational Regulations, in *Kuo-min cheng-fu chün-shih wei-yuan-hui pao-kao,* pp. 8–9.

36. Yang Yung-t'ai, *Yen-lun chi,* p. 52.

37. Wang Tz'u-p'u, p. 6.

38. Ma Wu, *Wo-ti sheng-huo shih,* p. 93. The author cites his experiences as the magistrate of Chiang-ling county, Hupeh.

39. *Ibid.*

40. Yang Yung-t'ai, *Yen-lun chi,* p. 58.

41. Hanwell, p. 48.

42. Yang Yung-t'ai, *Yen-lun chi,* p. 58.

43. *Ibid.,* pp. 58–59.   44. Whitney, p. 84.

45. *Chiang-hsi nien-chien,* p. 462.   46. Wei-chin Mu, p. 215.

Chapter Seven

1. Fang Tung-ying, no. 54, p. 14.

2. *Ibid.,* p. 15.

3. Jerome Ch'en, "Defining Chinese Warlords," p. 576.

4. *Ibid.,* p. 468.

5. Hatano Yoshihiro, p. 194.

6. T'ang Leang-li, p. 213; F. F. Liu, p. 74.

7. F. F. Liu, p. 15.

8. Landis, p. 155.

9. F. F. Liu, p. 11.

10. *Lu-chün chün-kuan hsüeh-hsiao hsiao-shih,* pp. 2230–31.

11. Figure calculated from *ibid.,* pp. 2501–57.

12. MacFarquhar, p. 162.   13. Hatano Yoshihiro, p. 373.

14. Ts'ang Cho, no. 63, p. 3.   15. *Ibid.,* no. 64, p. 5.

16. Li Tsung-huang, "Lu-chün ssu hsiao chi-lu," p. 31. Li was the man chosen by Sun to set up the association, and he was a key figure in it throughout the years 1918–29.

17. Li Tsung-huang, "Pao-ting hsüeh-hsiao," p. 24.

18. *Ibid.,* p. 35.

19. Ts'ang Cho, no. 71, p. 18.

20. Ch'ao Chü-jen, p. 28. They included Li P'in-hsien, Liu Hsing, Ho Chien, Yeh Ch'i, and Chou Lan.

21. Ts'ang Cho, no. 63, p. 2.

22. *Lu-chün ta-hsüeh-hsiao t'ung-hsüeh lu,* pp. 1–2.

23. Huang Hsü-ch'u, "Kuei chi lu-ta t'ung-hsüeh yu to-shao," pp. 14–16.

24. *Ibid.,* p. 14.

25. Since the Military Staff College was founded at Paoting, it is sometimes confused with the Paoting Military Academy. Thus some of its earlier graduates have been mistakenly referred to as Paoting alumni. Jerome

Ch'en makes this mistake with Li Chi-shen in "Defining Chinese War-lords," pp. 576, 595.

26. Sheridan, p. 243.   27. F. F. Liu, pp. 71–74.
28. Chang Chin-ch'ien, p. 32.   29. *Ibid.*, p. 34.
30. *Ibid.*, p. 31.   31. Ch'en Kuo-fu, pp. 104–5.

32. *Ibid.*, p. 14. Other reforms were attempted in Kiangsu and Chekiang as well. In 1932 Chiang Kai-shek instructed Ku Chu-t'ung, the governor of Kiangsu, to call on some of the faculty and graduates of the Central Political Academy to administer an experimental program in a county in that province. Kiang-ning county was chosen, and Mei Ssu-p'ing, a faculty member at the academy, was made county magistrate. In P'ing-fu county in Chekiang, Wang Hao, a professor of land administration at the academy was appointed magistrate. See Huang Shao-hung, p. 324.

33. Shih Yang-ch'eng, p. 97.

34. *Nei-cheng t'ung-chi chi-k'an* (Statistics quarterly of the Interior), no. 1, 1936, p. 234. Here are the numbers of local administrative function-aries trained in the provinces by 1936: Kiangsu, 213; Hupeh, 140; Sze-chwan, 125; Shantung, 493; Honan, 759; Hopei, 631; Shensi, 164; Tsing-hai, 71; Yunnan, 138; Kweichow, 356; and Chahar, 56. *Nei-cheng nien-chien*, 1936, pp. (B)328–34.

35. *Nei-cheng t'ung-chi chi-k'an* (Statistics quarterly of the Interior), no. 1, 1936, p. 2. The cities were Nanking, Shanghai, and Tsingtao; the provinces were Kiangsu, Chekiang, Fukien, Anhwei, Hupeh, Honan, Shan-tung, Shensi, Hunan, Shansi, Szechwan, Kweichow, Yunnan, Kiangsi, and Kwangsi. The number of trainees from each province and city is not spe-cified.

Chapter Eight

1. Ch'eng Fang, vol. 2, p. 133. For additional details see *Nei-cheng nien-chien*, 1935, pp. (B)303–6.

2. *Nei-cheng nien-chien*, 1935, pp. (B)832–33.

3. *Chung-hua nien-chien*, vol. 1, p. 522.

4. *Nei-cheng nien-chien*, 1935, p. (B)302.

5. Chao Ju-heng, p. 29.

6. Yang Yung-t'ai, "Nan-ch'ang hsing-ying tsung-p'ing," p. 2.

7. Shang Hsi-hsien, p. 1057.   8. Sheridan, p. 261.

9. Whitney, p. 124.   10. Ch'eng Fang, vol. 2, p. 131.

11. *Min-kuo erh-shih-erh nien chien-she*, p. 35.

Chapter Nine

1. *Chung-hua nien-chien*, vol. 2, p. 1970.

2. *Hu-nan nien-chien*, 1932, p. 492.

3. "Kuang-tung t'ung-chi tsu chih," p. 231.

4. Young, *China's Nation-Building Effort*, p. 83. Young makes some as-

sessment of the differing sets of data on pages 81–84 but omits figures from the Comptroller's Office.

5. For details see Boorman, *Biographical Dictionary*, vol. 2, pp. 191–92, and Shen I-yün, pp. 501–25.

6. Taylor, p. 310.

7. Cheng Chen-yü, pp. 967–69. Tsinghai, however, did not put its bureau into operation until later.

8. *Ibid.*, p. 969.

9. Cited in Whitney, *China*, p. 102.

10. *Ibid.*

11. For details see Robert Kapp, *Provincial Militarism and Central Authority in China: Szechwan Province, 1911–1938*, forthcoming from Yale University Press.

12. Between 1916 and 1935 there was at least one major war every year. It is estimated that during the 1912–33 period 479 battles were fought in the province. See Fang Ch'iu-wei, pp. 56–58.

13. Lü P'ing-teng, p. 478.

14. Jerome Ch'en, "Historical Background," p. 32.

15. Lü P'ing-teng, p. 460.

16. Chen Han-seng, *Landlord*, p. 82.

17. Shou Yü, p. 8.

18. *Ibid.*

19. *Ibid.*

20. Chen Han-seng, "P'o-ch'an chung ti Han-chung nung-min," p. 70.

21. Feng Ho-fa, pp. 494–96.

22. *Ibid.*

23. Cited in Wang Yuan-pi, p. 127. The original source is *Chung-yang jih-pao* (Central daily, Nanking), Sept. 7, 1935.

24. Wan Kuo-ting, p. 148.

25. *Ibid.*, p. 145. The traditional titles were *ch'en-shu, chuang-shu, li-shu, she-shu, ch'ing-shu, liang-fang, hu-fang,* and *ching-chao*. Some new titles were used as well: *szu-ts'e sheng, tsao-ts'e sheng,* and *kuan-ts'e sheng*.

26. Sun Hsiao-ts'un, p. 19.

27. Quoted in Hanwell, pp. 59–60.

28. *Ibid.*, p. 60.   29. Sun Hsiao-ts'un, pp. 24–26.

30. *Ibid.*, p. 24.   31. Sun Huai-jen, p. 122.

32. *Ibid.*, p. 140. For further details on surcharges in the provinces, see pp. 132–49.

33. *Ts'ai-cheng nien-chien*, vol. 2 (1935), pp. 2017–18.

34. Wan Kuo-ting, p. 158.

35. C. M. Chang, p. 32.

36. Ch'eng Fang, vol. 1, pp. 160–61.

37. *Chiang-su sheng nung-ts'un tiao-ch'a*, p. 63.

38. *Chün-shih wei-yuan-hui pao-kao*, p. 86.

39. *Ibid.*

40. Chuang Ch'ing-hua, p. 281. According to this source the Ministry of Finance also approved reductions for Peking. Since my analysis does not include cities, however, I have omitted the figures for Peking from the calculations.

41. Chen Han-seng, "P'o-ch'an chung ti Han-chung nung-min," p. 70.

42. *Agrarian China*, p. 150.

43. *Ibid.*, p. 103.

44. *Ibid.*

45. Chen Han-seng, "Economic Disintegration," p. 178.

46. Sun Huai-jen, p. 88.

47. Young, *China's Nation-Building Effort*, p. 79.

Bibliography

Bibliography

The following abbreviations are used in the Bibliography: *CC* for *Ch'un-ch'iu* (Spring and autumn), *TFTC* for *Tung-fang tsa-chih* (Eastern miscellany), and *TLPL* for *Tu-li p'ing-lun* (Independent critic).

Agrarian China. Selected Chinese source materials compiled and translated by the China Institute of Pacific Relations. Shanghai, 1938.

Almond, Gabriel, and G. Bingham Powell, Jr. *Comparative Politics: A Developmental Approach*. Boston, 1966.

Biographies of Kuomintang Leaders. Committee on International and Regional Studies, Harvard University. Cambridge, Mass., 1948.

Bloch, Kurt. "Warlordism: A Transitory Stage in Chinese Government," *American Journal of Sociology*, 43: 5 (1938).

Boorman, Howard L. "Wang Ching-wei: China's Romantic Radical," *Political Science Quarterly*, 79: 4 (1964).

——, ed. *Biographical Dictionary of Republican China*. 4 vols. New York, 1967–71.

——, ed. *Men and Politics in Modern China*. New York, 1960.

Buck, John Lossing. *Land Utilization in China*. 3 vols. Shanghai, 1937.

Cavendish, Patrick. "The 'New China' of the Kuomintang," in Gray, ed. (q.v.).

Chang Chin-ch'ien. "Pen hsiao chiao-yü ti fa-chan" (The development of education at Chengchi University), in *Cheng-ta ssu-shih nien* (Forty years of Chengchi University). Taipei, 1969.

Chang Chun-ku. *Tu Yüeh-sheng chuan* (A biography of Tu Yüeh-sheng), vol. 1. Taipei, 1967.

Chang, C. M. *A New Government for Rural China: The Political Aspect of Rural Reconstruction*. Data paper for the China Institute of Pacific Relations. Shanghai, 1936.

Chang Fo-ch'üan. "K'ao-ch'üan chih-tu yü hsing-cheng hsiao-lü" (The civil examination system and administrative efficiency), *Kuo-wen chou-pao*, (Kuowen weekly, illustrated), 12: 20 (1935).

Chang, Ray. "Trends in Chinese Public Administration," *Information Bulletin* (Council of International Affairs), 3: 5 (1937).

Chao Feng-yin. "Nung-ts'un chiu-chi ti fa-lü wen-t'i" (Legal problems of rural relief), *Ch'ing-hua hsüeh-pao* (Tsinghwa journal), 9: 2 (1934).

Chao Ju-heng, ed. *Chiang-su sheng-chien* (Kiangsu provincial yearbook), vol. 1. Chinkiang, 1935.

Ch'ao Chü-jen. *Chiang Pai-li p'ing-chuan* (A critical biography of Chiang Pai-li). Hong Kong, 1963.

Che-chiang sheng nung-ts'un tiao-ch'a (Rural survey of Chekiang province). Joint Commission on Rural Reconstruction of the Executive Yuan. Nanking, 1935.

Chen Han-seng [Ch'en Han-sheng]. "Economic Disintegration in China," *Pacific Affairs*, 6: 4–5 (1933).

———. *Landlord and Peasant in China*. New York, 1936.

———. "Po-ch'an chung ti Han-chung nung-min" (Peasants of Hanchung in bankruptcy), *TFTC*, 30: 1 (1933).

Ch'en Chih-mai. *Chung-kuo cheng-fu* (Chinese government), vol. 1. Chungking, 1944.

———. "Chung-kuo ti kuan" (Chinese officials), *She-hui k'o-hsüeh* (Social sciences), 1: 3 (1936).

———. "Kuo-min-tang ti cheng-chih wei-yuan-hui" (The Political Council of the Kuomintang), *She-hui k'o-hsüeh* (Social sciences), 2: 4 (1937).

———. "Sheng-fu ho-shu pan-kung" (Consolidating departmental offices of the provincial government), *TLPL*, no. 230, 1935.

Ch'en, Jerome. "Defining Chinese Warlords and Their Factions," *Bulletin of the School of Oriental and African Studies*, vol. 31 (1968).

———. "Historical Background," in Gray, ed. (q.v.).

———. "The Left Wing Kuomintang — A Definition," *Bulletin of the School of Oriental and African Studies*, vol. 25 (1962).

Ch'en Kung-po. *Ssu-nien ts'ung-cheng lu* (A record of four years of administrative experience). Shanghai, 1936.

Ch'en Kuo-fu. *Su-cheng hui-i* (Reminiscences of administration in Kiangsu). Taipei, 1951.

Ch'en Shao-hsiao. *Hei wang lu* (A record of the Black Net). Hong Kong, 1966.

Cheng Chen-yü. "Chin-nien lai ch'uan-kuo t'u-ti hsing-cheng ti fa-chan" (The development of national land administration in the past year), *Ti-cheng yüeh-k'an* (Land administration monthly), 4: 6 (1936).

Cheng-chih hui-i kung-tso pao-kao (Report of the Central Political Council). Nanking, 1935.

Ch'eng Fang. *Chung-kuo hsien-cheng kai-lun* (On Chinese county administration). 2 vols. Shanghai, 1939.

Chi Ch'ao-ting. *Key Economic Areas in Chinese History*, 2d ed. New York, 1963.